The
Knowledge-Creating
Company

The Knowledge-Creating Company

How Japanese Companies Create the Dynamics of Innovation

Ikujiro Nonaka and Hirotaka Takeuchi

New York   Oxford
OXFORD UNIVERSITY PRESS
1995

Oxford University Press

Oxford   New York
Athens   Auckland   Bangkok   Bombay
Calcutta   Cape Town   Dar es Salaam   Delhi
Florence   Hong Kong   Istanbul   Karachi
Kuala Lumpur   Madras   Madrid   Melbourne
Mexico City   Nairobi   Paris   Singapore
Taipei   Tokyo   Toronto

and associated companies in
Berlin   Ibadan

Copyright © 1995 by Oxford University Press, Inc.

Published in 1995 by Oxford University Press, Inc.
198 Madison Avenue, New York, New York 10016-4314

Oxford is a registered trademark of Oxford University Press

Library of Congress Cataloging-in-Publication Data
Nonaka, Ikujiro, 1935–
The knowledge-creating company: how Japanese companies create
the dynamics of innovation / Ikujiro Nonaka and Hirotaka Takeuchi.
p. cm.   Includes bibliographical references and index.
ISBN 0-19-509269-4
1. Communication in organizations—Japan.   2. Industrial
management—Japan.   I. Takeuchi, Hirotaka.   II. Title.
HD30.3.N66   1995
658.4'5—dc20   94-40408

10 12 14 16 18 19 17 15 13 11
Printed in the United States of America
on acid-free paper

To
Sachiko Nonaka
and Nobuko Takeuchi

PREFACE

The roots of this book go back 12 years. We were asked by the late Professor William J. Abernathy to submit a paper for the 75th Anniversary Colloquium of the Harvard Business School on the unique features of the new product development process within Japanese companies. The ideas generated in that study became the basis for our 1986 *Harvard Business Review* article, "The New New Product Development Game." In that article, we used the "rugby" metaphor to describe the speed and flexibility with which Japanese companies developed new products—as in rugby, the ball gets passed within the team as it moves up the field as a unit.

In retrospect, that study had touched on the roots of why Japanese companies became successful in the 1970s and 1980s. Let's continue the rugby analogy and focus our attention on the "ball" to describe what we mean. The ball being passed around in the team contains a shared understanding of what the company stands for, where it is going, what kind of a world it wants to live in, and how to make that world a reality. Highly subjective insights, intuitions, and hunches are also embraced. That's "what" the ball contains—namely, ideals, values, and emotions.

Now, let's focus on "how" the ball gets passed around in rugby. Unlike how a baton gets passed from one runner to the next in a relay race, the ball does not move in any defined or structured manner. Unlike relay, it does not move linearly or sequentially. Ball movement in rugby is borne out of the team members' interplay on the field. It is determined on the spot ("here and now"), based on direct experience and trial and error. It requires an intensive and laborious interaction among members of the team.

This interactive process is analogous to how knowledge is created organizationally within Japanese companies. As we shall see in this book, creating organizational knowledge is as much about bodily experience and trial and error as it is about mental modeling and learning from others. Similarly, it is as much about ideals as it is about ideas.

We contend in this book that Japanese companies have become successful because of their skills and expertise at "organizational knowledge creation." By organizational knowledge creation we mean the capability of a company as a whole to create new knowledge, disseminate it throughout the organization, and embody it in products, services, and systems. Herein lies the roots. Other theories of why Japanese companies have become successful abound, but our explanation hits at the most basic and universal component of the organization—human knowledge.

The study of human knowledge is as old as human history itself. It has been a central subject matter of philosophy and epistemology since the Greek period. Knowledge has also begun to gain a new wave of attention in recent years. Not only socio-economic theorists such as Peter Drucker and Alvin Toffler call for our attention to the importance of knowledge as management resource and power, but also an increasing number of scholars in the fields of industrial organization, technology management, management strategy, and organizational theory have begun to theorize about management of knowledge.

In this book, we take knowledge as the basic unit of analysis for explaining firm behavior. In discussing knowledge in the business organization, this book calls for a fundamental shift in thinking about what the business organization does with knowledge. More specifically, this book starts from the belief that the business organization not merely "processes" knowledge but "creates" it as well. Knowledge creation by the business organization has been virtually neglected in management studies. Years of research on Japanese firms, however, convinces us that knowledge creation has been the most important source of their international competitiveness.

In this book, we classify human knowledge into two kinds. One is *explicit knowledge,* which can be articulated in formal language including grammatical statements, mathematical expressions, specifications, manuals, and so forth. This kind of knowledge thus can be transmitted across individuals formally and easily. This has been the dominant mode of knowledge in the Western philosophical tradition. However, we shall argue, a more important kind of knowledge is *tacit knowledge,* which is hard to articulate with formal language. It is personal knowledge embedded in individual experience and involves intangible factors such as personal belief, perspective, and the value system. Tacit knowledge has been overlooked as a critical component of collective human behavior. At the same time, however, tacit knowledge is an important source of Japanese companies' competitiveness. This is probably a major reason that Japanese management is seen as an enigma among Western people.

In this book, we focus on explicit knowledge and tacit knowledge as basic building blocks in a complementary relationship. More importantly, the interaction between these two forms of knowledge is the key *dynamics* of knowledge creation in the business organization. "Organizational knowledge creation" is a spiral process in which the above interaction takes place repeatedly.

In the dominant Western philosophy, the individual is the principal agent who possesses and processes knowledge. In this study, however, we shall show that the individual interacts with the organization through knowledge. Knowledge creation takes place at three levels: the individual, the group, and the organizational levels. Therefore, our discussion of organizational knowledge creation consists of two major components: the forms of knowledge interaction and the levels of knowledge creation. The two forms of interactions—between tacit knowledge and explicit knowledge and between the individual and the organization—will then bring about four major processes of knowledge conversion, which all together constitute knowledge creation: (1) from tacit to explicit; (2) from explicit to explicit; (3) from explicit to tacit; and (4) from tacit to tacit.

The goal of this study is to formalize a generic model of organizational knowledge creation. Our discussion will mostly involve Japanese companies for two major reasons. First, Japanese companies provide a most challenging laboratory to develop and test the model of organizational knowledge creation as they have become most competitive over a short period of time. Second, we have been conducting an in-depth investigation of Japanese firms for a number of years. This long history offers a rich data pool for our present intellectual undertaking, which should be shared with Western readers at some point. In short, Japanese companies are analyzed in this book as representative case studies rather than as "success stories."

In fact, some may contend that the recent setback of Japanese companies in international competition could undermine our model. But, faced with the longest and most severe recession in recent history in the early 1990s, we are observing how Japanese companies are trying to break away from what worked in the past and move into new and untried territories of opportunity. The pressure of the current crisis and the need to globalize even further are forcing Japanese companies to turn to a more advanced form of knowledge creation, which we may want to write about sometime in the future.

On a more personal note, the roots of the authors' relationship go back 24 years. The two first met at the University of California, Berkeley, in 1970. Jiro, as Ikujiro Nonaka was called in Berkeley, was finishing up his Ph.D. program in marketing and organizational theory. Hiro, short for Hirotaka, had just started the MBA program. It was an encounter that changed Hiro's life for good. Jiro persuaded Hiro to enter the Ph.D. program in marketing. At Berkeley, both were inspired by the late Dean E. T. Grether, from whom they learned industrial organization. They both minored in sociology, studying under Professors Neil J. Smelser and Arthur L. Stinchcombe. Jiro wrote his thesis under Professor Francesco M. Nicosia and Hiro under Professor Louis P. Bucklin.

Berkeley has had a profound impact on the two of us. The University of California, Berkeley, was founded under the vision to become the "Athens of the Pacific." The founding fathers wanted to replicate the Athens of Aristotle and Plato, the Athens of Pericles at Berkeley. The city of Berkeley itself was named after Bishop George Berkeley, an Irish philosopher, who wrote "Principles of Human Knowledge" in 1710. We inherited this philosophical tradition, as evidenced from the ample references made to Greek philosophy and epistemology throughout the book. We also inherited the intellectual tradition of the Berkeley Ph.D. program, which is bent on developing theory. Our attempt to formalize a generic model of organizational knowledge creation is an indicator of this theoretical tradition.

Besides Berkeley, we have something else in common. Both of us had worked in business right after graduating a Japanese university. Jiro worked for an electronics manufacturer for nine years and Hiro for an advertising agency for two years. It is this shared experience that compels us to become practical and seek reality in the front line of business. The case studies in the book are indicators of this practical bent. In this book, we hope to combine our theoretical and practical bents. After all, as in the words of Kurt Lewin, "There is nothing so practical as a good theory."

After leaving Berkeley, Jiro returned to Japan to teach at Nanzan University and later at the National Defense Academy, where he conducted research on contingency theory based on the information-processing paradigm. Hiro went on to teach at the Harvard Business School, where he was exposed to case studies. Their paths crossed again, when Jiro joined Hitotsubashi University in 1982 and Hiro a year later. Ken-ichi Imai was instrumental in recruiting us to Hitotsubashi. Imai, who is now a research director at Stanford Japan Center in Kyoto, was also a co-researcher of the study we conducted for the 75th Anniversary Colloquium of the Harvard Business School.

As you can see, the roots for this book and our personal relationship go back a long time. Our only regret is that it has taken us so long to complete this book. Had we done so sooner, we would have been able to show Dean E. T. Grether, who passed away this year, that his two former students are keeping the Berkeley spirit alive across the Pacific, developing new theory out of Japan.

Tokyo   I. N.
December 1994   H. T.

ACKNOWLEDGMENTS

We have had the opportunity to interact with a large number of people in writing this book. This book, to a large extent, is the product of our interactions with managers, colleagues, graduate students and research assistants, and editors.

Our interactions with managers from Honda, Canon, Matsushita, Sharp, Nissan, Kao, Shin Caterpillar Mitsubishi, NEC, Mazda, Fuji Xerox, Seven-Eleven Japan, Asahi Breweries, Fujitsu, General Electric, and 3M have formed that knowledge base of this book. We are greatly indebted to all the managers we interviewed, who so willingly shared their tacit and explicit knowledge with us, and to the companies that gave us the opportunity to test our ideas.

Our interactions with our colleagues stimulated our thinking and oftentimes opened up our eyes. In addition to our mentors and colleagues mentioned above, we owe an enormous intellectual debt to Hiroyuki Itami, Iwao Nakatani, Kiyonori Sakakibara, Seiichiro Yonekura, Tsuyoshi Numagami, Kazuo Ichijo, Hisanaga Amikura, Shigemi Yoneyama, Tadao Kagono, Akihiro Okumura, Yoshiya Teramoto, Toshihiro Kanai, Noboru Konno, Kohichiro Tokuoka, Michael E. Porter, John A. Quelch, Alan M. Webber, Noel M. Tichy, David A. Aaker, David J. Teece, James R. Lincoln, Johny K. Johansson, Martin Kenney, D. Eleanor Westney, Gunnar Hedlund, Fabio Corno, Michael A. Brimm, Philippe Byosiere, and many others throughout the world.

Our interactions with graduate students and research assistants served as the engine for progress. Sung-Joon Roh, Taek-Whan Chung,

Yaichi Aoshima, Takaya Kawamura, all of whom are Jiro's graduate students, and Timothy Ray of Manchester University provided substantial research support in the early stages of our research. Yoshinori Fujikawa, Emi Osono, both of whom are Hiro's graduate students, and Katsuhiro Umemoto, a Ph.D. candidate at George Washington University, provided key research support toward the end. It was the dedication and commitment of Fujikawa, Osono, and Umemoto that finally drove the book to its completion. Noriko Morimoto of Hitotsubashi University provided administrative support through all the phases of our research. Our sincere *arigato* to all our support staff.

Our interactions with editors were truly a satisfying experience. As with explicit and tacit knowledge, the authors and the editors functioned as building blocks in a complementary relationship. Robert Howard, who was with the *Harvard Business Review* and now serves as an independent editor, did a heroic job of reading our earlier drafts and suggesting ingenious ways of reorganizing our materials. The current storyline of the book is due largely to his insights. Our editor at the Oxford University Press, Herbert J. Addison, also deserves a lot of credit. He was the first to "buy into" our ideas and constantly encouraged us to never lose sight of our uniqueness. As a result, what you are holding in your hands turned out to be a very unique book that covers the span from Plato to Zen Buddhism and from rugby to American football.

As a result of all the interactions mentioned above, our interface with our family members was kept at a suboptimal level while this book was being produced. On their part, many weekends and holidays were spent watching their husband/father work on the book. Our wives, Sachiko and Nobuko, understood our ideals and watched us with patience. Our children watched our backs with silence. In Japan, they say that's how children mature. Hopefully, our children, Miho, Yukiho, Yumeko, and Kohtaro, were able to share a tacit knowledge that will benefit them in the future. That's our way of saying "Thanks."

CONTENTS

The
Knowledge-Creating
Company

1

Introduction to Knowledge in Organizations

Japanese companies remain an enigma to most Westerners. They are not terribly efficient, entrepreneurial, or liberated. Yet, slowly but surely, they have advanced their position in international competition.

Why have Japanese companies become successful? In this book we offer a new explanation. We argue that the success of Japanese companies is not due to their manufacturing prowess; access to cheap capital; close and cooperative relationships with customers, suppliers, and government agencies; or lifetime employment, seniority system, and other human resources management practices—although all of these factors, of course, are important. Instead, we make the claim that Japanese companies have been successful because of their skills and expertise at "organizational knowledge creation." By organizational knowledge creation we mean the capability of a company as a whole to create new knowledge, disseminate it throughout the organization, and embody it in products, services, and systems. Organizational knowledge creation is the key to the distinctive ways that Japanese companies innovate. They are especially good at bringing about innovation continuously, incrementally, and spirally.

This view goes against the grain of the way most Western observers think of Japanese companies. The common view is that Japanese companies, while extremely successful at imitation and adaptation, are not really all that innovative, especially when "knowledge" plays a big role in gaining competitive advantage. Take, for example, the debate about

3

competitiveness in the computer and semiconductor industries. Five years ago everyone was afraid of the Japanese, but only a few are today. The general feeling is that the U.S. computer and semiconductor companies regained their strength by developing new architectures and designs. Others would contend that the Japanese have never been a major threat in the telecommunications and software industries.

These views have been reinforced by the recent setback of Japanese companies, which have been faced with the longest and most severe recession in recent history. We agree that Japanese companies have been slowed down, but at the same time we contend that they will emerge stronger from the current recession. Faced with a crisis, Japanese companies have historically turned to organizational knowledge creation as a means of breaking away from the past and moving them into new and untried territories of opportunity.

For at least the past 50 years, Japanese companies existed in an environment in which the only certainty was uncertainty. Following the devastating effects of World War II, they were confronted with two wars in their own region (the Korean War and the Vietnam War) and numerous economic crises, including the two "oil shocks," the "Nixon shock," the "yen crisis," and, more recently, the bursting of the "bubble economy." In addition to this uncertainty in the external environment, Japanese companies saw markets shifting, technology proliferating, competitors multiplying, and products becoming obsolete almost overnight.

Coping with uncertainty was a matter of life or death even for the more successful Japanese companies. Honda, for example, might not be in the automobile industry today had it not developed an energy-efficient engine prior to the oil shocks. In the camera industry, Canon bet the future of the company on the AE-1, the first single-lens reflex camera with a built-in electronic brain. Similarly, Sony could have gone into oblivion had it not pursued an aggressive export strategy during the days when "Made in Japan" was still synonymous with being "cheap and shoddy."

As latecomers into international competition, none of the Japanese companies ever achieved the dominance and success once enjoyed by such companies as IBM, General Motors, or Sears Roebuck. Competition was a constant uphill battle for Japanese companies. In retrospect, that was fortunate, since they did not acquire the usual encumbrances of success—including complacency and arrogance—that have come to plague the three monarchs mentioned above. No single Japanese company ever dominated a business the way IBM once ruled the computer business or the way General Motors and Sears once dominated the automobile and retailing industries, respectively. As rulers of their own fiefdoms, these companies sat comfortably on their laurels, becoming increasingly numb and blind to changes taking place around them. Certainty, not uncertainty, became the norm.

In contrast, Japanese companies struggled against international competition with dogged determination, often in the face of tough obstacles and adversities. Until recently, they could not afford to relax or become complacent. The fear of losing and the hope of catching up propelled them to anticipate change and to come up with something new—a new technology, a new product design, a new production process, a new marketing approach, a new form of distribution, or a new way of servicing customers. For instance, Japanese motorcycle manufacturers anticipated the growing needs of the emerging baby-boom segment in the United States and offered smaller, lower-capacity models that other competitors disdained as less profitable and less important.

But innovation was not a one-act drama for successful Japanese companies. One innovation led to another, bringing about continuous improvement and upgrading, which is precisely what took place in the Japanese automobile industry:

> They initially penetrated foreign markets with inexpensive compact cars of adequate quality, and competed on the basis of lower labor costs. Even while their labor-cost advantage persisted, however, the Japanese companies were upgrading. They invested aggressively to build modern plants to reap economies of scale. Then they became innovators in process technology, pioneering just-in-time production and a host of other quality and productivity practices. This led to better product quality, repair records, and customer satisfaction ratings than foreign rivals. Most recently, Japanese auto makers have advanced to the vanguard of product technology and are introducing new, premium brand names. (Porter, 1990, p. 75)

Continuous innovation of this sort has also been characteristic of successful Japanese companies in other businesses, including motorcycles, consumer electronics, sewing machines, and air-conditioning equipment.

How do Japanese companies bring about continuous innovation? One way is to look outside and into the future, anticipating changes in the market, technology, competition, or product. We have argued thus far that living in a world of uncertainty worked in favor of Japanese companies, since they were constantly forced to make their existing advantages obsolete. In fact, this trait—the willingness to abandon what has long been successful—is found in all successful companies, not only those in Japan. To these companies, change is an everyday event and a positive force. Contrast this mindset to that of the three monarchs mentioned earlier, who became preoccupied with defending their advantages and treated change with the fear that there was much to lose. They became insular, seeking predictability and stability.

Times of uncertainty often force companies to seek knowledge held by those outside the organization. Japanese companies have continually turned to their suppliers, customers, distributors, government agencies, and even competitors for any new insights or clues they may have to offer. Just as the proverbial "drowning man will catch at a straw," these companies accumulate knowledge from the outside almost in desperation during times of uncertainty. What is unique about the way Japanese companies bring about continuous innovation is the linkage between the outside and the inside. Knowledge that is accumulated from the outside is shared widely within the organization, stored as part of the company's knowledge base, and utilized by those engaged in developing new technologies and products. A conversion of some sort takes place; it is this conversion process—from outside to inside and back outside again in the form of new products, services, or systems—that is the key to understanding why Japanese companies have become successful. It is precisely this dual internal and external activity that fuels continuous innovation within Japanese companies. Continuous innovation, in turn, leads to competitive advantage, as shown.

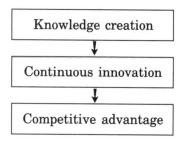

The New Focus on "Knowledge" as a Competitive Resource

The focus of this book is on knowledge *creation,* not on knowledge per se. But before we can embark on the task of trying to master an understanding of the Japanese techniques of knowledge creation, a close examination of knowledge itself is in order.

A keen interest in the subject of knowledge has been developing in the West. An explosion of sorts has occurred in the business press in recent years, with prominent authors such as Peter Drucker, Alvin Toffler, James Brian Quinn, and Robert Reich leading the field. In their own ways, they all herald the arrival of a new economy or society, referred to as the "knowledge society" by Drucker, which distinguishes itself from the past in the key role knowledge plays within society. Drucker (1993) argues in his latest book that in the new economy, knowledge is not just another resource alongside the traditional factors of production—labor, capital, and land—but the only meaningful resource today. The fact that knowledge has become *the* resource, rather than *a* resource, is what makes the new society unique, he contends.

Toffler (1990) echoes Drucker's contention, proclaiming that knowledge is the source of the highest-quality power and the key to the *powershift* that lies ahead. Toffler observes that knowledge has gone from being an adjunct of money power and muscle power to being their very essence, and that is why the battle for the control of knowledge and the means of communication is heating up all over the world. He believes that knowledge is the ultimate replacement of other resources.

Quinn (1992) shares with Drucker and Toffler the similar view that the economic and producing power of a modern corporation lies more in its intellectual and service capabilities than in its hard assets, such as land, plant, and equipment. He goes a step further by pointing out that the value of most products and services depends primarily on how "knowledge-based intangibles"—like technological know-how, product design, marketing presentation, understanding of the customer, personal creativity, and innovation—can be developed.

These authors also agree that the future belongs to people endowed with knowledge. In a society based on knowledge, says Drucker, the "knowledge worker" is the single greatest asset. Included in his definition of a knowledge worker is a knowledge executive who knows how to allocate knowledge to productive use, just as the capitalist knew how to allocate capital to productive use. Quinn notes that the capacity to manage what he calls "knowledge-based intellect" is fast becoming the critical executive skill of this era. Reich (1991) contends that the only true competitive advantage will reside among those he calls "symbolic analysts," who are equipped with the knowledge to identify, solve, and broker new problems.

The same message is beginning to appear in the popular press as well. A recent feature article entitled "Knowledge Is Power" (*Newsweek,* June 14, 1993) predicts in no uncertain terms that the future belongs to people who use their heads instead of their hands. *Newsweek* ends its article by pointing out how countries like South Korea and Singapore are educating their workers to new standards of excellence, and how international competition will be defined in terms of the advantage in knowledge a nation creates in the future.

The realization that knowledge is the new competitive resource has hit the West like lightning. But all this talk about the importance of knowledge—for both companies and countries—does little to help us understand how knowledge gets created. Despite all the attention by leading observers of business and society, none of them has really examined the mechanisms and processes by which knowledge is created. This distinction is what separates the Japanese approach from theirs. More important, it is for this reason that the Japanese experience is especially interesting and useful.

The Distinctive Japanese Approach
to Knowledge Creation

There is a reason why Western observers tend not to address the issue of organizational knowledge creation. They take for granted a view of the organization as a machine for "information processing." This view is deeply ingrained in the traditions of Western management, from Frederick Taylor to Herbert Simon. And it is a view of knowledge as necessarily "explicit"—something formal and systematic. Explicit knowledge can be expressed in words and numbers, and easily communicated and shared in the form of hard data, scientific formulae, codified procedures, or universal principles. Thus knowledge is viewed synonymously with a computer code, a chemical formula, or a set of general rules. When Drucker (1993, p. 38) observes that "within a few years after Taylor began to apply knowledge to work, productivity began to rise at a rate of 3.5 and 4 percent compound a year," he is actually referring to the application of quantifiable data to work. Similarly, Toffler (1990) uses the words "data," "information," and "knowledge" interchangeably throughout his book "to avoid tedious repetition."

Japanese companies, however, have a very different understanding of knowledge. They recognize that the knowledge expressed in words and numbers represents only the tip of the iceberg. They view knowledge as being primarily "tacit"—something not easily visible and expressible. Tacit knowledge is highly personal and hard to formalize, making it difficult to communicate or to share with others. Subjective insights, intuitions, and hunches fall into this category of knowledge. Furthermore, tacit knowledge is deeply rooted in an individual's action and experience, as well as in the ideals, values, or emotions he or she embraces.

To be more precise, tacit knowledge can be segmented into two dimensions. The first is the technical dimension, which encompasses the kind of informal and hard-to-pin-down skills or crafts captured in the term "know-how." A master craftsman, for example, develops a wealth of expertise "at his fingertips" after years of experience. But he is often unable to articulate the scientific or technical principles behind what he knows.

At the same time, tacit knowledge contains an important cognitive dimension. It consists of schemata, mental models, beliefs, and perceptions so ingrained that we take them for granted. The cognitive dimension of tacit knowledge reflects our image of reality (what is) and our vision for the future (what ought to be). Though they cannot be articulated very easily, these implicit models shape the way we perceive the world around us.

The distinction between explicit knowledge and tacit knowledge is the key to understanding the differences between the Western approach to knowledge and the Japanese approach to knowledge. Explicit knowledge can easily be "processed" by a computer, transmitted electronically, or stored in databases. But the subjective and intuitive nature of tacit knowledge makes it difficult to process or transmit the acquired knowledge in any systematic or logical manner. For tacit knowledge to be communicated and shared within the organization, it has to be converted into words or numbers that anyone can understand. It is precisely during the time this conversion takes place—from tacit to explicit, and, as we shall see, back again into tacit—that organizational knowledge is created.

Although Western managers have been more accustomed to dealing with explicit knowledge, the recognition of tacit knowledge and its importance has a number of crucially relevant implications. First, it gives rise to a whole different view of the organization—not as a machine for processing information but as a living organism. Within this context, sharing an understanding of what the company stands for, where it is going, what kind of a world it wants to live in, and how to make that world a reality becomes much more crucial than processing objective information. Highly subjective insights, intuitions, and hunches are an integral part of knowledge. Knowledge also embraces ideals, values, and emotion as well as images and symbols. These soft and qualitative elements are crucial to an understanding of the Japanese view of knowledge.

The Japanese have come to realize that tacit knowledge cannot be easily communicated to others. Everyone in Japan would agree that Shigeo Nagashima, nicknamed "Mr. Baseball" in Japan, is one of the greatest baseball players of all time. Having had the opportunity of meeting him in person, we asked him why he was so successful in rising to the occasion and hitting so many game-winning runs in tight moments. He used a lot of figurative language and body movement, but couldn't explain exactly what he meant. His words were not very logical or systematic. In the end, Nagashima simply said, "You have to feel it."

This episode questions the premise widely held in the West that knowledge can be taught through education and training. As Levitt (1991) points out, "The most precious knowledge can neither be taught nor passed on." Levitt uses another metaphor to drive home his point that not everything that is learned is done so consciously:

> A young child screams with pain upon touching a hot stove. A little comfort and mild medication soon make things well, except for a small blister. That evening the parent, returning home, greets the child as usual: "Hi— and what did you learn today?" "Nothing," comes the cheerful response. But never again will the child touch the burner, except cautiously, even when the stove is cold. (Levitt, 1991, p. 17)

In fact, the most powerful learning comes from direct experience. A child learns to eat, walk, and talk through trial and error; she or he learns with the *body,* not only with the mind.

Similarly, managers in Japan emphasize the importance of learning from direct experience as well as through trial and error. Like a child learning to eat, walk, and talk, they learn with their *minds* and *bodies.* This tradition of emphasizing the oneness of body and mind has been a unique feature of Japanese thinking since the establishment of Zen Buddhism. It stands in sharp contrast to the thinking behind the "learning organization," a phrase that has become a conceptual catch-all of the new business organization. Peter Senge (1990), the apostle of the learning organization, utilizes "systems thinking" to shift the mind from seeing the parts to seeing the whole. Systems thinking, according to Senge, is a conceptual framework, a body of knowledge and tools that has been developed over the past 50 years in the West to help people see the full patterns more clearly. The focus of the learning organization is clearly on learning with the *mind,* not with the body. Senge goes a step further and says that trial-and-error learning is a delusion, since the most critical decisions made in an organization have systemwide consequences stretching over years and decades, a time frame that makes learning from direct experience an impossibility.

The second implication of tacit knowledge follows naturally from the first. Once the importance of tacit knowledge is realized, then one begins to think about innovation in a whole new way. It is not just about putting together diverse bits of data and information. It is a highly individual process of personal and organizational self-renewal. The personal commitment of the employees and their identity with the company and its mission become indispensable. In this respect, the creation of new knowledge is as much about ideals as it is about ideas. And that fact fuels innovation. The essence of innovation is to re-create the world according to a particular ideal or vision. To create new knowledge means quite literally to re-create the company and everyone in it in an ongoing process of personal and organizational self-renewal. It is not the responsibility of the selected few—a specialist in research and development, strategic planning, or marketing—but that of everyone in the organization.

Creating new knowledge is also not simply a matter of learning from others or acquiring knowledge from the outside. Knowledge has to be built on its own, frequently requiring intensive and laborious interaction among members of the organization. New-product development team members at Canon, for example, hold "camp sessions" at a local hotel over a weekend to brainstorm through a critical problem or issue. In this respect, the Japanese approach is at variance with the "best" and "benchmarking" practices carried out at companies like GE, AT&T, Xerox, and Milliken that are bent on learning from others.

Milliken calls its practice SIS, for "Steal ideas shamelessly." The Japanese approach also runs counter to the basic premise of the "modular" or "virtual" corporation, which uses the knowledge of outside partners—suppliers, customers, rivals, and outside specialists—in lieu of its own. Companies in Japan believe that new and proprietary knowledge cannot be created without an intensive outside-inside interaction. To create knowledge, the learning that takes place from others and the skills shared with others need to be internalized—that is, reformed, enriched, and translated to fit the company's self-image and identity.

A third important implication that can be drawn from the above discussion is that Western managers need to "unlearn" their old view of knowledge and grasp the importance of the Japanese view. They need to get out of the old mode of thinking that knowledge can be acquired, taught, and trained through manuals, books, or lectures. Instead, they need to pay more attention to the less formal and systematic side of knowledge and start focusing on highly subjective insights, intuitions, and hunches that are gained through the use of metaphors, pictures, or experiences. Doing so will enable Western managers to understand what successful Japanese companies are doing right. And indeed, our theory will help them do just that.

Making Tacit Knowledge Explicit: The Honda City Example[1]

The explanation of how Japanese companies create new knowledge boils down to *the conversion of tacit knowledge to explicit knowledge.* Having an insight or a hunch that is highly personal is of little value to the company unless the individual can convert it into explicit knowledge, thus allowing it to be shared with others in the company. Japanese companies are especially good at realizing this exchange between tacit and explicit knowledge during the product development phase.

Take Honda as a case in point. In 1978, top management at Honda inaugurated the development of a new-concept car with the slogan, "Let's gamble." The phrase expressed senior executives' conviction that Honda's Civic and Accord models were becoming too familiar. Managers also realized that along with a new postwar generation entering the car market, a new generation of young product designers was coming of age with unconventional ideas about what made a good car.

The business decision that followed from the "Let's gamble" slogan was to form a new-product development team of young engineers and designers (the average age was 27). Top management charged the team with two—and only two—instructions: first, to come up with a product concept fundamentally different from anything the company had ever done before; and second, to make a car that was inexpensive but not cheap.

This mission might sound vague, but in fact it provided the team with an extremely clear sense of direction. For instance, in the early days of the project, some team members proposed designing a smaller and cheaper version of the Honda Civic—a safe and technologically feasible option. But the team quickly decided this approach contradicted the entire rationale of its mission. The only alternative was to invent something totally new.

Project team leader Hiroo Watanabe coined another slogan to express his sense of the team's ambitious challenge: "Automobile Evolution." The phrase described an ideal. In effect, it posed the question: If the automobile were an organism, how should it evolve? As team members argued and discussed what Watanabe's slogan might mean, they came up with an answer in the form of yet another slogan: "man-maximum, machine-minimum." This captured the team's belief that the ideal car should somehow transcend the traditional human-machine relationship. But that required challenging what Watanabe called "the reasoning of Detroit," which had sacrificed comfort for appearance.

The "evolutionary" trend the team articulated eventually came to be embodied in the image of a sphere—a car simultaneously "short" (in length) and "tall" (in height). Such a car, they reasoned, would be lighter and cheaper, but also more comfortable and more solid than traditional cars. A sphere provided the most room for the passenger while taking up the least amount of space on the road. What's more, the shape minimized the space taken up by the engine and other mechanical systems. This gave birth to a product concept the team called "Tall Boy," which eventually led to the Honda City, the company's distinctive urban car.

The Tall Boy concept contradicted the conventional wisdom about automobile design at the time, which emphasized long, low sedans. But the City's revolutionary styling and engineering were prophetic. The car inaugurated a whole new approach to design in the Japanese auto industry based on the man-maximum, machine-minimum concept, which had led to the new generation of "tall and short" cars now quite prevalent in Japan.

Three Key Characteristics of Knowledge Creation

The story of the Honda City illustrates the way Japanese managers approach the process of making tacit knowledge explicit. It also suggests three other characteristics of knowledge creation that relate to how tacit can be made explicit. First, to express the inexpressible, heavy reliance is placed on figurative language and symbolism. Second, to disseminate knowledge, an individual's personal knowledge has to be shared with others. Third, new knowledge is born in the midst of ambiguity and redundancy. We shall elaborate on each of these characteristics below.

Metaphor and Analogy

First, the story of the Honda City suggests how Japanese managers use figurative language to articulate their intuitions and insights. Figurative language, which is especially prominent in product development, can take the form of metaphor or analogy. A metaphor or an analogy—such as "Automobile Evolution," "man-maximum, machine-minimum," or "Tall Boy"—is a distinctive method of perception. It is a way for individuals grounded in different contexts and with different experiences to understand something intuitively through the use of imagination and symbols. No analysis or generalization is needed. Through metaphors, people put together what they know in new ways and begin to express what they know but cannot yet say. As such, metaphor is highly effective in fostering direct commitment to the creative process in the early stages of knowledge creation.

An analogy is much more structured than a metaphor in making a distinction between two ideas or objects. It clarifies how the two ideas or objects are alike and not alike. In this respect, analogy is an intermediate step between pure imagination and logical thinking. In the Honda City example, recall how some team members proposed designing a smaller and cheaper version of the Civic. But the team quickly realized that this approach contradicted the rationale of its mission and decided to make a distinction by trying to invent something totally new. By exploring how the City and the Civic are actually alike and not alike, the team was able to postulate a breakthrough concept.

From Personal to Organizational Knowledge

Second, the story of the Honda City suggests how new knowledge always starts with an individual—Hiroo Watanabe in this case—and how an individual's personal knowledge is transformed into organizational knowledge valuable to the company as a whole (i.e., Tall Boy). Other examples of this sort of transformation may include a brilliant researcher's insight leading to a new patent or a shop-floor worker's long years of experience resulting in a new process innovation.

Although we use the term "organizational" knowledge creation, the organization cannot create knowledge on its own without the initiative of the individual and the interaction that takes place within the group. Knowledge can be amplified or crystallized at the group level through dialogue, discussion, experience sharing, and observation. Recall how the new-product development team at Honda discussed what Watanabe's slogan might possibly mean before coming up with a metaphor of its own, "man-maximum, machine-minimum." This example illustrates the central role teams play in the knowledge-creation process—they provide a shared context in which individuals can interact with each other. Team members create new points of view through dialogue and discussion. This dialogue can involve considerable conflict and disagreement, but it is precisely such conflict that pushes employees to question existing premises and to make sense of their experience in a new way. This kind of dynamic interaction facilitates the transformation of personal knowledge into organizational knowledge.

Ambiguity and Redundancy

Third, the story of the Honda City suggests how certain organizational conditions can enhance the knowledge-creation process. It may sound paradoxical, but the confusion created within the product development team by the ambiguity of the mission handed down by Honda's top management provided an extremely clear sense of direction to the team. Ambiguity can prove useful at times not only as a source of a new sense of direction, but also as a source of alternate meanings and a fresh way of thinking about things. In this respect, new knowledge is born out of chaos.

Another organizational condition worth mentioning here is redundancy. To Western managers, the term "redundancy," with its connotation of unnecessary duplication and waste, may sound unappealing. And yet, the building of a redundant organization plays an important role in management of the knowledge-creation process. Redundancy is important because it encourages frequent dialogue and communication. This helps create a "common cognitive ground" among employees and thus facilitates the transfer of tacit knowledge. Since members of the organization share overlapping information, they can sense what others are struggling to articulate. Redundancy, which takes place primarily in information sharing, also spreads new explicit knowledge through the organization so that it can be internalized by employees.

The organizational logic of redundancy helps explain why Japanese companies manage product development as an overlapping process in which different functional divisions work together in a shared division of labor (Takeuchi and Nonaka, 1986). At many Japanese companies, redundant product development goes one step further. A product development team is divided into competing subgroups that develop different approaches to the same project and then argue over the advantages and disadvantages of their proposals. This redundancy encourages the team to look at a project from a variety of perspectives. Under the guidance of a team leader, the team eventually develops a common understanding of the "best" approach.

The Key Players in Knowledge Creation

Who is responsible for creating new knowledge? Another unique feature of Japanese companies is the fact that no one department or group of experts has the exclusive responsibility for creating new knowledge.

Front-line employees, middle managers, and senior managers all play a part. But this is not to say that there is no differentiation among these three roles. In fact, the creation of new knowledge is the product of a dynamic interaction among them.

Front-line employees are immersed in the day-to-day details of particular technologies, products, or markets. Most members of the Honda City development team were front-line employees who qualified as genuine car maniacs. Recalls Hiroshi Honma, "It's incredible how the company called in young engineers like ourselves to design a car with a totally new concept and gave us the freedom to do it our way." Giving them the freedom makes sense, since no one is more expert in the realities of a company's business than they are. But while these employees have an abundance of highly practical information, they often find it difficult to turn that information into useful knowledge. For one thing, signals from the marketplace can be vague and ambiguous. For another, employees can become so caught up in their own narrow perspective that they lose sight of the broader context. Moreover, even when employees do develop meaningful ideas or insights, they may find it difficult to communicate the importance of that information to others. People do not just receive new knowledge passively; they interpret it actively to fit their own situation and perspective. Thus what makes sense in one context can change or even lose meaning when communicated to people in a different context. As a result, there is continual confusion as new knowledge is diffused in an organization.

The major job of managers is to direct this confusion toward purposeful knowledge creation. Both senior and middle managers do this by providing employees with a conceptual framework that helps them make sense of their own experience. Senior managers provide a sense of direction by creating grand concepts that identify the common features linking seemingly disparate activities or businesses into a coherent whole. The Honda City project, for example, began with the slogan, "Let's gamble." These slogans provide employees with a sense of direction by establishing the criteria for estimating the value of the knowledge being created. Does the idea embody the company's vision? Is it an expression of top management's aspirations and ideals? Nobuhiko Kawamoto, the current president of Honda who was a vice president in charge of the City project at the time, kept on rejecting the team's too-conservative designs in the early phase of development. Recalls Hiroshi Honma, "Senior managers are romantics who go in quest of the ideal."

Middle managers serve as a bridge between the visionary ideals of the top and the often chaotic reality of those on the front line of business. Middle managers mediate between the "what should be" mindset of the top and the "what is" mindset of the front-line employees by creating mid-level business and product concepts. As team leaders of the product development team, for example, middle managers are in a position to remake reality according to the company's vision. Thus, at Honda, top management's vision of coming up with something completely new became a reality at the level of Hiroo Watanabe and his team in the form of the Tall Boy product concept.

Middle managers play a key role in the knowledge-creation process. They synthesize the tacit knowledge of both front-line employees and senior executives, make it explicit, and incorporate it into new products and technologies. It is people such as Hiroo Watanabe at Honda who actually manage the knowledge-creation process within Japanese companies.

The Journey Ahead

This book has several ambitious objectives. Succinctly, they are as follows. One is to present a new theory of organizational knowledge creation developed in Japan to researchers and managers in the West. The second is to provide a new explanation for why certain Japanese companies have been continuously successful in innovation. The third is to develop a universal model of how a company should be managed, based on the converging of management practices found in Japan and the West.

Given these ambitions, our journey will be covering a great deal of ground. It will traverse a wide territory marked by sharp contrasts— from Greek philosophy to Zen Buddhism, from neo-classical economists to modern-day management gurus, from pure theory to practical cases, from Matsushita to 3M, and from new-product development to human-resources management. But despite this breadth of coverage, we will be singularly focused throughout our journey on the topic of organizational knowledge creation.

To Western managers, the anecdotes and figurative language used in this book may seem odd or even incomprehensible. Consider the examples we have seen thus far. How is the slogan "Automobile Evolution" a meaningful design concept for a new car, or "man-maximum, machine-minimum" a useful ideal? These cryptic slogans may sound just plain silly to a Western manager, but are in fact highly effective tools for creating new knowledge in Japanese companies.

Western managers will also come across new and strange-sounding "road signs" throughout the journey. Many of the key concepts used throughout this book—for example, "oneness of body and mind," "knowledge conversion," "knowledge spiral," "self-organizing teams," "middle-up-down management style," or "hypertext organization"—are not everyday terms. Not only are they new, but they are foreign in origin and theoretical in nature as well. Thus many of the ideas in the pages that follow are difficult, but necessarily so. Managers in any country can no longer afford to be satisfied with simplistic ideas about knowledge and its creation. Our goal is to develop as rigorous and robust a theory about knowledge creation in the modern corporation as others have developed for corporate finance or business strategy.

We shall visit with close to 20 organizations during our journey. Most of these are companies based in Japan—Canon, Honda, Matsushita, NEC, Nissan, Kao, Sharp, Mazda, Fuji Xerox, Shin Caterpillar Mitsubishi, and Fujitsu—but some are based in the United States— 3M, GE, the U.S. Marines. We conducted in-depth personal interviews with approximately 130 managers in these companies to collect the necessary field data for this book.

Most of the research was conducted in the 1980s. At the time, the Japanese economy was strong and Japanese companies appeared to be a competitive juggernaut. Today, the Japanese economy is in trouble and Japanese companies appear considerably less invincible. Does this change of affairs invalidate our theory of knowledge creation?

We don't think so. Indeed, it is the skills of Japanese companies at creating systematic organizational knowledge that has allowed them again and again to innovate their way out of crisis. After all, the current situation is not the first time observers have noted the "crisis" of the Japanese economy. During the Nixon shock of 1971 and the oil shock of the 1970s, similar concerns were raised about the sustainability of the Japanese miracle. But in both cases, Japanese companies used knowledge creation to turn economic crisis into competitive opportunity. We fully expect them to do so again.

As a case in point, just look at how Honda innovated itself out of a crisis with the development of the 1994 Accord. When Kawamoto took over as Honda's president in 1990, the year sales of autos in the Japanese market began to slide, American and European engineers and marketers were flown into Tokyo to help with early-stage planning for the new model, something that Honda had never done before. Similarly, for the first time ever, nearly 60 American production engineers and their families began moving to Japan for two- to three-year stints working with development engineers at Honda's Sayama assembly plant and Wako engine plant. One of their key roles was to make sure that each part could be easily and cheaply manufactured at Honda's plants in Marysville, Ohio. Furthermore, Honda carried out a contest among Honda's design studios in Japan, the United States, and Europe to choose the 1994 Accord design—again, a company first. What Honda did was to create new knowledge on a global scale, with the American team making major contributions, to develop a jazzier looking and more affordable 1994 Accord. Looking at the brisk sales of the new Accord in the United States since its September 1993 introduction, this case may offer another example of how a Japanese company may emerge from a crisis stronger than ever before.

Road Map to the Rest of the Book

Our journey will take us through seven more chapters. Chapter 2 discusses the theoretical foundation of knowledge and its application to management. Our discussion of knowledge is embedded in three divergent theoretical foundations—the theory of knowledge (epistemology), organizational theory, and the theory of innovation. We will review existing theories of knowledge in the Western philosophical tradition and contrast them with the Japanese philosophical tradition. We will also review and critique economic and management theories of knowledge that are strongly influenced by Western epistemology.

Chapter 3 presents the core concepts of knowledge creation, centered around tacit and explicit knowledge. Four modes of knowledge conversion—from tacit to tacit, from tacit to explicit, from explicit to explicit, and from explicit to tacit—will be presented, sprinkled with examples from companies such as NEC, Canon, Asahi Breweries, and Fuji Xerox. We will explore how a key idea for Canon's epoch-making personal copier was the product of a conversation about a beer can. We will also present a process model of organizational knowledge creation in this chapter. Organizational conditions for promoting the spiral process upon which knowledge is created are discussed as well.

Chapter 4 uses Matsushita to illustrate the theoretical arguments presented in the two preceding chapters. The case shows that knowledge creation takes place continuously and at all levels of the organization. The example focuses on the product development story of Home Bakery, the world's first fully automatic home bread-making machine, and demonstrates how personal knowledge was converted to organizational knowledge through a seemingly never-ending iterative process. But the case also shows that knowledge creation did not end with the development of Home Bakery. In fact, it triggered major changes in other parts of the company, which started yet another round of iterations involving the corporation at large.

Chapter 5 shows that the two traditional styles of management, the top-down model and the bottom-up model, are not all that effective in fostering the dynamic interaction necessary to create organizational knowledge. We propose a new management style, which we call "middle-up-down management," that is more conducive to creating knowledge organizationally than the two traditional models. Under the new model, middle managers play the central role in managing the knowledge-creation process, taking the initiative to involve managers located "up" on the organizational ladder as well as front-line employees at the "bottom" of the organization. The chapter draws on three mini-cases—GE, 3M, and Canon—to compare and contrast the three management models. It also describes the expected roles of the three key players—top, middle, and front-line employees—under the middle-up-down model.

Chapter 6 discusses the organizational structure most conducive to knowledge creation. It argues that neither a formal hierarchy nor a flexible task force alone is the appropriate organizational structure in which knowledge creation can flourish, using the Japanese military and the U.S. Marines as examples. We propose a new organizational structure that can take best advantage of the efficiency inherent in a hierarchal structure and a flexible task force. We call this new structure a "hyptertext" organization and show how certain Japanese companies have already adopted it, using Sharp and Kao as case studies.

Chapter 7 shows that knowledge creation can be extended on a global scale. Two experiences of global knowledge creation are presented, one inside a Japanese company (Nissan) and the other involving a U.S.-Japanese alliance (Shin Caterpillar Mitsubishi). Nissan's experience in developing its first global car, Primera, with its British subsidiary is an example of how intracompany knowledge creation can take place across national boundaries. Shin Caterpillar Mitsubishi's experience, on the other hand, shows how knowledge creation not only can cross boundaries but can cut across different companies as well. To use our terminology, knowledge creation can take place "inter-organizationally."

Chapter 8, the culmination of our journey, summarizes the major findings of the book and presents two kinds of implications drawn from our study. The first is a set of practical managerial implications intended for the business reader. They take the form of our recommendations on "what" companies in the West should do to convert themselves into *knowledge-creating companies*. One of our recommendations, for example, is to treat every employee as a member of the "knowledge crew." The second set of implications is conceptual and theoretical in nature. Written primarily for the academic reader, our discussion here revolves around our observation that organizational knowledge is created by *transcending* a multitude of dichotomies presented throughout our book. In this introductory chapter alone, several of these dichotomies—such as body vs. mind, tacit vs. explicit, individual vs. organization, East vs. West—have already been mentioned.

With this preview of the following chapters, we are now ready to embark on a journey that should provide a new insight into how Japanese companies engage themselves in a never-ending process of continuous innovation. For practitioners who are in a hurry and are not theoretically inclined, Chapter 4 may be the most appropriate place to start. For practitioners who are theoretically inclined but cannot get excited about Plato or Descartes, Chapter 3 will most likely serve as the best starting platform. All others should come on board, starting with the following chapter on the theory of knowledge.

Note

1. This section is taken largely from Nonaka (1991, p. 100).

2

Knowledge
and Management

In Chapter 1, we sketched a basic difference in the way Western and Japanese managers approach "knowledge creation," which is deeply rooted in the intellectual traditions of the two cultures. To understand the difference, we need to examine fundamental assumptions about what knowledge is and how knowledge comes about. The philosophical inquiry of knowledge is known as "epistemology." Thus we begin our journey in this chapter with a brief look at the contrasting approaches to epistemology in the Western and Japanese intellectual traditions.

We encounter a paradox right away. While there is a rich epistemological tradition in Western philosophy, there is almost none to speak of in Japan. Yet this is in itself a reflection of the very different ways that the two cultures think about knowledge. In Western philosophy there has long been a tradition separating the subject who knows from the object that is known. This tradition was given a solid methodological basis by Descartes, who posited the "Cartesian split" between subject (the knower) and object (the known), mind and body, or mind and matter. And, as we will see below, the history of Western philosophy in the past two centuries can be seen as an unsuccessful effort to overcome this Cartesian dualism.

This history is important because the Western philosophical tradition has fundamentally shaped the disciplines of economics, management, and organization theory, which in turn have affected managerial thinking about knowledge and innovation. Contrasting this Western philosophical tradition with the Japanese intellectual tradition, where the split between subject and object has not been as deeply rooted, goes a long way toward understanding Western and Japanese managerial approaches today. This is not to say that we see only an either-or choice between the Western and Japanese approaches to knowledge creation. Indeed, our theory is based on the idea that these two perspectives are mutually complementary. We maintain that any adequate theory of knowledge creation must contain elements of both.

We start this chapter by examining the history of Western epistemology. Here again we encounter two opposing yet complementary traditions. One is "rationalism," which essentially says that knowledge can be obtained deductively by reasoning. The other is "empiricism," which essentially says that knowledge can be attained inductively from sensory experiences. We will follow these two dominant epistemological traditions by contrasting Plato with Aristotle and then Descartes with Locke. We will go on to argue that philosophers in the eighteenth and nineteenth centuries such as Kant, Hegel, and Marx attempted to synthesize the two traditions. Then we will briefly examine some twentieth-century attempts to overcome the Cartesian split. Finally, we will look briefly at the Japanese intellectual tradition in order to highlight differences from the Western philosophical tradition, but we will argue that they are mutually complementary.

What Is Knowledge?

The history of philosophy since the ancient Greek period can be seen as the process of searching for an answer to the question, "What is knowledge?"[1] Despite the fundamental differences between rationalism and empiricism, Western philosophers have generally agreed that knowledge is "justified true belief," a concept that was first introduced by Plato in his *Meno, Phaedo, and Theaetetus*.[2] However, the definition of knowledge is far from perfect in terms of logic.[3] According to this definition, our belief in the truth of something does not constitute our true knowledge of it, so long as there is a chance, however slight, that our belief is mistaken. Therefore, the pursuit of knowledge in Western philosophy is heavily laden with skepticism, which has induced numerous philosophers to search for the method to help them establish the ultimate truth of knowledge beyond all doubt. They have aimed to discover "fundamental knowledge without proof or evidence," on which all other knowledge could be grounded.

As noted above, there are two great epistemological traditions in Western philosophy. Rationalism argues that true knowledge is not the product of sensory experience but some ideal mental process. According to this view, there exists a priori knowledge that does not need to be justified by sensory experience. Rather, absolute truth is deduced from rational reasoning grounded in axioms. Mathematics is a classic example of this kind of reasoning. In contrast, empiricism claims that there is no a priori knowledge and that the only source of knowledge is sensory experience. According to this view, everything in the world has an intrinsically objective existence; even when one has an illusory perception, the very fact that something is perceived is significant. Experimental science is the classic example of this view.

Thus the two dominant approaches to epistemology, rationalism and empiricism, differ sharply with regard to what constitutes the actual source of knowledge.[4] Another fundamental difference lies in the method by which knowledge is obtained. Rationalism argues that knowledge can be attained *deductively* by appealing to mental constructs such as concepts, laws, or theories. Empiricism, on the other hand, contends that knowledge is derived *inductively* from particular sensory experiences.

Plato vs. Aristotle: Foundation of Western Epistemology

It was Plato who first built up an elaborate structure of thought on knowledge from a rationalistic perspective.[5] He developed the theory of "idea," which is a "form" seen through the pure mental eye, and at the same time the ultimate ideal that the human spirit aspires to know. Plato argued:

> Would not that man do this most perfectly who approaches each thing, so far as possible, with the reason alone, not introducing sight into his reasoning nor dragging in any of the other senses along with his thinking, but who employs pure, absolute reason in his attempt to search out the pure, absolute essence of things, and who removes himself, so far as possible, from eyes and ears, and, in a word, from his whole body, because he feels that its companionship disturbs the soul and hinders it from attaining truth and wisdom? Is not this the man, Simmias, if anyone, to attain to the knowledge of reality?[6]

Thus, for Plato, the physical world is a mere shadow of the perfect world of "ideas." Human beings aspire toward the eternal, unchanging, and perfect "ideas" that cannot be known through sensory perception but only through pure reason.

Aristotle, a student of Plato, criticized his mentor. He contended that Plato's conceptualization of "idea" as "form" or an eternal and supersensible object was wrong. Idea, or more precisely form, cannot be isolated from a physical object, nor does it have an existence independent from sensory perception. Rather, an individual thing consists of its form and physical object or matter, and knowledge of forms is always occasioned by sensory perception. From an empiricistic perspective, he argued as follows:

So out of sense-perception comes to be what we call memory, and out of frequently repeated memories of the same thing develop experience; for a number of memories constitute a single experience. From experience again—i.e., from the universal now stabilized in its entirety within the soul, the one besides the many which is a single identity within them all— originate the skill of the craftsman and the knowledge of the man of science, skill in the sphere of coming to be and science of being. We conclude that these stages of knowledge are neither innate in a deterministic form, nor developed from other higher states of knowledge, but from sense-perception.[7]

Thus he stressed the importance of observation and the clear verification of individual sensory perception.[8]

Descartes vs. Locke: Continental Rationalism vs. British Empiricism

The Platonic and Aristotelian views were inherited through intermediate philosophers[9] by modern epistemology's two mainstreams: the Continental rationalism and the British empiricism. René Descartes, a Continental rationalist, proposed four general rules for rational thinking:

The first of these was to accept nothing as true which I did not clearly recognize to be so: that is to say, carefully to avoid precipitation and prejudice in judgments, and to accept in them nothing more than what was presented to my mind so clearly and distinctly that I could have no occasion to doubt it.

The second was to divide up each of the difficulties which I examined into as many parts as possible, and as seemed requisite in order that it might be resolved in the best manner possible.

The third was to carry on my reflections in due order, commencing with objects that were the most simple and easy to understand, in order to rise little by little, or by degrees, to knowledge of the most complex, assuming an order, even if a fictitious one, among those which do not follow a natural sequence relatively to one another.

The last was in all cases to make enumerations so completely and reviews so general that I should be certain of having omitted nothing.[10]

Descartes also devised the "method of doubt," questioning all beliefs in an attempt to create his own philosophy from scratch. His methodological skepticism is reflected in the following question: "What can I hold as true beyond any doubt?" He discovered that one could question all beliefs except the existence of the questioner, which was expressed by the famous phrase, "I think, therefore I am" *(cogito, ergo sum)*. He argued that ultimate truth can be deduced only from the real existence of a "thinking self." He went a step further to assume that the "thinking self" is independent of body or matter, because while a body or matter does have an "extension" (or existence we can see and touch) in space, but does not think, a mind has no extension, but thinks. As for his epistemology, Descartes argued that honey wax's qualities, such as taste, scent, color, and size, which are apparent to the senses, change if we put it near fire; therefore, wax itself cannot be sensible. Thus true knowledge about external things can be obtained by the mind, not by the senses.

Descartes's rationalism was criticized by John Locke, the founder of British empiricism. In Locke's view, things existing in the real world are objective in nature. Even if the sensory perception of things is illusory, it is undoubtedly evident that something can be perceived. He compared the human mind to a *tabula rasa,* or "white paper, void of all characters," which has no a priori idea. With this metaphor he rejected the rationalist argument that the human mind is already furnished with innate ideas or concepts. He argued that only experience can provide the mind with ideas and that there are two kinds of experience: sensation and reflection. By sensation Locke meant the sensory perception, which is the "great source of most of our ideas," and by reflection "the perception of the operation of our own mind within us," which is "the other fountain from which experience furnisheth the understanding with ideas."[11]

Kant, Hegel, and Marx: Attempts at a Synthesis

The two streams of rationalism and empiricism were brought together by the eighteenth-century German philosopher Immanuel Kant. He agreed that the basis of knowledge is experience, but did not accept the empiricist argument that experience is the sole source of all knowledge. In his words: "Though all our knowledge begins with experience, it does not follow that it all arises out of experience."[12] He argued that knowledge arises only when both the logical thinking of rationalism and sensory experience of empiricism work together. For Kant, the human mind is not the passive *tabula rasa* but active in ordering sensory experiences in time and space and supplying concepts as tools for understanding them (Russell, 1961, p. 680). Therefore, his position is closer to rationalism than to empiricism. However, Kant believed that we could only know the "phenomenon" or our sensory perception of the "transcendental object" or "thing in itself," which transcends experience. For this reason, his philosophy is often called "transcendental idealism."

Rejecting the concept of the "thing in itself" in Kantian philosophy, Georg W. F. Hegel argued that both mind and matter are derived from the "Absolute Spirit" through a dynamic, dialectical process. According to Hegel, dialectics is the creation of a synthesis by reconciling thesis and antithesis or rejecting what is not rational and retaining what is rational. For Hegel, knowledge begins with sensory perception, which becomes more subjective and rational through a dialectic purification of the senses, and at last reaches the stage of self-knowledge of the "Absolute Spirit" (Russell, 1961, p. 704). The self-consciousness of the "Absolute Spirit" is the highest form of knowledge. In this sense, his position is closer to rationalism than to empiricism. With this absolute idealism, he attempted to overcome the Cartesian dualism between subject and object.

Karl Marx made another attempt at a synthesis between rationalism and empiricism by integrating Hegel's dialectical dynamics and the emerging social sciences of the day. He refuted Hegel's abstract and idealistic philosophy because it could not explain the dynamic and interactive relationship between man and his environment.[13] According to Marx, perception is an interaction between the knower (subject) and the known (object). In the pursuit of knowledge, both subject and object are in a continual and dialectic process of mutual adaptation. Object is transformed in the process of becoming known. As for subject, what the British empiricists conceived as "sensation" would be better called "noticing" to imply activity. We notice things in the process of acting on them. Thus knowledge is obtained by handling things, or "action," and its truth should be demonstrated in practice. However, Marx's interest was not in knowledge itself. His real task was not to interpret the world but to change it (Russell, 1961, pp. 749–750).

Twentieth-Century Challenges to the Cartesian Split

The Cartesian dualism of subject and object or mind and body followed from the assumption that the essence of a human being lies in the rational thinking self. This thinking self seeks knowledge by isolating itself from the rest of the world and other human beings. But contemporary challenges to the Cartesian split have emphasized the importance of some form of interaction between the self and the outside world in seeking knowledge. We will briefly describe the contributions made by Husserl, Heidegger, Sartre, Merleau-Ponty, Wittgenstein, James, and Dewey.

Edmund Husserl, a German philosopher, focused on the relationship between the thinking self and the world. He built the foundation of phenomenology, which is a philosophical inquiry into human consciousness of self and other objects. He contrasted the physical objectivism of modern science since Galileo with the transcendental idealism established by Kant, and highlighted the importance of conscious, direct experience. He argued that certain knowledge is possible only by describing the interactions between "pure consciousness" and its objects. "Pure consciousness" can be reached through "phenomenological reduction," a method whereby all factual knowledge and reasoned assumptions about a phenomenon are set aside so that pure intuition of its essence may be analyzed.[14]

Martin Heidegger, a student of Husserl, used the phenomenological method to analyze the mode of human "being in the world" *(Dasein)*. According to Heidegger, we are a "being in the world" by "having to do with something," such as "producing something" or "making use of something." These "practical" behaviors or actions "must employ theoretical cognition."[15] In other words, our *Dasein* is characterized by active relationships with other things in the world. For Heidegger, therefore, *Dasein* is not a detached spectator like Descartes's thinking self, but someone who has a close relationship between knowledge and action. He thus rejected the Cartesian dualism between the thinking subject and the objective world.

The relationship between knowledge and action was further emphasized by a philosophical and literary movement known as "existentialism," an inquiry into individual human existence and living experience (Russell, 1989, pp. 302–304). While most phenomenologists argue that knowledge can be obtained through reflection, existentialists stress that if we want to know the world, we must act toward an end. Jean-Paul Sartre, a French existentialist, stated: "For human reality, to be is to act . . . the act must be defined by an *intention*. . . . Since the intention is a choice of the end and since the world reveals itself across our conduct, it is the intentional choice of the end which reveals the world" [italics in original].[16]

The Cartesian split between mind and body was refuted by Maurice Merleau-Ponty, a French phenomenologist, who contended that perception is a bodily cognitive action aimed at something and that consciousness is "not a matter of 'I think that' but of 'I can.' "[17] It is through body that we can perceive things and understand other people. In this sense, a body is "ambiguous" in that it is subject and, at the same time, object. The body subject does not just exist but dwells in the world here and now, and contains knowledge of such bodily habits as driving a car, a blind person's use of a cane, and typing. Despite this empiricistic tendency, Merleau-Ponty was a rationalist at heart. He reproached empiricists for "deducing the datum from what happens to be furnished by the sense organs" and asserted that empirical theories based on such data "could never be the equivalent of knowledge."[18]

While phenomenology has tried to describe and analyze phenomena, or how the Kantian "things in themselves" appear to our consciousness, another twentieth-century philosophical movement called "analytical philosophy" has focused on the language with which people describe phenomena. Ludwig Wittgenstein, an Austrian philosopher, is the most influential figure of this philosophical movement. In his earlier days Wittgenstein viewed language as a "picture" of reality that corresponds exactly to logic, and rejected metaphysics as "nonsensical" with his famous saying: "What we cannot speak about we must pass over in silence" (quoted by Ayer, 1984, p. 112). In his later days, however, he viewed language as a "game" or interaction played by multiple persons following rules. Moreover, knowing is a bodily action with a will to bring about changes in the state of affairs rather than with a detached stance toward the world. Thus Wittgenstein argued:

> The grammar of the word "knows" is evidently closely related to that of "can," "is able to." But also closely related to that of "understands." But there is also *this* use of the word "to know": we say "Now I know!"—similarly "Now I can do it!" and "Now I understand!" [19]

The emphasis on the relationship between knowledge and action can also be found in pragmatism, an American philosophical tradition. In *Pragmatism* (1907), William James argued that if an idea works, it is true; insofar as it makes a difference to life in terms of cash value, it is meaningful. This pragmatic standpoint was further developed by John Dewey, who opposed the spectator theory of knowledge that separates "theory and practice, knowledge and action." He maintained that "ideas are worthless except as they pass into actions which rearrange and reconstruct in some way, be it little or large, the world in which we live" (Dewey, 1929, p. 138). Thus, pragmatism has attempted to develop an interactive relationship between human beings and the world by means of human action, experiment, and experience.

The Japanese Intellectual Tradition

In this section, we introduce the Japanese intellectual tradition. No major Japanese philosophical tradition has become widely known, nor has one been described in any systematic way.[20] And scarcely can a trace of Cartesian rationalism be found in Japanese thinking. But there exists some "Japanese" approach to knowledge that integrates the teachings of Buddhism, Confucianism, and major Western philosophical thoughts. We will briefly discuss three distinctions of the Japanese intellectual tradition: (1) oneness of humanity and nature; (2) oneness of body and mind; and (3) oneness of self and other. These traits have formed the foundation of the Japanese view toward knowledge as well as the Japanese approach toward management practices.

Oneness of Humanity and Nature

The most important characteristic of Japanese thinking can be termed a "oneness of humanity and nature." Examples of this trait include: (1) the sympathy to nature depicted in the *Manyohshu;*[21] (2) the notion of "the beauty of change and transition" *(mono no aware)* described in the famous *Tale of Genji;* [22] (3) the delicate sentiment conveyed by the *Kokin-wakashu;* [23] and (4) the stylish *(iki)* lifestyle and art in the urban culture of eighteenth- and nineteenth-century Yedo (old name of Tokyo). Yujiro Nakamura (1967), a contemporary Japanese philosopher, dubbed this tradition "emotional naturalism." According to this tradition, the Japanese perception is oriented toward objects in nature that are subtle but, at the same time, visual and concrete. While Japanese epistemology has nurtured a delicate and sophisticated sensitivity to nature, it has prevented the objectification of nature and the development of "sound skepticism." Nakamura argued that the Japanese had failed to build up a rational thought of clear universality, because they did not succeed in the separation and objectification of self and nature. [24]

Basic attitudes associated with the "oneness of humanity and nature" in Japanese epistemology can also be found in the structural characteristics of the Japanese language. According to Kumakura (1990), a Japanese linguist, physical and concrete images of objects are indispensable for Japanese expression; an essential epistemological pattern for the Japanese is to think visually and manipulate tangible images. In the Japanese language, statements made by the speaker articulate certain concrete images. These images, irrespective of whether they belong to the world of reality or the imagination, are all realistic to the speaker because they exist as a reality within the mind of the speaker the moment they are spoken. Even when the speaker narrates a past experience, the concrete images of the experience are revived within himself or herself. Put simply, the Japanese language is characterized by visual concepts that are highly context-specific in terms of both time and space.

The inherent characteristics of the Japanese language reveal a unique view of time and space. The Japanese see time as a continuous flow of a permanently updated "present." Many Japanese novels do not have any fixed time point in their plots, and traditional Japanese poems are free from any fixed time perspective. In contrast, Westerners have a sequential view of time and grasp the present and forecast the future in a historical retrospection of the past. The Japanese view of time is more circular and momentalistic. Everything appears and disappears occasionally and ultimate reality is confined to "here and now." To the Japanese, emphasis is given to leaving their existence to the flow of time and placing a high value on being flexible in accordance with the flux and transition of the world. The Japanese view of space is also free from a fixed perspective, as is clearly depicted in traditional Japanese art. Although Western drawings view things from a fixed standpoint, Japanese drawings do not fix the artist's viewpoint. In the traditional Japanese woodcut print *ukiyoe,* for example, the rendition of the parts is realistic but the distance is not determined from one fixed point. Since the perspective is not fixed, there is no need to draw shadows.

The basic attitude of the "oneness of humanity and nature" found in the Japanese language and the flexible view of time and space clearly illustrates a Japanese tendency to deal with sensitive emotional movements rather than to abide by any fixed worldview or metaphysics. The Japanese have a tendency to stay in their own world of experience without appealing to any abstract or metaphysical theory in order to determine the relationship between human thought and nature. Such a basic attitude of the "oneness of human and nature" is one of the most important characteristics of the Japanese intellectual tradition. We do not regard this tradition as underdeveloped, but believe it can complement the Cartesian separation of man and nature in which Western philosophical traditions are deeply rooted.

Oneness of Body and Mind

Another important intellectual tradition of Japan is the emphasis on the "whole personality" as opposed to the Western sense of knowledge, which is separated from human philosophical and epistemological development. For the Japanese, knowledge means wisdom that is acquired from the perspective of the entire personality. This orientation has provided a basis for valuing personal and physical experience over indirect, intellectual abstraction.

This tradition of emphasizing bodily experience has contributed to the development of a methodology in Zen Buddhism dubbed "the oneness of body and mind" by Eisai, one of the founders of Zen Buddhism in medieval Japan. It is the ultimate ideal condition that Zen practitioners seek by means of internal meditation and disciplined life. Zen profoundly affected *samurai* education, which sought to develop wisdom through physical training. In his famous book *Bushido,* Inazo Nitobe (1899), a Japanese Christian educator, pointed out that in traditional *samurai* education, knowledge was acquired when it was integrated into one's "personal character." *Samurai* education placed a great emphasis on building up character and attached little importance to prudence, intelligence, and metaphysics. Being a "man of action" was considered more important than mastering philosophy and literature, although these subjects constituted a major part of the *samurai*'s intellectual education.[25]

In the Meiji era (1868–1912), Kitaro Nishida, Japan's first theoretical philosopher, built up a philosophy through the logical articulation of Zen experience. For Nishida, ultimate reality and existence lay only in the acquisition of "fact from pure experience" (Yuasa, 1987, p. 65). Nishida interpreted it as experience direct to subject:

Pure experience is an animated state with maximum freedom in which there is not the least gap between the will's demand and its fulfillment. . . . [I]t is in such occasions as a person's scaling a cliff, holding on for dear life, or a musician's playing a composition he has mastered. . . . [W]hen our mind, forgetting both self and things, is lost in a sublime music, the entire world becomes a single melodious sound.[26]

As these examples indicate, Nishida believed that true "directness" is realized only within the living reality of experience prior to the separation of subject and object. This philosophy is in stark contrast to the Western philosophical tradition of the body-mind separation.[27] According to Nishida's philosophy, true knowledge cannot be obtained by theoretical thinking but only through one's total mind and body (Yuasa, 1987, pp. 25–26). Nishida (1990, p. 26) also held that the perfect truth "cannot be expressed in words."[28] The Western philosophical tradition is compared with Nishida's philosophy as follows:

Modern Western philosophy regards the problem of action, namely, that of the will, to be an issue for practical ethics, but not theoretical epistemology. . . . This is because modern Western philosophy seeks human essence in rational, thinking subject; its epistemology excludes the problem of the body. This attitude obviously originates in the rationalistic view of the human being and from Descartes' mind-body dualism. In contrast, Nishida's theory of acting intuition grasps the human being-in-the-world as originally having the character of *action;* the essential mode is to act on the world, not to cognize it. Persons are subjects qua action before they are thinking, cognizing subjects. The former implies the latter. So it is clear why Nishida rejects both the rationalistic view of being human represented by modern epistemology as well as the mode of thinking that puts the subject and object in opposition to each other [italics in original]. (Yuasa, 1987, p. 68)

The belief that a person is a subject of action can be seen in the training style of the Zen temple, where a mentor and students live together. Although this tradition is also evident in the Western tradition of the "academy," which started in the ancient Greek period, the method for pursuing truth is different. The dialectic used since Socrates and Plato is completely different from the practice of Zen Buddhism. While the Zen master uses a question-and-answer conversation to evaluate the student's ability to explore paradoxical issues, this style of conversation is nonlogical, metaphorical, and abductive rather than being deductive or inductive. In Zen Buddhist training, students are required to devote themselves to the world of nonlogic throughout their learning process.

As we have discussed earlier, Western epistemology tends to accord the highest values to abstract theories and hypotheses, which have contributed to the development of science. The backdrop of this tendency is the long tradition of valuing precise, conceptual knowledge and systematic sciences, which can be traced back to Descartes. In contrast, Japanese epistemology tends to value the embodiment of direct, personal experience. The emphasis of "on-the-spot" personal experience in Japanese management is a real manifestation of such an epistemological tendency.

Oneness of Self and Other

The two major traditions of the oneness of humanity and nature and the oneness of body and mind have led the Japanese to value the interaction between self and other. While most Western views of human relationships are atomistic and mechanistic, the Japanese view is collective and organic. It is within this context of an organic worldview that the Japanese emphasize subjective knowledge and intuitive intelligence. While a typical Western individual "conceptualizes" things from an objective vantage point, a Japanese person does so by relating her- or himself to other things or persons. Therefore, the Japanese perspective is "tactile" and "interpersonal." The structure of the Japanese language shows the sympathetic unity of self and other people. In the Japanese language, a message is often communicated through the use of context, not solely by the self-complete grammatical code. The ambiguous nature of the Japanese language thus asks one to be equipped with some tacit knowledge of each context.[29]

This ambiguity can be seen from the fact that verbs in the Japanese language do not conjugate with the subject of the sentence. In Indo-European languages, verbs basically conjugate in accordance with the subject because the meaning of a verb differs when used with a different subject. A Japanese can easily gain sympathy and agreement with a statement because verbs are always used in the same form in any context. The perspective of the Japanese speaker, therefore, can be shared naturally and smoothly by the group, and sometimes by larger society, because of this sympathetic nature of the verb. This also means, however, that it is difficult for the Japanese to express their own thoughts and feelings directly. For the Japanese, you and I are two parts of a whole, that is, two sides of the same coin. To be an independent individual and to respect others is such a difficult concept for the Japanese that they sometimes misunderstand the Western notion of "public." While Western societies promote the realization of the individual self as the goal of life, the Japanese ideal of life is to exist among others harmoniously as a collective self. For the Japanese, to work for others means to work for oneself. The natural tendency for the Japanese is to realize themselves in their relationship to others.

The above review of the Japanese intellectual tradition suggests that the ultimate reality for the Japanese lies in the delicate, transitional process of permanent flux, and in visible and concrete matter, rather than in an eternal, unchanging, invisible, and abstract entity. They see reality typically in the physical interaction with nature and other human beings. These basic attitudes are clearly different from the prevailing Western view that the thinking self seeks the eternal ideal as a detached spectator. Although contemporary Western philosophy seems to be getting closer to the Japanese intellectual tradition that has emphasized body and action, the view of knowledge in sciences and in Western management practices is still dominated by the Cartesian dualism between subject and object, mind and body, or mind and matter. Following the Japanese intellectual tradition, however, we do not see these distinctions as an either-or dichotomy, but as mutually complementary.

Knowledge in Economic and Management Theories

The separation of "subject," "mind," and "self" from "object," "body," and "other" lies at the root of Western social sciences, including economics, management, and organization theory. As will be illustrated below, the century-long history of Western management thought can be seen as repeated challenges against the "scientific" view of knowledge by the "humanistic" one. This history reflects the entire effort of Western philosophy in the past two centuries to overcome the Cartesian split between the knower and known.

In this section we will critically review major economic and management thinkers of the West in terms of how they have treated knowledge, covering the span from Alfred Marshall to Peter Senge. We contend that none of the thinkers has articulated the dynamic notion that human beings can actively create knowledge to change the world, implicitly suggesting that our view of knowledge and theory of organizational knowledge creation provide a fundamentally new economic and management perspective that can overcome the limitations of existing theories bounded by the Cartesian split.

Knowledge in Economic Theories

Most economic theories have treated knowledge, either implicitly or explicitly, as an important factor in economic phenomena.[30] However, the way knowledge is treated differs depending on the emphasis put on knowledge, the type of knowledge to which attention is paid, and the ways to acquire and utilize it. In this section we will examine the treatment of knowledge in the neoclassical economics of Marshall, the Austrian school of economics by Hayek and Schumpeter, the economic theory of firm by Penrose, and the evolutionary model of technological change by Nelson and Winter.[31]

Marshall vs. Hayek and Schumpeter

Although classical economists treated knowledge as a "disturbance" category in their model specifications, Alfred Marshall, a forefather of today's tradition of neoclassical economics, was among the first to state explicitly the importance of knowledge in economic affairs. According to Marshall (1965), "Capital consists in a great part of knowledge and organization. . . . Knowledge is our most powerful engine of production . . . organization aids knowledge" (p. 115).[32] But neoclassical economists were concerned with the utilization of existing knowledge, which is represented by price information. Under market mechanism, every firm has the same fixed knowledge that enables profit maximization, rather than having different knowledge created by each firm. Thus, neoclassical economists neglected a huge amount of both tacit and explicit knowledge held by economic subjects that is not represented in the form of price information. They were not concerned with the creation of knowledge and did not position the firm as a knowledge creator.

The Austrian school of economics, represented by Frederich von Hayek and Joseph A. Schumpeter, paid more attention to knowledge in economic affairs. They argued that knowledge is "subjective" and cannot be treated as fixed. In contrast to the neoclassical economists, both Hayek and Schumpeter tried to describe the dynamics of economic change by focusing their attention on the unique knowledge held by each economic subject rather than on the common knowledge shared by economic subjects.

Hayek was a pioneer in drawing attention to the importance of implicit, context-specific knowledge. He classified knowledge into scientific knowledge (i.e., knowledge of general rules) and knowledge of the particular circumstances of time and place, arguing that changing circumstances continually redefine the relative advantage of knowledge held by different individuals. According to Hayek (1945):

> The peculiar character of the problems of a rational economic order is determined precisely by the fact that the knowledge of the circumstances of which we must make use never exist in concentrated or integrated form, but solely as the dispersed bits of incomplete and frequently contradictory knowledge which all the separate individuals possess. The economic problem of society is thus not merely a problem of how to allocate "given" resources . . . it is a problem of the utilization of knowledge not given to anyone in its totality. (pp. 519–520)

Hayek posited that the function of the price mechanism is to communicate information and that the market is the process through which individual knowledge is mobilized socially. However, he failed to grasp the important role of the conversion of such context-specific knowledge, which is "tacit" in large part, into explicit knowledge. Despite his original intention to develop a dynamic theory of market as the continuous process of change, Hayek ended up with a "static" interpretation, arguing for simply the efficient "utilization" of "existing" knowledge.

Schumpeter, who developed a dynamic theory of economic change, was concerned primarily with the tentative and unfolding nature of the capitalist economy. According to Schumpeter, "Capitalism . . . is by nature a form or method of economic change and not only never is but never can be stationary" (1952, p. 82) and the fundamental impulse of capitalism development is "new combinations" (1951, p. 66). Schumpeter emphasized the importance of combining explicit knowledge. In fact, he pointed out that the emergence of new products, production methods, markets, materials, and organizations resulted from new "combinations" of knowledge. However, "combination" is only one mode of knowledge creation, as we will see in the next chapter.

The Firm as a Knowledge Repository: Penrose, Nelson, and Winter

While Schumpeter was primarily concerned with the process of change in the economy as a whole, Edith P. Penrose (1959) focused on the growth of individual firms. She viewed the firm as "both an administrative organization and a collection of productive resources, both human and material" (p. 31). According to Penrose, "it is never *resources* themselves that are the 'inputs' in the production process, but only the *services* that resources can render [italics in original]" (p. 25). Services are a function of the experience and knowledge accumulated within the firm, and thus firm specific. In essence, the firm is a repository of knowledge.

Moreover, Penrose (1959) considered the planning process as a central determinant of the growth of firms. She argued that corporate planners create "images" or mental models of the firm and its environment by appraising the firm's strengths and weaknesses in terms of its productive services and the environment's opportunities and constraints. And these images emerge from the experience and knowledge within the firm. Although Penrose pointed out the importance of experience and knowledge accumulated within the firm, she did not elaborate on the organizational mechanism or the process through which members of a firm can accumulate knowledge.

Nelson and Winter (1977, 1982) and Winter (1988) also viewed the firm as a repository of knowledge in their evolutionary theory of economic and technological change. Echoing the Hayekian view of knowledge, Winter (1988) argued as follows:

> Fundamentally, business firms are organizations that know how to do things. . . . In fact . . . a particular firm at a particular time is a repository for a quite specific range of productive knowledge, a range that often involves idiosyncratic features that distinguish it even from superficially similar firms in the same line(s) of business. (p. 175)

According to Nelson and Winter, such knowledge is stored as "regular and predictable behavioral patterns" of business firms, or what they called "routines" and equated with "genes." Innovation is an inherently unpredictable "mutation" of routines (1982, pp. 14–18). Nelson and Winter also devised a concept of "natural trajectory," a path of technological evolution that is decided by a "technology regime" broadly defined as "*cognitive beliefs* about what is feasible or at least worth attempting [italics added]" as well as technological imperatives (1982, pp. 258–259). Thus they recognized that the essence of technology is knowledge, but they did not explicitly link the creation of technological knowledge to broader organizational processes.

Knowledge in Management and Organization Theories

One of the reasons why economists have tended to focus on existing knowledge and to neglect the "active and subjective creation" of new knowledge by economic subjects may be found in the strong orientation toward the "scientification" of economics. Economists tend to accept the Cartesian view of knowledge that separates economic knowledge from the economic subject. While we find a similar trend in management theories, there is another strong orientation toward "humanization." This "humanistic" approach may have come from management researchers' strong interest in management practices, in contrast to economists' primary concern with the building of abstract models. Management literature in the past century can be divided along two developmental lines. On the one hand is the "scientific" line, from Taylor to Simon to contemporary preoccupation with the "scientification" of strategy. On the other hand is the "humanistic" line, from Mayo to Weick to recent attention to "organizational culture." In fact, the century-long history of management studies can be seen as a series of controversies between the two camps and unsuccessful attempts at a synthesis between them (e.g., Barnard, 1938), which seems to be very similar to the development process of Western philosophy discussed earlier.

"Scientific Management" vs. Human Relations Theory

Scientific management was founded by Frederick W. Taylor, who tried to eliminate the "soldiering" of workers and to replace "rules of thumb" with science, thereby increasing efficiency in production. He prescribed "scientific" methods and procedures to organize and operate work, the most important of which was time and motion study to find "the best method" for implementing a job. The "scientific management" was an attempt to formalize workers' experiences and tacit skills into objective and scientific knowledge. However, it failed to perceive the experiences and judgments of the workers as a source of new knowledge. Consequently, the creation of new work methods became the responsibility of managers only. Managers were shouldered with the chore of classifying, tabulating, and reducing the knowledge into rules and formulae and applying them to daily work (Taylor, 1911, p. 36).[33]

The rapid diffusion of scientific management gave rise to the human relations theory, which highlighted the importance of human factors in management. In the 1920s and 1930s, a group of management scholars at Harvard University, headed by George Elton Mayo, conducted a series of experiments at the Hawthorn plant of Western Electric. The so-called "Hawthorn experiments" showed that social factors such as morale, a "sense of belonging" to a work group, and interpersonal skills to understand human (especially group) behavior improved productivity (Roethlisberger and Dickson, 1939).[34]

Based on this finding, Mayo developed a new management theory of "human relations," in collaboration with F. J. Roethlisberger and others. They criticized the Taylorist view of management for treating the worker as an atomized "economic man," and argued that human beings are social animals who should be understood and treated in the context of the social group. Mayo (1933) contended that managers should develop "social human skills" to facilitate interpersonal communication within formal and informal groups of the work organization.

The human relations theory suggested that human factors played a significant role in raising productivity through the continuous improvement of practical knowledge held by workers on the shop floor. It did not develop clear-cut theoretical constructs that differentiated it from the Taylorist view. As a result, it was later absorbed into more "scientific" theories of human group and social interaction similar to Taylor's—such as group dynamics and operational behaviorism—that tended to treat human beings as stimulus-response machines with little capability of knowledge creation.

Barnard's Attempt at a Synthesis

Chester I. Barnard attempted to synthesize the management theories of the two camps—mechanistic rationality stressed by "scientific management" and the human factors highlighted by the human relations theory—at the organizational level. Barnard, who tried to build a science of organization based on his own experience as president of the New Jersey Bell Telephone Company, was one of the first to recognize clearly the importance of the organization in business management. Although knowledge was not a central issue in Barnard's management concept, his views of knowledge can be condensed into the following two points. First, knowledge consists not only of logical, linguistic content, but also of "behavioral," nonlinguistic content.[35] Second, leaders create values, beliefs, and ideas in order to maintain the soundness of knowledge system within the organization as well as to manage the organization as a cooperative system.

Barnard emphasized the importance of "behavioral knowledge" in the management processes, which is different from scientific knowledge. According to Barnard, leaders use both scientific knowledge obtained from logical mental processes and behavioral knowledge extracted from nonlogical mental processes. Barnard (1938) argued that the latter is more important for the following reason:

> The essential aspect of the executive process is the sensing of organization as a whole and the total situation relevant to it. It transcends the capability of merely intellectual methods, and the techniques of discriminating the factors of the situation. The terms pertinent to it are "feeling," "judgement," "sense," "proportion," "balance," and "appropriateness." It is a matter of art rather than science, and is aesthetic rather than logical. For this reason it is recognized rather than described and is known by its effects rather than by analysis. (p. 235)

The essence of the "problem of organizing," according to Barnard, is to transform the actors who strategically pursue mutually conflicting goals into a rational cooperative system. And knowledge is essential to securing cooperative rationality because of our limited capability to process information.

Barnard recognized the importance of the integration of the logical and nonlogical processes of human mental activity, of scientific and behavioral knowledge, and of the managerial and moral functions of executives. But since the creation of knowledge was not his central concern, Barnard's treatment of the executive's role in creating knowledge was rather general, leaving the organizational process of knowledge creation largely unexplained.[36] The important questions concerning how to convert organizational members' implicit, behavioral knowledge into organizational knowledge and how best to implement this knowledge in acting on the environment remained unanswered by Barnard's analysis of the organization.

Simon's Information-Processing Paradigm

The Barnardian attempt to synthesize the scientific and humanistic views of management laid the foundation of organization theory. Inspired by Barnard's insights on the importance of the role of executive managers in the organization, Herbert Simon saw the essential function of executives as that of decision making. Strongly influenced by the development of the computer and cognitive science, Simon investigated the nature of human problem solving and decision making and developed a view of organization as an "information-processing machine."

The task Simon undertook in *Administrative Behavior* (1945) and *Organizations* (1958) (coauthored with J. March) was to build a scientific theory of problem solving and decision making based on the assumption that human cognitive capacity is inherently limited. In other words, he contended that we have only a limited ability to process information over a short period of time. Using this concept of "bounded rationality," Simon built a computer model of the human thought process as a form of information processing. According to this model, human beings act as information-processing systems that extract "meaning structures" from information inputs through sensory organs, and store these meaning structures as new knowledge or use them in deciding courses of action. It is knowledge that selects a limited number of, or ideally a single set of, consequences correlated with each strategy from all possible consequences. Simon further argued that the basic features of organizational structure and function are derived from the characteristics of human problem-solving processes and rational choices. Thus, Simon (1973) concluded that an organization facing a complex environment should design itself in a way that minimizes the need for information distribution among its units, in order to reduce the information load on them.

Simon, however, overemphasized the logical aspect of the human reasoning and of organizational decision-making processes, and the limitations of human cognitive capacity. He attempted to formalize information and knowledge by disregarding the "nonlinguistic mental process" or "behavioral knowledge" discussed by Barnard and the "tacit knowledge" emphasized by Polanyi (1966).[37] For Simon, implicit knowledge is nothing more than noise, and the logical content of human reasoning and decision making is far more important than such things as value and meaning. Nor did he pay sufficient attention to the role of the ambiguity and diversity that resides in a problem, or to the importance of redundancy of information in the organization. Simon argued that effective information processing was possible only when complex problems were simplified and only when organizational structures were specialized so that units did not have any unnecessary interaction with each other. This Cartesian-like rationalist view led him to neglect the human potential for creating knowledge both at the individual and organizational levels; he failed to see human beings as those who actively discover problems and create knowledge to solve them.

In addition, Simon viewed the organization's relation to its environment as passive. He argued that the business organization reacts to the environment mainly by adjusting the information-processing structure. What he missed was the proactive aspect of the organization's action on the environment. The organization acting on the environment not only performs effective information processing but also creates information and knowledge by itself. This process involves not merely a strategy of reducing the information-processing burden; it also requires the organization to evolve itself by amplifying its own diversity, destroying the existing patterns of thought and behavior, and creating new patterns.

Garbage Can Model and the Theory of Sensemaking

The Simonian paradigm was challenged by the "garbage can model" of organization proposed by Cohen, March, and Olsen (1972) and March and Olsen (1976), who emphasized the irrational and ambiguous nature of human problem solving and decision making. They argued that an organization is a collection of choices looking for problems, issues and feelings seeking decision situations in which they may be aired, solutions searching for issues to which they may be the answer, and decision makers looking for work (Cohen, March, and Olsen 1972, p. 2).

In this model, selection opportunities are equated with "garbage," and problems, solutions, and decision makers with "garbage can." This model also characterizes the organization as a system of perception that assigns meaning to what happened retrospectively, rather than as a system of planning and deductive decision making. In contrast with choice theories dominant in economics and decision science, March (1978) argued that preferences may emerge as a consequence of action rather than guiding such action a priori, an argument consonant with Karl Weick's (1969) discussion of retrospective rationality.

The garbage can model noted the role of ambiguity or disorder in the organization, but contained no valid insight on the learning that takes place among individuals and organizations. The model did not throw light on the importance of active knowledge creation within an organization and neglected to integrate organizational behavior with systematic organizational learning. If learning takes place only at the individual level, as March and Olsen (1976) indicated, the learner would produce knowledge only on a limited range of activity, and the resulting knowledge could be relevant only to those who produced it. An organizational knowledge base could hardly emerge because of the difficulty of establishing links among the knowledge produced by different individuals. In addition, the model assumed that individuals involved in organizational learning hit on relevant ideas more or less randomly. When they do, and when they can manage to establish a case of cause and effect, organizational knowledge may increase. Such a very limited view of organizational learning cannot provide a basis for describing a systematic organizational learning process (Duncan and Weiss, 1979, p. 90).

The view of knowledge underlying the garbage can model can also be found in Weick's theory of organizational "sensemaking." According to Weick (1993):

> The basic idea of sensemaking is that reality is an ongoing accomplishment that emerges from efforts to create order and make retrospective sense of what occurs. . . . Sensemaking emphasizes that people try to make things rationally accountable to themselves and others. (p. 635)

Weick viewed the organization in terms of cycles of structured behaviors, which can be better expressed by the term "organizing" (Weick, 1969, 1979). He argued that shared information and meaning become structured in organizations as well as in behaviors. It is through the development of shared meaning and understanding that the cycles of structured behaviors themselves become sensible and meaningful. Organized actions occur in the face of various interpretations and dissensions around one dimension of meaning, as long as there is consensus around another (Fiol, forthcoming). Reaching convergence among members characterizes the act of organizing (Weick, 1969) and enables the organization to interpret the convergence as a system (Daft and Weick, 1984). Weick (1969) also emphasized the importance of the "enactment" of organizations on their environment. From our perspective, however, Weick's view is still passive and lacks a proactive view of organization that includes a notion of "creative chaos" that is critical to the process of organizational knowledge creation.

Science of Business Strategy

While the Simonian scientific view of organization as information-processing machine was challenged by the humanistic view that sees organization as the process of sensemaking and nonrational decision making, another debate between the scientific and humanistic views of management has taken place between theories of strategic management and organizational culture. The scientification of business strategy started from the concept of the "experience curve effect" that was suggested by the Boston Consulting Group (BCG). In the 1960s, management scholars and consultants argued that business strategy should not be concerned merely with production cost but with total cost.[38] To cut total cost quickly, they argued that a firm should produce as much as possible and increase market share. BCG refined this idea into a strategic planning technique called Product Portfolio Management (PPM), a system in which the flow of funds for a product or a business is determined by a combination of market growth rate and relative market share.[39]

Another technique called Profit Impact of Marketing Strategy (PIMS) was created in 1960 by a project team at General Electric (GE) to find better methods of explaining and forecasting business results.

The PIMS model (Buzzell and Gale, 1987) was based on factors that had contributed to higher return on investment (ROI) rates in many of GE's markets or businesses.

Porter (1980) developed a framework for understanding how firms create and sustain competitive advantage. He argued that a firm had to make two choices with regard to competitive strategy: (1) industry attractiveness and (2) competitive positioning within an industry. To analyze the attractiveness of an industry, Porter devised the famous "five-forces" model, which provided an understanding of the structure of an industry and how it is changing by examining five competitive forces (entry barriers, bargaining power of buyers, bargaining power of suppliers, threat of substitute products or services, and rivalry among existing competitors). Porter (1985) proposed another framework called the "value chain" model to analyze the sources of competitive advantage. The value chain is a systematic theory of examining all the activities a firm performs and how they are linked with each other.

The techniques and frameworks developed in the field of strategy implicitly assumed the importance of strategic knowledge, but it is unrealistic to expect the notion of knowledge creation to come up in this field. The major limitations of the view of knowledge in the science of strategy can be summarized by the following three points. First, the science of business strategy is not able to deal with questions of value and belief and has precluded the possibility of the creation of knowledge or vision from its theoretical domain. The preoccupation with explicit information makes researchers ignore the creation of a new vision or value system.[40] Second, the science of strategy presupposes the top-down style of management, in which only top management is assumed to think or manipulate existing explicit knowledge. A huge amount of tacit knowledge held by all other organizational members tends to be unutilized. Third, prevailing strategic management concepts do not pay due attention to the role of knowledge as a source of competitiveness. As society is becoming more knowledge based, the lack of attention to knowledge weakens the otherwise strong appeal of this approach.

In sum, the view of knowledge in the science of strategy is similar to that of Taylorism. Emphasis is put on logical and analytical (i.e., deductive or inductive) thinking as well as on the use of existing explicit knowledge at the top of the organization. Unquantifiable human factors, such as values, meanings, and experiences, are excluded from formal business planning and deployment of strategic resources.[41] As we will see below, this lack of attention to the human aspect of knowledge was supplemented by studies on "organizational culture" similarly to the way that the human relations theory supplemented "scientific management."

Studies of Organizational Culture

Many Western firms preoccupied with the "scientific," quantitative approach to strategy making and inflicted with the "analysis paralysis" syndrome began to lose their dynamism and competitiveness in the early 1980s. In response to the demand for an alternative to the "scientific" approach, Peters and Waterman (1982) proposed a "humanistic" approach to management. They observed that "excellent companies" had made a variety of efforts to promote the sharing of values among employees. Each excellent company has created its own unique "corporate culture," which determines how a company thinks and behaves.

Schein (1985) argued, "There has to have been enough *shared experience* to have led to a *shared view,* and this shared view has to have worked for long enough to have come to be taken for granted and to have dropped out of awareness. Culture, in this sense, is a learned product of *group experience* [italics added]" (p. 7).[42] He defined culture as "a pattern of basic assumptions—invented, discovered, or developed by a given group as it learns to cope with its problems of external adaptation and internal integration—that has worked well enough to be considered valid and therefore, to be taught to new members as the correct way to perceive, think, and feel in relation to those problems" (p. 9).[43] Pfeffer (1981), on the other hand, stressed the importance of beliefs. He considered organizations as "systems of shared meanings and beliefs, in which a critical administrative activity involves the construction and maintenance of belief systems which assure continued compliance, commitment, and positive effect on the part of participants" (p. 1). Thus, organizational culture can be seen as consisting of beliefs and knowledge shared by members of the organization.[44]

Studies of organizational culture have been able to shed light on the organization as an epistemological system. In addition, they have underscored the importance of such human factors as values, meanings, commitments, symbols, and beliefs, and paved the way for more elaborate research on the tacit aspect of knowledge. Furthermore, they have recognized that the organization, as a shared meaning system, can learn, change itself, and evolve over time through the social interaction among its members and between itself and the environment.

While the studies of organizational culture have recognized the importance of knowledge, they have not given it its due place. From our point of view, there seem to be three common shortcomings with this line of research. First, most of these studies have not paid enough attention to the potential and creativity of human beings. Second, the human being, in most cases, is seen as an information processor, not as an information creator. And third, the organization is portrayed as rather passive in its relation to the environment, neglecting its potential to change and to create.

Toward a New Synthesis

Barnard attempted to synthesize scientific and humanistic views of knowledge. Two camps subsequently pursued divergent paths, with the scientific approach further advanced by the information-processing paradigm and the science of strategy, and the humanistic approach by the garbage can model, the theory of organizational sensemaking, and studies of organizational culture. But since the mid-1980s, a new attempt at synthesizing the scientific and humanistic approaches has appeared along three strands of literature. They consist of: (1) conjectures about the "knowledge society"; (2) theories of organizational learning; and (3) resource-based (core-competence or core-capability) approaches to strategic management.

Drucker on the Knowledge Society

Of course, society has been subject to continual change and evolution over time. The manufacturing-based industrial society of the postwar period has evolved more and more into a service society,[45] and more recently into the so-called information society. According to the leading management thinkers, the manufacturing, service, and information sectors will be based on knowledge in the coming age, and business organizations will evolve into knowledge creators in many ways.

Peter Drucker is one of the earliest thinkers who noticed a sign of this great transformation. He coined the terms "knowledge work" or "knowledge worker" around 1960 (Drucker, 1993, p. 5). According to his most recent book, *Post-Capitalist Society* (1993), we are entering "the knowledge society," in which "the basic economic resource" is no longer capital, or natural resources, or labor, but "is and will be knowledge," and where "knowledge workers" will play a central role (p. 7).

Drucker (1993) suggested that one of most important challenges for every organization in the knowledge society is to build systematic practices for managing a self-transformation. The organization has to be prepared to abandon knowledge that has become obsolete and learn to create new things through: (1) continuing improvement of every activity; (2) development of new applications from its own successes; and (3) continuous innovation as an organized process. Drucker (1991) also points out that an organization has to raise productivity of knowledge and service workers in order to meet the challenge:

> The single greatest challenge facing managers in the developed countries of the world is to raise the productivity of knowledge and service workers. This challenge, which will dominate the management agenda for the next several decades, will ultimately determine the competitive performance of

companies. Even more important, it will determine the very fabric of society and the quality of life in every industrialized nation. (p. 69)

Drucker (1993) seems to have recognized the importance of tacit knowledge when he argues that a skill (*techne* in Greek) "could not be explained in words, whether spoken or written. It could only be demonstrated," and therefore "the only way to learn a techne was through apprenticeship and experience" (p. 24). At the same time, Drucker believes that such methodologies as scientific and quantitative methods can convert "*ad hoc* experience into system . . . anecdotes into information, and skill into something that can be taught and learned" (p. 42). He does not argue for the need of human interaction in the knowledge-conversion process, or of knowledge sharing among a group of persons. He may thus be closer to the "scientific" camp than to the "humanistic" camp at heart.

Organizational Learning

The need for organizations to change continuously, which was emphasized by Drucker, has long been the central concern of organizational learning theorists.[46] Just as with individuals, organizations must always confront novel aspects of their circumstances (Cohen and Sproull, 1991). The need is growing in this era of turbulent economy and accelerated technological change. It is widely agreed that learning consists of two kinds of activity. The first kind of learning is obtaining know-how in order to solve specific problems based upon existing premises. The second kind of learning is establishing new premises (i.e., paradigms, schemata, mental models, or perspectives) to override the existing ones. These two kinds of learning have been referred to as "Learning I" and "Learning II" (Bateson, 1973) or "single-loop learning" and "double-loop learning" (Argyris and Schön, 1978). From our viewpoint, the creation of knowledge certainly involves interaction between these two kinds of learning, which forms a kind of dynamic spiral.

Senge (1990) recognized that many organizations suffer from "learning disabilities." To cure the diseases and enhance the organization's capacity to learn, he proposed the "learning organization" as a practical model. He argued that the learning organization has the capacity for both generative learning (i.e., active) and adaptive learning (i.e., passive) as the sustainable sources of competitive advantage. According to Senge, managers must do the following in order to build a learning organization: (1) adopt "systems thinking"; (2) encourage "personal mastery" of their own lives; (3) bring prevailing "mental models" to the surface and challenge them; (4) build "a shared vision"; and (5) facilitate "team learning."

Among these five "disciplines," Senge (1990) emphasized the importance of "systems thinking" as "the discipline that integrates the disciplines, fusing them into a coherent body of theory and practice" (p. 12). He also suggested that systems thinking is "a philosophical alternative to the pervasive 'reductionism' in Western culture—the pursuit of simple answers to complex issues" (p. 185). He argues:

> At the heart of a learning organization is a shift of mind—from seeing ourselves as separate from the world to connected to the world, from seeing problems as caused by someone or something "out there" to seeing how our own actions create the problems we experience. A learning organization is a place where people are continually discovering how they create their reality. And how they can change it. (pp. 12–13)

Senge may not have intended to build a new synthesis between scientific and humanistic approaches to management, but he seems to be trying to overcome the Cartesian dualism. He says that "Systems thinking may hold a key to integrating reason and intuition" (p. 168) and that systems thinking fuses the five disciplines "into a coherent body of theory and practice" (p. 12). Judging from the entire argument of his book, more specifically from such terms as "mental models," "a shared vision," "team learning," and the above quotation, his practical model of "learning organization" has some affinity with our theory of knowledge creation, which we will present in the next chapter. However, he rarely uses the word "knowledge" and does not present any ideas on how knowledge can be created.

Despite the affinity with our own thinking, there are some critical limitations often found in the literature on "organizational learning." First, as seen in Senge (1990), organizational learning theories basically lack "the view that knowledge development constitutes learning" (Weick, 1991, p. 122). Most of them are trapped in a behavioral concept of "stimulus-response." Second, most of them still use the metaphor of individual learning (Weick, 1991; Dodgson, 1993). In the accumulation of over 20 years of studies, they have not developed a comprehensive view on what constitutes "organizational" learning. Third, there is widespread agreement that organizational learning is an adaptive change process that is influenced by past experience, focused on developing or modifying routines, and supported by organizational memory.[47] As a result, the theories fail to conceive an idea of knowledge creation.[48] The fourth limitation is related to the concept of "double-loop learning" or "unlearning" (Hedberg, 1981) as well as to a strong orientation toward organizational development, which we will discuss below.

Following the development of Argyris and Schön's (1978) theory of organizational learning, it has been widely assumed implicitly or explicitly that double-loop learning—the questioning and rebuilding of existing perspectives, interpretation frameworks, or decision premises—can be very difficult for organizations to implement by themselves. In order to overcome this difficulty, the learning theorists argue that some kind of artificial intervention, such as the use of an organizational development program, is required. The limitation of this argument is that it assumes that someone inside or outside an organization "objectively" knows the right time and method for putting double-loop learning into practice. A Cartesian-like view of organization lies behind this assumption. Seen from the vantage point of organizational knowledge creation, double-loop learning is not a special, difficult task but a daily activity for the organization. Organizations continuously create new knowledge by reconstructing existing perspectives, frameworks, or premises on a daily basis. In other words, the capacity for double-loop learning is built into the knowledge-creating organization without the unrealistic assumption of the existence of a "right" answer.

A New Resource-Based Approach to Strategy

A new paradigm of corporate strategy, which we call the "resource-based approach," has emerged to help companies compete more effectively in the ever-changing and globalizing environment of the 1990s. In contrast to the structural approach, which we discussed under the science of strategy, the new approach sees competencies, capabilities, skills, or strategic assets as the source of sustainable competitive advantage for the firm. The literature on the resource-based approach to competitive strategy has been increasing in recent years,[49] with Prahalad and Hamel's (1990) article on "core competence" and Stalk, Evans, and Shulman's (1992) article on "capabilities-based competition" representing the field. Conceptually, the new approach is rooted in Penrose's (1959) theory of the firm, which we discussed earlier.

Proponents of the resource-based approach contend that the competitive environment of the 1990s has changed dramatically, making the structural approach, represented by Porter's competitive-forces framework, obsolete. Stalk, Evans, and Shulman (1992) observed as follows:

> When the economy was relatively static, strategy could afford to be static. In a world characterized by durable products, stable consumer needs, well-defined national and regional markets, and clearly identified competitors, competition was a "war of position" in which companies occupied competitive space like squares on a chessboard. . . .
>
> Competition is now a "war of movement" in which success depends on anticipation of market trends and quick response to changing customer needs. Successful competitors move quickly in and out of products, markets, and sometimes even entire businesses—a process more akin to an interactive video game than to chess. In such an environment, the essence of strategy is *not* the structure of a company's products and markets but the dynamics of its behavior [italics in original]. (p. 62)

The dynamic nature of strategy was also emphasized by Teece, Pisano, and Shuen (1991), who developed the concept of "dynamic *capabilities,*" or the "ability of an organization to learn, adapt, change, and renew over time," which "involves search, problem finding, and problem solving (at the organizational level)" (p. 20). Prahalad and Hamel (1990) provided a similar but less dynamic definition of core competence: "the collective learning in the organization, especially how to coordinate diverse production skills and integrate multiple streams of technologies" (p. 82).

As the above definitions show, the distinction between core competence and capabilities has not been clear. Both concepts emphasize "behavioral" aspects of strategy, namely "how" a company chooses to compete rather than "where" it chooses to compete. But whereas Prahalad and Hamel (1990) focused on corporatewide technologies and production skills that underlie a company's myriad product lines in defining core competence, Stalk, Evans, and Shulman (1992) took a broader view of the skill base and focused on business processes, which encompass the entire value chain, in defining capabilities.

Prahalad and Hamel (1990) referred to the following examples to illustrate the importance of corporatewide technologies and production skills in gaining competitive advantage:

> In NEC, digital technologies, especially VLSI and systems integration skills, are fundamental. In the core competence underlying them, disparate businesses become coherent. It is Honda's core competence in engines and power trains that gives it a distinctive advantage in car, motorcycle, lawn mower, and generator businesses. Canon's core competencies in optics, imaging, and microprocessor controls have enabled it to enter, even dominate, markets as seemingly diverse as copiers, laser printers, cameras, and image scanners. (p. 83)

According to Stalk, Evans, and Shulman (1992), however, it is broader skills that can transform a company's key business processes into strategic capabilities, thereby leading to competitive success. Taking Honda as an example, they point out that the innovative designs of its products or the way they were manufactured are not the only factors underlying Honda's success. They believe that the company's ability to train and support its dealer network with operating procedures and policies for merchandising, selling, floor planning, and service management—its expertise in the "dealer management" process—is equally as important. This expertise, which was first developed for its motorcycle business, has since been replicated in lawn mowers, outboard motors, and automobiles.

Despite this distinction, there are a number of similarities between Prahalad and Hamel and Stalk, Evans, and Shulman. First, both groups of authors make extensive use of Japanese companies as case studies of exemplary behavior, as shown above. Second, they both observe that larger companies today are suffering from the "tyranny" of the strategic business unit (SBU) and need to overcome it by developing corporatewide or organizational skills in moving competencies or capabilities from one business unit to another. Third, they both believe that the process of identifying and building competencies or capabilities involves a top-down process, with the CEO and top management playing the key role. And finally, they both contend that competitive advantage should be found in resources and skills "inside" the company, as opposed to the market environment "outside" the company, as in the structural approach.

At first glance, these characteristics may give the impression that our theory of organizational knowledge creation resembles the resource-based view of strategy. Indeed, both are concerned with (1) how innovation takes place, (2) how Japanese companies have gained competitive advantage, (3) organizational skills rather than individual skills, (4) the role of top management as a key player, and (5) what takes place inside the company. But there are several fundamental differences between our theory and the resource-based approach to strategy.

First, while we are explicitly concerned with *knowledge,* Prahalad and Hamel and Stalk, Evans, and Shulman treat knowledge only implicitly. Although several authors have recently incorporated the notion of knowledge into the resource-based approach,[50] the focus is still blurred because of the lack of agreed-upon and well-defined definitions of terms. According to Teece, Pisano, and Shuen (1991): "There remains a substantial level of ambiguity surrounding such terms as resources, capabilities, skills . . . and the conceptual framework is overdetermined in that there are too many competing explanations for the phenomena identified" (pp. 17–18).

Second, although Prahalad and Hamel and Stalk, Evans, and Shulman make extensive use of Japanese case examples, these examples do not shed much light on how the companies actually went about *building* core competence or capabilities. In contrast, our primary research interest is in how Japanese companies go about creating knowledge organizationally. We will discuss the knowledge-creation process in the next chapter and then identify the management process and the organizational structure most conducive to the process in later chapters. Our in-depth field research of selected Japanese companies provides a unique inside look at how Japanese companies actually go about the knowledge-creation process.

Third, regarding middle managers, Stalk, Evans, and Shulman (1992) argue as follows: "Because capabilities are cross-functional, the change process [associated with building capabilities] can't be left to middle managers. It requires the hands-on guidance of the CEO and the active involvement of top line managers" (p. 65). Prahalad and Hamel (1990) also assign the key role of identifying, developing, and managing competencies or capabilities to top management; the responsibilities of middle managers and front-line workers are not made clear in their approach. In contrast, middle managers play a key role in our theory, acting as "knowledge engineers" within the company. They function as facilitators of knowledge creation, involving top management and front-line workers in a management process we call "middle-up-down" management (more on this topic in Chapter 5).

And finally, the resource-based approach has not yet reached the stage of being able to build a comprehensive theoretical framework. Our intent in this book is to build a new theory, something Porter was able to do in the field of strategy. We will progress a step at a time, identifying elements of knowledge creation, building an interactive model, and eventually coming up with a dynamic model that incorporates three different dimensions—epistemological, ontological, and temporal. What is missing in the resource-based approach is a comprehensive framework that shows how various parts within the organization interact with each other over time to create something new and unique.

Need for the Theory of Organizational Knowledge Creation

In this chapter we have critically reviewed the major economic, management, and organization theories. We have found a paradox in that most of these theories scarcely mention knowledge itself, while they supposedly pursue scientific, objective knowledge under the strong influence of the Western epistemological tradition. Even though many of the new management theories since the mid-1980s have pointed to the importance of knowledge to society and organizations in the coming era, there are very few studies on how knowledge is created within and between business organizations. At the core of concern of these theories is the acquisition, accumulation, and utilization of *existing* knowledge; they lack the perspective of "creating new knowledge." This may be due to the fact that they have not followed modern and contemporary philosophical discussions on how the Cartesian dualism between subject and object or body and mind can be transcended. The subjective, bodily, and tacit aspects of knowledge are still largely neglected. Recent studies on product development (Davis, 1986; von Hippel, 1994) have begun to shed light on the tacitness of knowledge, but their primary research interest is still focused on the transfer or articulation of tacit knowledge for information sharing, particularly in the product development process. As a result, the creation of explicit knowledge from tacit knowledge is still beyond their reach.

Organizations deal with uncertain environments not merely through passive adaptation, but through active interaction. Organizations can transform themselves. Yet, many existing views of organization are passive and static. The organization that wishes to cope dynamically with the changing environment needs to be one that creates information and knowledge, not merely processes them efficiently. Furthermore, the organizational members must not be passive, but must rather be active agents of innovation. As we will see in the next chapter, our view of the organization is one in which the organization re-creates itself by destroying the existing knowledge system and then innovating new ways of thinking and doing things.

Simon (1986) once criticized Barnard for being too preoccupied with strategic factors and thus failing to provide a "general treatment of the design process." He continued:

> A major target for research in organizations today is to understand how organizations acquire new products, new methods of manufacture and marketing, and new organizational forms. This is the unfinished business that Chester Barnard has left for us. (p. 16)

Understanding how organizations create new products, new methods, and new organizational forms is important. A more fundamental need is to understand how organizations create new knowledge that makes such creations possible. This is the unfinished business that Herbert Simon has left for us. In the next chapter we will embark upon this challenging task.

Notes

1. For the history of Western epistemology, see Russell (1961, 1989), Moser and Nat (1987), and Jordan (1987); for a review of contemporary epistemology, see Ayer (1984) and Dancy (1985).

2. In traditional epistemological accounts, knowledge must satisfy the following conditions. In order for individual A to have knowledge of something (that is, a proposition, hereafter P), the following are necessary and sufficient conditions of A's knowledge of P:

    (a) P is true (the truth condition);
    (b) A must believe that P is true (the belief condition); and
    (c) A's belief that P is true must be justified (the justification condition).

According to the first truth condition, an individual's knowledge of something does not exist unless its proposition is true. Therefore, a statement like "I know P, but P is not true" is simply self-contradictory. A true proposition describes reality, which is true in the past, the present, and the future.

The belief condition requires not only that a statement must be true, but also that we must believe that the statement is true. While the truth condition is an objective requirement, the belief condition is a subjective requirement. Therefore, when we claim the knowledge of P, we must assume a certain attitude toward P. Assuming an attitude toward P means that we believe in P. Nevertheless, believing P is not a defining characteristic of P's being true. It is possible to say that "I believe in P, but P is not true"; yet the proposition "I know P is true, but I do not believe P is true" is a self-contradiction. In short, knowledge contains belief, but belief does not contain knowledge.

The justification condition calls for evidence for proving the truthfulness of knowledge. Belief, which reveals an attitude toward P, does not justify P itself; it needs evidence of truth. Belief formed without valid evidence does not constitute knowledge, even though it could happen to be true in some circumstances.

3. The famous "Gettier counter-examples" provide a good case in point. Suppose one holds a belief grounded in valid assumptions. Despite the fact that the belief could be wrong in reality, it could give birth to another belief that is true. Based upon this observation, Gettier noted that a wrong belief that satisfies the above three conditions cannot produce knowledge. This is an important criticism of the imperfect nature of the mainstream conception of knowledge.

4. Western epistemology has been loaded with contending arguments about three major problems: (1) the nature of knowledge; (2) the origin of knowledge; and (3) the reliability of knowledge.

5. His epistemology was partly derived from previous philosophers, particularly from Parmenides—the belief that reality is eternal and therefore all changes must be illusory; from Heraclitus—the doctrine that there is nothing permanent in the sensible world; and from his mentor Socrates—the theory of "idea" or "form."

6. Plato, *Phaedo,* 65e, in *Plato I,* trans. H. N. Fowler (Cambridge, Mass.: Harvard University Press, The Loeb Classical Library, 1953), p. 229.

7. Aristotle, *Analytica Posteriora,* II 19 (100a), from *The Oxford Translation of Aristotle,* Vol. 1, trans. G. R. G. Mure, ed. W. D. Ross (Oxford: Oxford University Press, 1928); quoted by Moser and Nat (1987), p. 59, and by Jordan (1987), p. 136.

8. It should be noted that while Aristotle's argument is empiricistic, he has been considered the authority on logic or rational reasoning. Moser and Nat (1987) considered Aristotle a rationalist, emphasizing that knowledge about the "forms" and their relationships can be acquired only by rational reasoning (p. 17).

9. Among others, St. Augustine was a rationalist influenced by Plato and held that "the sensible world is inferior to the eternal" (Russell, 1961, p. 356). Disliking Platonism in St. Augustine, St. Thomas Aquinas became an ardent follower of Aristotle, i.e., an empiricist (ibid., p. 445). Taking the middle course between Plato and Aristotle, William of Occam, a Franciscan philosopher, argued that abstract knowledge presupposes perception or intuitive knowledge, which is caused by individual things (ibid., p. 464).

10. René Descartes, *Discourses on the Methods,* trans. E. S. Haldane and G. R. T. Ross, in *The Philosophical Works of Descartes,* Vol. 1 (Cambridge: Cambridge University Press, 1911), p. 92.

11. John Locke, *An Essay Concerning Human Understanding,* Book II: i, 3–4; quoted by Moser and Nat (1987), p. 133.

12. Immanuel Kant, *Critique of Pure Reason,* trans. Norman Kemp Smith (New York: St. Martin's Press, 1965), p. 41.

13. Marx was strongly influenced by "dialectical materialism" of Ludwig A. Feuerbach, a critical student of Hegel, who contended that the physical and material life of human beings determines human consciousness and thought, thus denying Hegel's idea that the mind is the source and reality of the world.

14. For Husserl's phenomenological method, see Part I of his *Ideas: General Introduction to Pure Phenomenology,* trans. W. R. Royce Gibson (London: Allen and Unwin, 1931).

15. Martin Heidegger, *Being and Time,* trans. John Macquarrie and Edward Robinson (Oxford: Basil Blackwell, 1962), pp. 83, 99.

16. Jean-Paul Sartre, *Being and Nothingness,* trans. H. E. Barnes (New York: Philosophical Library, 1956), p. lxvi.

17. Maurice Merleau-Ponty, *Phenomenology of Perception,* trans. Colin Smith (London: Routledge and Kegan Paul, 1962), p. 137.

18. Ibid., pp. 21–22.

19. Ludwig Wittgenstein, *The Blue and Brown Books* (Oxford: Basil Blackwell, 1958), p. 150.

20. Chohmin Nakae, a liberal thinker who led the "freedom and people's right movement" in the Meiji era (1868–1912), once lamented, "Japan has never created any philosophy since its foundation" (quoted in Nakamura, 1967, p. 174).

21. The earliest extant collection of poetry, compiled ca. A.D. 770.

22. One of the most distinguished Japanese novels, written by Lady Murasaki in ca. A.D. 1010.

23. The first official collection of Japanese poetry, compiled by the order of Emperor Daigo in ca. A.D. 905.

24. Nakamura's criticism against the Japanese intellectual tradition is based on his study of modern French philosophy.

25. Thus Nitobe (1899) lamented: "Our lack of abstruse philosophy—while some of our young men have already gained international reputation in scientific researches, no one has achieved anything in philosophical lines—is traceable to the neglect of metaphysical training under Bushido regimen of education" (p. 176).

26. Quoted by Yuasa (1987), p. 65. While Nishida borrowed the term "pure experience" from psychological philosophies of Wilhelm Wundt and William James, he criticized their philosophical expression of "pure experience" and reconceptualized it by shifting the basis of metaphysics from speculation to factuality. In the introduction of the English language edition (1990) of Nishida's *An Inquiry into the Good,* Masao Abe summarized Nishida's criticism as follows: "they (Wundt and James) grasp pure experience not from within but from without, thus missing the true reality of pure experience. To see it from without means to analyze the concrete, dynamic whole of pure experience into abstract psychological elements like perception, feeling, and representation, and then to reconstruct them. In this explanation, living individual experience is generalized . . . true pure experience is . . . direct to the subject. But in the . . . psychological philosophies (of Wundt and James), the observed consciousness and the observing consciousness stand dualistically opposed" (p. xv).

27. Varela, Thompson, and Rosch (1991) argued, "From Descartes on, the guiding question in Western philosophy has been whether body and mind are one or two distinct substances (properties, levels of description, etc.) and what the ontological relation between them is. . . . Descartes's conclusion that he was a thinking thing was the product of his question, and that question was a product of specific practices—those of disembodied, unmindful reflection" (p. 28).

28. Nishida (1990) also asserted that "scientific truth cannot be considered perfect truth" (p.26). It is, however, the Western orientation toward rigorous questioning and doubting that gave birth to modern science.

29. Kumakura (1990), pp. 64–65. Pascale and Athos (1981) observed as follows: "In the Japanese language, verbs appear at the ends of sentences, so the listener doesn't know where the speaker is headed until he gets there. The speaker can change his verbs in response to the listener's expression. So pronounced, in fact, is their desire for concurrence that the Japanese sometimes avoid the definitiveness of verbs altogether. The listener's receptivity or hesitancy in responding to a few key nouns sets the stage for a choreography of consensus. The Japanese employ open discussions with generalities that leave room for movement and compromise. They have nineteen ways of saying no— suggestive of the extreme finesse with which their language navigates the shoals of conflict, avoiding it if possible" (p. 98).

30. According to Penrose (1959), "Economists have, of course, always recognized the dominant role that increasing knowledge plays in economic process but have, for the most part, found the whole subject of knowledge too slippery to handle" (p. 77). Finally, however, some economists started building the economics of knowledge in the form of growth theory. Examples include Romer (1986, 1990a, 1990b) of the University of California, Berkeley.

31. For a review of economic thought from the viewpoint of knowledge, see Fransman (1993). Our argument concerning knowledge in economic theories draws partly on this paper.

32. Marshall was aware of the contradiction between the increasing fragmentation of knowledge implied by the process of the division of labor and the need for the integration of this knowledge. He thus identified a number of different forms of organization that aid the development and use of knowledge.

33. It should be noted that Taylor himself had a humanitarian interest in workers' fair wages and productive development. In practice, however, techniques he and his followers developed to increase labor productivity were often misused, with dehumanizing effects on workers.

34. This kind of phenomenon, which arises from persons being noticed, has become known as the "Hawthorn effect."

35. Barnard (1938) divided mental processes into logical and nonlogical processes. Logical processes refer to the conscious thinking or reasoning process that can be expressed in terms of words and signals. Nonlogical processes involve inexpressible mental processes such as judgments, decisions, or actions in practical affairs. These processes are unconscious, and behavioral knowledge stems from them. He argued that the words and signals, even though they are correct, constitute only the top layer of the huge system of human knowledge, given that human rationality is incomplete itself (p. 303). These nonlogical processes are essential even in the most rigorous scientific work (pp. 303–306).

36. According to Levitt and March (1990), Barnard did not attempt to define exactly what these nonlogical processes consist of, but one thing he had in mind was "the coding of experience and knowledge"; Barnard described the advantages and limitations of nonlogical processes, and some circumstances in which such nonlogical "good judgment" or "good sense" had an advantage over rationality (p. 14).

37. For this very reason, Barnard found Simon's decision-making process too mathematical and called attention to the importance of nonlogical mental processes.

38. From its analysis of thousands of products, BCG found that total cost depended on empirical observations regarding the marginal reduction of costs.

39. The PPM technique was later expanded to include organization and human resource aspects in the deployment of resources. As such, "strategic management" came to include a wide variety of areas including the functions, goals, strategies, structure, and control systems of the business organization.

40. As a counter argument, Ohmae (1982) stressed the importance of insight in business strategy. He argued that insight contains creativity and from time to time involves the breakdown of the status quo. Therefore, the plans that stem from insight cannot be "analyzed" in quantitative terms. In a similar vein, Tregoe et al. (1989) highlighted the role of vision in the establishment of long-term plans, which is usually missing from theories preoccupied with the immediateness of activity.

41. Mintzberg (1994) criticized three assumptions of strategic planning as fundamental fallacies: (1) formalization that assumes systems can make strategy better than human beings; (2) detachment that assumes thought, strategy, ostensible thinkers, and strategists should be detached from action, operations, real doers, and the objects of their strategies; and (3) predetermination that assumes the process of strategy making and strategies themselves can be predetermined because context of strategy making is predictable.

42. Traditionally, anthropologists and sociologists view culture as webs of meaning, organized in terms of symbols and other ways of representation. They see human beings as makers of meaning, creating their world through symbols.

43. According to Schein (1985), moreover, a key part of every culture is a set of assumptions about what is "real," how one determines or discovers what is real, and "how members of a group take an action, how they determine what is relevant information, and when they have enough of it to determine whether to act and what to do" (p. 89).

44. From our viewpoint, culture is important to organizational knowledge creation. A good part of our knowledge has been learned as culture from older generations.

45. Quinn (1992) observed that the U.S. economy today is fundamentally restructured by service industries, and up to 95 percent of a manufacturing firm's employees are engaged in service activities. He stressed the importance of focusing strategy on core intellectual and service competencies and leveraging knowledge- and service-based strategies through strategic outsourcing. He also proposed organizational strategies that yield knowledge-based services and illustrated the way to reconstruct manufacturing-service interfaces. This new management paradigm was summarized under the concept of an "intelligent enterprise" that manages professional, innovative, and mass-service intellect to achieve high service productivity.

46. For a detailed review, see Dodgson (1993).

47. Literature reviews on organizational learning revealed that the terms "adaptation" and "learning" are sometimes used interchangeably (Levitt and March, 1988; Huber, 1991).

48. Duncan and Weiss (1979), Daft and Weick (1984), Brown and Duguid

(1991), and Fiol (forthcoming) are among the few exceptions on this point. They study organizational learning from the viewpoint of organizational interpretation or collective sensemaking and define knowledge development as the outcome of learning.

49. For example, Itami (1987) pointed to the importance of information-based resources or "invisible assets," such as customer trust, brand images, and management skills; Aaker (1989) distinguished between an asset and a skill—an asset is "something your firm *possesses* such as a brand name or retail location that is superior to the competition" and a skill is "something that your firm *does* better than competitors such as advertising or efficient manufacturing [italics added]" (p. 91); Dierickx and Cool (1990) called "stocks" such as technological expertise and brand loyalty "strategic assets," which are accumulated over time.

50. For example, Leonard-Barton (1992) defined "a core capability as the knowledge set that distinguishes and provides a competitive advantage" (p. 113) and argued that there are four dimensions to a knowledge set: (1) employee knowledge and skills; (2) technical systems; (3) managerial systems; and (4) values and norms; Spender (1993) classified tacit knowledge into three categories: conscious, automatic, and communal, each of which has different strategic implications.

3

Theory of Organizational Knowledge Creation

In the previous chapter, we saw that the distinctive approach of Western philosophy to knowledge has profoundly shaped the way organizational theorists treat knowledge. The Cartesian split between subject and object, the knower and the known, has given birth to a view of the organization as a mechanism for "information processing." According to this view, an organization processes information from the external environment in order to adapt to new circumstances. Although this view has proven to be effective in explaining how organizations function, it has a fundamental limitation. From our perspective, it does not really explain innovation. When organizations innovate, they do not simply process information, from the outside in, in order to solve existing problems and adapt to a changing environment. They actually create new knowledge and information, from the inside out, in order to redefine both problems and solutions and, in the process, to re-create their environment.

To explain innovation, we need a new theory of organizational knowledge creation. Like any approach to knowledge, it will have its own "epistemology" (the theory of knowledge), although one substantially different from the traditional Western approach. The cornerstone of our epistemology is the distinction between tacit and explicit knowledge. As we will see in this chapter, the key to knowledge creation lies in the mobilization and conversion of tacit knowledge. And because we are concerned with organizational knowledge creation, as opposed to individual knowledge creation, our theory will also have its own distinctive "ontology," which is concerned with the levels of knowledge-creating entities (individual, group, organizational, and inter-organizational). In this chapter we present our theory of knowledge creation, keeping in mind the two dimensions—epistemological and ontological—of knowledge creation. Figure 3-1 presents the epistemological and ontological dimensions in which a knowledge-creation "spiral" takes place. A spiral emerges when the interaction between tacit and explicit knowledge is elevated dynamically from a lower ontological level to higher levels.

The core of our theory lies in describing how such a spiral emerges. We present the four modes of knowledge conversion that are created when tacit and explicit knowledge interact with each other. These four modes—which we refer to as socialization, externalization, combination, and internalization—constitute the "engine" of the entire knowledge-creation process. These modes are what the individual experiences. They are also the mechanisms by which individual knowledge gets articulated and "amplified" into and throughout the organization. After laying out these four modes and illustrating them with examples, we will describe five conditions that enable or promote this spiral model of organizational knowledge creation. We also present a five-phase process through which knowledge is created over time within the organization.

Knowledge and Information

Before delving into our theory, we first turn to describing how knowledge is similar to and different from information. Three observations

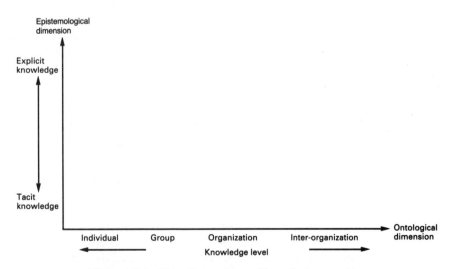

Figure 3-1. Two dimensions of knowledge creation.

become apparent in this section. First, knowledge, unlike information, is about *beliefs* and *commitment.* Knowledge is a function of a particular stance, perspective, or intention. Second, knowledge, unlike information, is about *action.* It is always knowledge "to some end." And third, knowledge, like information, is about *meaning.* It is context-specific and relational.

In our theory of organizational knowledge creation, we adopt the traditional definition of knowledge as "justified true belief." It should be noted, however, that while traditional Western epistemology has focused on "truthfulness" as the essential attribute of knowledge, we highlight the nature of knowledge as "justified belief." This difference in focus introduces another critical distinction between the view of knowledge of traditional Western epistemology and that of our theory of knowledge creation. While traditional epistemology emphasizes the absolute, static, and nonhuman nature of knowledge, typically expressed in propositions and formal logic, we consider knowledge as *a dynamic human process of justifying personal belief toward the "truth."*

Although the terms "information" and "knowledge" are often used interchangeably, there is a clear distinction between information and knowledge. As Bateson (1979) put it, "information consists of differences that make a difference" (p. 5). Information provides a new point of view for interpreting events or objects, which makes visible previously invisible meanings or sheds light on unexpected connections. Thus information is a necessary medium or material for eliciting and constructing knowledge. It affects knowledge by adding something to it or restructuring it (Machlup, 1983). Similarly, Dretske (1981) argued as follows: "Information is commodity capable of yielding knowledge, and what information a signal carries is what we can learn from it. . . . Knowledge is identified with information-produced (or sustained) belief" (pp. 44, 86).

Information can be viewed from two perspectives: "syntactic" (or volume of) and "semantic" (or meaning of) information. An illustration of syntactic information is found in Shannon and Weaver's (1949) analysis of information flow measured without any regard to inherent meaning, although Shannon himself admitted that his way of viewing information is problematic.[1] The semantic aspect of information is more important for knowledge creation, as it focuses on conveyed meaning. If one limits the span of consideration to the syntactic aspect alone, one cannot capture the real importance of information in the knowledge-creation process. Any preoccupation with the formal definition of information will lead to a disproportionate emphasis on the role of information processing, which is insensitive to the creation of new meaning out of the chaotic, equivocal sea of information.

Thus information is a flow of messages, while knowledge is created by that very flow of information, anchored in the beliefs and commitment of its holder. This understanding emphasizes that *knowledge is essentially related to human action.*[2] Searle's (1969) discussion of the "speech act" also points out the close relationship between language and human action in terms of "intention" and the "commitment" of speakers. As a fundamental basis for the theory of organizational knowledge creation, we focus attention on the active, subjective nature of knowledge represented by such terms as "commitment" and "belief" that are deeply rooted in individuals' value systems.

Finally, both information and knowledge are context-specific and relational in that they depend on the situation and are created dynamically in social interaction among people. Berger and Luckmann (1966) argue that people interacting in a certain historical and social context share information from which they construct social knowledge as a reality, which in turn influences their judgment, behavior, and attitude. Similarly, a corporate vision presented as an equivocal strategy by a leader is organizationally constructed into knowledge through interaction with the environment by the corporation's members, which in turn affects its business behavior.

Two Dimensions of Knowledge Creation

Although much has been written about the importance of knowledge in management, little attention has been paid to how knowledge is created and how the knowledge-creation process is managed. In this section we will develop a framework in which traditional and nontraditional views of knowledge are integrated into the theory of organizational knowledge creation. As mentioned earlier, our basic framework contains two dimensions—epistemological and ontological (see Figure 3-1).

Let us start with the ontological dimension. In a strict sense, knowledge is created only by individuals. An organization cannot create knowledge without individuals. The organization supports creative individuals or provides contexts for them to create knowledge. Organizational knowledge creation, therefore, should be understood as a process that "organizationally" amplifies the knowledge created by individuals and crystallizes it as a part of the knowledge network of the organization. This process takes place within an expanding "community of interaction," which crosses intra- and inter-organizational levels and boundaries.[3]

As for the epistemological dimension, we draw on Michael Polanyi's (1966) distinction between *tacit knowledge* and *explicit knowledge*. Tacit knowledge is personal, context-specific, and therefore hard to formalize and communicate. Explicit or "codified" knowledge, on the other hand, refers to knowledge that is transmittable in formal, systematic language. Polanyi's argument on the importance of tacit knowledge in human cognition may correspond to the central argument of Gestalt psychology, which has asserted that perception is determined in terms of the way it is integrated into the overall pattern or *Gestalt*. However, while Gestalt psychology stresses that all images are intrinsically integrated, Polanyi contends that human beings acquire knowledge by actively creating and organizing their own experiences. Thus, knowledge that can be expressed in words and numbers represents only the tip of the iceberg of the entire body of knowledge. As Polanyi (1966) puts it, "We can know more than we can tell" (p. 4).[4]

In traditional epistemology, knowledge derives from the separation of the subject and the object of perception; human beings as the subject of perception acquire knowledge by analyzing external objects. In contrast, Polanyi contends that human beings create knowledge by involving themselves with objects, that is, through self-involvement and commitment, or what Polanyi called "indwelling." To know something is to create its image or pattern by tacitly integrating particulars. In order to understand the pattern as a meaningful whole, it is necessary to integrate one's body with the particulars. Thus indwelling breaks the traditional dichotomies between mind and body, reason and emotion, subject and object, and knower and known. Therefore, scientific objectivity is not a sole source of knowledge. Much of our knowledge is the fruit of our own purposeful endeavors in dealing with the world.[5]

While Polanyi argues the contents of tacit knowledge further in a philosophical context, it is also possible to expand his idea in a more practical direction. Tacit knowledge includes cognitive and technical elements. The cognitive elements center on what Johnson-Laird (1983) calls "mental models," in which human beings create working models of the world by making and manipulating analogies in their minds. Mental models, such as schemata, paradigms, perspectives, beliefs, and viewpoints, help individuals to perceive and define their world. On the other hand, the technical element of tacit knowledge includes concrete know-how, crafts, and skills. It is important to note here that the cognitive elements of tacit knowledge refer to an individual's images of reality and visions for the future, that is, "what is" and "what ought to be." As will be discussed later, the articulation of tacit mental models, in a kind of "mobilization" process, is a key factor in creating new knowledge.

Some distinctions between tacit and explicit knowledge are shown in Table 3-1. Features generally associated with the more tacit aspects of knowledge are listed on the left, while the corresponding qualities related to explicit knowledge are shown on the right. For example, knowledge of experience tends to be tacit, physical, and subjective, while knowledge of rationality tends to be explicit, metaphysical, and objective. Tacit knowledge is created "here and now" in a specific, practical context and entails what Bateson (1973) referred to as "analog" quality. Sharing tacit knowledge between individuals through communication is an analog process that requires a kind of "simultaneous processing" of the complexities of issues shared by the individuals. On

Table 3-1. Two Types of Knowledge

Tacit Knowledge (Subjective)	Explicit Knowledge (Objective)
Knowledge of experience (body)	Knowledge of rationality (mind)
Simultaneous knowledge (here and now)	Sequential knowledge (there and then)
Analog knowledge (practice)	Digital knowledge (theory)

the other hand, explicit knowledge is about past events or objects "there and then" and is oriented toward a context-free theory.[6] It is sequentially created by what Bateson calls "digital" activity.

Knowledge Conversion: Interaction Between Tacit and Explicit Knowledge

As discussed in Chapter 2, the history of Western epistemology can be seen as a continuous controversy about which type of knowledge is more truthful. While Westerners tend to emphasize explicit knowledge, the Japanese tend to stress tacit knowledge. In our view, however, tacit knowledge and explicit knowledge are not totally separate but mutually complementary entities. They interact with and interchange into each other in the creative activities of human beings. Our dynamic model of knowledge creation is anchored to a critical assumption that human knowledge is created and expanded through social interaction between tacit knowledge and explicit knowledge. We call this interaction "knowledge conversion." It should be noted that this conversion is a "social" process *between* individuals and not confined *within* an individual.[7] According to the rationalist view, human cognition is a deductive process of individuals, but an individual is never isolated from social interaction when he or she perceives things. Thus, through this "social conversion" process, tacit and explicit knowledge expand in terms of both quality and quantity (Nonaka, 1990b).

The idea of "knowledge conversion" may be partially consonant with the ACT model (Anderson, 1983; Singley and Anderson, 1989) developed in cognitive psychology. This model hypothesizes that for cognitive skills to develop, all declarative knowledge, which corresponds to explicit knowledge in our theory, has to be transformed into procedural knowledge, which corresponds to tacit knowledge, used in such activities as riding a bicycle or playing the piano.[8] But as Singley and Anderson admit, the ACT model has one limitation. It views the transformation as a special case, because this model's research interest is focused on the acquisition and transfer of procedural (tacit) knowledge, not declarative (explicit) knowledge. In other words, proponents of this model consider knowledge transformation as mainly unidirectional from declarative (explicit) to procedural (tacit), whereas we argue that the transformation is interactive and spiral.

Four Modes of Knowledge Conversion

The assumption that knowledge is created through the interaction between tacit and explicit knowledge allows us to postulate four different modes of knowledge conversion. They are as follows: (1) from tacit knowledge to tacit knowledge, which we call socialization; (2) from tacit knowledge to explicit knowledge, or externalization; (3) from explicit knowledge to explicit knowledge, or combination; and (4) from explicit knowledge to tacit knowledge, or internalization.[9] Three of the four types of knowledge conversion—socialization, combination, and internalization—have been discussed from various perspectives in organizational theory. For example, socialization is connected with the theories of group processes and organizational culture; combination has its roots in information processing; and internalization is closely related to organizational learning. However, externalization has been somewhat neglected.[10] Figure 3-2 shows the four modes of knowledge conversion. Each of these four modes of knowledge conversion will be discussed in detail below, along with actual examples.

Socialization: From Tacit to Tacit

Socialization is a process of sharing experiences and thereby creating tacit knowledge such as shared mental models and technical skills.[11] An individual can acquire tacit knowledge directly from others without

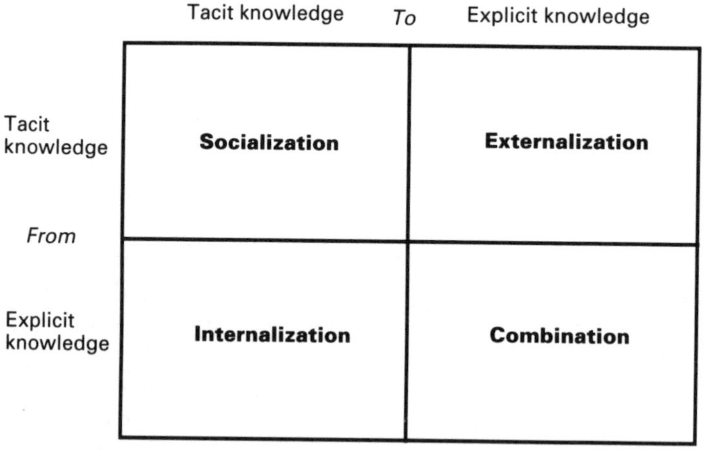

Figure 3-2. Four modes of knowledge conversion.

using language. Apprentices work with their masters and learn crafts-manship not through language but through observation, imitation, and practice. In the business setting, on-the-job training uses basically the same principle. The key to acquiring tacit knowledge is experience. Without some form of shared experience, it is extremely difficult for one person to project her- or himself into another individual's thinking process. The mere transfer of information will often make little sense, if it is abstracted from associated emotions and specific contexts in which shared experiences are embedded. The following three examples illustrate how socialization is employed by Japanese companies within the product development context.

The first example of socialization comes from Honda, which set up "brainstorming camps" *(tama dashi kai)*—informal meetings for de-tailed discussions to solve difficult problems in development projects. The meetings are held outside the workplace, often at a resort inn where participants discuss difficult problems while drinking *sake,* sharing meals, and taking a bath together in a hot spring. The meet-ings are not limited to project team members but are open to any em-ployees who are interested in the development project under way. In these discussions, the qualifications or status of the discussants are never questioned, but there is one taboo: criticism without constructive suggestions. Discussions are held with the understanding that "mak-ing criticism is ten times easier than coming up with a constructive alternative." This kind of brainstorming camp is not unique to Honda but has been used by many other Japanese firms. It is also not unique to developing new products and services but is also used to develop managerial systems or corporate strategies. Such a camp is not only a forum for creative dialogue but also a medium for sharing experience and enhancing mutual trust among participants.[12] It is particularly effective in sharing tacit knowledge and creating a new perspective. It reorients the mental models of all individuals in the same direction, but not in a forceful way. Instead, brainstorming camps represent a mechanism through which individuals search for harmony by engag-ing themselves in bodily as well as mental experiences.

The second example, which shows how a tacit technical skill was socialized, comes from the Matsushita Electric Industrial Company. A major problem at the Osaka-based company in developing an auto-matic home bread-making machine in the late 1980s centered on how to mechanize the dough-kneading process, which is essentially tacit knowledge possessed by master bakers. Dough kneaded by a master baker and by a machine were x-rayed and compared, but no meaning-ful insights were obtained. Ikuko Tanaka, head of software develop-ment, knew that the area's best bread came from the Osaka Interna-tional Hotel. To capture the tacit knowledge of kneading skill, she and several engineers volunteered to apprentice themselves to the hotel's head baker. Making the same delicious bread as the head baker's was not easy. No one could explain why. One day, however, she noticed that the baker was not only stretching but also "twisting" the dough, which turned out to be the secret for making tasty bread. Thus she socialized the head baker's tacit knowledge through observation, imitation, and practice.

Socialization also occurs between product developers and customers. Interactions with customers before product development and after market introduction are, in fact, a never-ending process of sharing tacit knowledge and creating ideas for improvement. The way NEC developed its first personal computer is a case in point. The new-product development process began when a group from the Semiconductor and IC Sales Division conceived of an idea to sell Japan's first microcomputer kit, the TK-80, to promote the sales of semiconductor devices. Selling the TK-80 to the public at large was a radical departure from NEC's history of responding to routine orders from Nippon Telegraph and Telephone (NTT). Unexpectedly, a wide variety of customers, ranging from high school students to professional computer enthusiasts, came to NEC's BIT-INN, a display service center in the Akihabara district of Tokyo, which is famous for its high concentration of electronic goods retailers. Sharing experiences and continuing dialogues with these customers at the BIT-INN resulted in the development of NEC's best-selling personal computer, the PC-8000, a few years later.

Externalization: From Tacit to Explicit

Externalization is a process of articulating tacit knowledge into explicit concepts. It is a quintessential knowledge-creation process in that tacit knowledge becomes explicit, taking the shapes of metaphors, analogies, concepts, hypotheses, or models. When we attempt to conceptualize an image, we express its essence mostly in language—writing is an act of converting tacit knowledge into articulable knowledge (Emig, 1983). Yet expressions are often inadequate, inconsistent, and insufficient. Such discrepancies and gaps between images and expressions, however, help promote "reflection" and interaction between individuals.

The externalization mode of knowledge conversion is typically seen in the process of concept creation and is triggered by dialogue or collective reflection.[13] A frequently used method to create a concept is to combine deduction and induction. Mazda, for example, combined these two reasoning methods when it developed the new RX-7 concept, which is described as "an authentic sports car that provides an exciting and comfortable drive." The concept was *deduced* from the car maker's corporate slogan: "create new values and present joyful driving pleasures" as well as the positioning of the new car as "a strategic car for the U.S. market and an image of innovation." At the same time, the new concept was *induced* from "concept" trips," which were driving experiences by development team members in the United States as well as from "concept clinics," which gathered opinions from customers and car experts. When we cannot find an adequate expression for an image through analytical methods of deduction or induction, we have to use a nonanalytical method. Externalization is, therefore, often driven by metaphor and/or analogy. Using an attractive metaphor and/or analogy is highly effective in fostering direct commitment to the creative process. Recall the Honda City example. In developing the car, Hiroo Watanabe and his team used a metaphor of "Automobile Evolution." His team viewed the automobile as an organism and sought its ultimate form. In essence, Watanabe was asking, "What will the automobile eventually evolve into?"

> I insisted on allocating the minimum space for mechanics and the maximum space for passengers. This seemed to be the ideal car, into which the automobile should evolve. . . . The first step toward this goal was to challenge the "reasoning of Detroit," which had sacrificed comfort for appearance. Our choice was a short but tall car . . . spherical, therefore lighter, less expensive, more comfortable, and solid.[14]

The concept of a tall and short car—"Tall Boy"—emerged through an analogy between the concept of "man-maximum, machine-minimum" and an image of a sphere that contains the maximum volume within the minimum area of surface, which ultimately resulted in the Honda City.

The case of Canon's Mini-Copier is a good example of how an analogy was used effectively for product development. One of the most difficult problems faced by the development team was producing at low cost a disposable cartridge, which would eliminate the necessity for maintenance required in conventional machines. Without a disposable cartridge, maintenance staff would have to be stationed all over the country, since the copier was intended for family or personal use. If the usage frequency were high, maintenance costs could be negligible. But that was not the case with a personal copier. The fact that a large number of customers would be using the machine only occasionally meant that the new product had to have high reliability and no or minimum maintenance. A maintenance study showed that more than 90 percent of the problems came from the drum or its surrounding parts. Aimed at cutting maintenance costs while maintaining the highest reliability, the team developed the concept of a disposable cartridge system in which the drum or the heart of the copier is replaced after a certain amount of usage.

The next problem was whether the drum could be produced at a cost low enough to be consistent with the targeted low selling price of the copier. A task force assigned to solve this cost problem had many heated discussions about the production of conventional photosensitive drum cylinders with a base material of aluminum-drawn tube at a low cost. One day Hiroshi Tanaka, leader of the task force, sent out for some cans of beer. Once the beer was consumed, he asked, "How much does it cost to manufacture this can?" The team then explored the possibility of applying the process of manufacturing the beer can to manufacturing the drum cylinder, using the same material. By clarifying similarities and differences, they discovered a process technology to manufacture the aluminum drum at a low cost, thus giving rise to the disposable drum.

These examples within Japanese firms clearly show the effectiveness of the use of metaphor and analogy in creating and elaborating a concept (see Table 3-2). As Honda's Watanabe commented, "We are more than halfway there, once a product concept has been created." In this sense, the leaders' wealth of figurative language and imagination is an essential factor in eliciting tacit knowledge from project members.

Among the four modes of knowledge conversion, externalization holds the key to knowledge creation, because it creates new, explicit concepts from tacit knowledge. How can we convert tacit knowledge into explicit knowledge effectively and efficiently? The answer lies in a sequential use of metaphor, analogy, and model. As Nisbet (1969) noted, "much of what Michael Polanyi has called 'tacit knowledge' is expressible—in so far as it is expressible at all—in metaphor" (p. 5). Metaphor is a way of perceiving or intuitively understanding one thing by imaging another thing symbolically. It is most often used in abductive reasoning or nonanalytical methods for creating radical concepts (Bateson, 1979). It is neither analysis nor synthesis of common attributes of associated things. Donnellon, Gray, and Bougon (1986)

Table 3-2. Metaphor and/or Analogy for Concept Creation in Product Development

Product (Company)	Metaphor/Analogy	Influence on Concept Creation
City (Honda)	"Automobile Evolution" (metaphor)	Hint of maximizing passenger space as ultimate auto development "Man-maximum, machine-minimum" concept created
	The sphere (analogy)	Hint of achieving maximum passenger space through minimizing surface area "Tall and short car (Tall Boy)" concept created
Mini-Copier (Canon)	Aluminum beer can (analogy)	Hint of similarities between inexpensive aluminum beer can and photosensitive drum manufacture "Low-cost manufacturing process" concept created
Home Bakery (Matsushita)	Hotel bread (metaphor)	Hint of more delicious bread
	Osaka International Hotel head baker (analogy)	"Twist dough" concept created

argue that "metaphors create novel interpretation of experience by asking the listener to see one thing in terms of something else" and "create new ways of experiencing reality" (pp. 48, 52). Thus, "metaphors are one communication mechanism that can function to reconcile discrepancies in meaning" (p. 48).[15]

Moreover, metaphor is an important tool for creating a *network* of new concepts. Because a metaphor is "two thoughts of different things . . . supported by a single word, or phrase, whose meaning is a resultant of their interaction" (Richards, 1936, p. 93), we can continuously relate concepts that are far apart in our mind, even relate abstract concepts to concrete ones. This creative, cognitive process continues as we think of the similarities among concepts and feel an imbalance, inconsistency, or contradiction in their associations, thus often leading to the discovery of new meaning or even to the formation of a new paradigm.

Contradictions inherent in a metaphor are then harmonized by analogy, which reduces the unknown by highlighting the "commonness" of two different things. Metaphor and analogy are often confused. Association of two things through metaphor is driven mostly by intuition and holistic imagery and does not aim to find differences between them. On the other hand, association through analogy is carried out by rational thinking and focuses on structural/functional similarities between two things, and hence their differences. Thus analogy helps us understand the unknown through the known and bridges the gap between an image and a logical model.[16]

Once explicit concepts are created, they can then be modeled. In a logical model, no contradictions should exist and all concepts and propositions must be expressed in systematic language and coherent logic. But in business terms, models are often only rough descriptions or drawings, far from being fully specific. Models are usually generated from metaphors when new concepts are created in the business context.[17]

Combination: From Explicit to Explicit

Combination is a process of systemizing concepts into a knowledge system. This mode of knowledge conversion involves combining different bodies of explicit knowledge. Individuals exchange and combine knowledge through such media as documents, meetings, telephone conversations, or computerized communication networks. Reconfiguration of existing information through sorting, adding, combining, and categorizing of explicit knowledge (as conducted in computer databases) can lead to new knowledge. Knowledge creation carried out in formal education and training at schools usually takes this form. An MBA education is one of the best examples of this kind.

In the business context, the combination mode of knowledge conversion is most often seen when middle managers break down and operationalize corporate visions, business concepts, or product concepts. Middle management plays a critical role in creating new concepts through networking of codified information and knowledge. Creative uses of computerized communication networks and large-scale databases facilitate this mode of knowledge conversion.[18]

At Kraft General Foods, a manufacturer of dairy and processed foods, data from the POS (point-of-sales) system of retailers is utilized not only to find out what does and does not sell well but also to create new "ways to sell," that is, new sales systems and methods. The company has developed an information-intensive marketing program called "micro-merchandizing," which provides supermarkets with timely and precise recommendations on the optimal merchandise mix and with sales promotions based on the analysis of data from its micromerchandising system. Utilizing Kraft's individual method of data analysis, including its unique classification of stores and shoppers into six categories, the system is capable of pinpointing who shops where and how. Kraft successfully manages its product sales through supermarkets by controlling four elements of the "category management" methodology—consumer and category dynamics, space management, merchandizing management, and pricing management.[19]

At the top management level of an organization, the combination mode is realized when mid-range concepts (such as product concepts) are combined with and integrated into grand concepts (such as a corporate vision) to generate a new meaning of the latter. Introducing a new corporate image in 1986, for example, Asahi Breweries adopted a grand concept dubbed "live Asahi for live people." The concept stood for the message that "Asahi will provide natural and authentic products and services for those who seek active minds and active lives." Along with this grand concept, Asahi inquired into the essence of what makes beer appealing, and developed Asahi Super Dry beer based on the new-product concept of "richness and sharpness." The new-product concept is a mid-range concept that made the grand concept of Asahi more explicitly recognizable, which in turn altered the company's product development system. The taste of beer was hitherto decided by engineers in the production department without any participation by the sales department. The "richness and sharpness" concept was realized through cooperative product development by both departments.

Other examples of interaction between grand concepts and mid-range concepts abound. For example, NEC's "C&C" (computers and communications) concept induced the development of the epoch-making PC-8000 personal computer, which was based on the mid-range concept of "distributed processing." Canon's corporate policy, "Creation of an excellent company by transcending the camera business," led to the development of the Mini-Copier, which was developed with the mid-range product concept of "easy maintenance." Mazda's grand vision, "Create new values and present joyful driving," was realized in the new RX-7, "an authentic sports car that provides an exciting and comfortable drive."

Internalization: From Explicit to Tacit

Internalization is a process of embodying explicit knowledge into tacit knowledge. It is closely related to "learning by doing." When experiences through socialization, externalization, and combination are internalized into individuals' tacit knowledge bases in the form of shared mental models or technical know-how, they become valuable assets. All the members of the Honda City project team, for example, internalized their experiences of the late 1970s and are now making use of that know-how and leading R&D projects in the company. For organizational knowledge creation to take place, however, the tacit knowledge accumulated at the individual level needs to be socialized with other organizational members, thereby starting a new spiral of knowledge creation.

For explicit knowledge to become tacit, it helps if the knowledge is verbalized or diagrammed into documents, manuals, or oral stories. Documentation helps individuals internalize what they experienced, thus enriching their tacit knowledge. In addition, documents or manuals facilitate the transfer of explicit knowledge to other people, thereby helping them experience the experiences of others indirectly (i.e., "re-experience" them). GE, for example, documents all customer complaints and inquiries in a database at its Answer Center in Louisville, Kentucky, which can be used, for example, by members of a new-product development team to "re-experience" what the telephone operators experienced. GE established the Answer Center in 1982 to process questions, requests for help, and complaints from customers on any product 24 hours a day, 365 days a year. Over 200 telephone operators respond to as many as 14,000 calls a day. GE has programmed 1.5 million potential problems and their solutions into its computerized database system. The system is equipped with an on-line diagnosis function utilizing the latest artificial intelligence technology for quick answers to inquiries; any problem-solution response can be retrieved by the telephone operator in two seconds. In case a solution is not available, 12 specialists with at least four years of repair experience think out solutions on site. Four full-time programmers put the solutions into the database, so that the new information is usually installed into the system by the following day. This information is sent to the respective product divisions every month. Yet, the product divisions also frequently send their new-product development people to the Answer Center to chat with the telephone operators or the 12 specialists, thereby "re-experiencing" their experiences.

Internalization can also occur even without having actually to "re-experience" other people's experiences. For example, if reading or listening to a success story makes some members of the organization feel the realism and essence of the story, the experience that took place in the past may change into a tacit mental model. When such a mental model is shared by most members of the organization, tacit knowledge becomes part of the organizational culture. This practice is prevalent in Japan, where books and articles on companies or their leaders abound. Freelance writers or former employees publish them, sometimes at the request of the companies. One can find about two dozen books on Honda or Soichiro Honda in major bookstores today, all of which help instill a strong corporate culture for Honda.

An example of internalization through "learning by doing" can be seen at Matsushita when it launched a companywide policy in 1993 to reduce yearly working time to 1,800 hours. Called MIT'93 for "Mind and Management Innovation Toward 1993," the policy's objective was not to reduce costs but to innovate the mindset and management by reducing working hours and increasing individual creativity. Many departments were puzzled about how to implement the policy, which was clearly communicated as explicit knowledge. The MIT'93 promotion office advised each department to experiment with the policy for one month by working 150 hours. Through such a bodily experience, employees got to know what working 1,800 hours a year would be like. An explicit concept, reducing working time to 1,800 hours, was internalized through the one-month experience.

Expanding the scope of bodily experience is critical to internalization. For example, Honda City project leader Hiroo Watanabe kept saying "Let's give it a try" to encourage the team members' experimental spirit. The fact that the development team was cross-functional enabled its members to learn and internalize a breadth of development experiences beyond their own functional specialization. Rapid prototyping also accelerated the accumulation of developmental experiences, which can lead to internalization.

Contents of Knowledge and the Knowledge Spiral

As already explained, socialization aims at the sharing of tacit knowledge. On its own, however, it is a limited form of knowledge creation. Unless shared knowledge becomes explicit, it cannot be easily leveraged by the organization as a whole. Also, a mere combination of discrete pieces of explicit information into a new whole—for example, a comptroller of a company collects information from throughout the company and puts it together in a financial report—does not really extend the organization's existing knowledge base. But when tacit and explicit knowledge interact, as in the Matsushita example, an innovation emerges. Organizational knowledge creation is a continuous and dynamic interaction between tacit and explicit knowledge. This interaction is shaped by shifts between different modes of knowledge conversion, which are in turn induced by several triggers (see Figure 3-3).

First, the socialization mode usually starts with building a "field" of interaction. This field facilitates the sharing of members' experiences and mental models. Second, the externalization mode is triggered by meaningful "dialogue or collective reflection," in which using appropriate metaphor or analogy helps team members to articulate hidden tacit knowledge that is otherwise hard to communicate. Third, the combination mode is triggered by "networking" newly created knowledge and existing knowledge from other sections of the organization, thereby crystallizing them into a new product, service, or managerial system. Finally, "learning by doing" triggers internalization.

The content of the knowledge created by each mode of knowledge conversion is naturally different (see Figure 3-4). Socialization yields what can be called "sympathized knowledge," such as shared mental models and technical skills. The tacit skill of kneading dough in the Matsushita example is a sympathized knowledge. Externalization outputs "conceptual knowledge." The concept of "Tall Boy" in the Honda example is a conceptual knowledge created through the metaphor of "Automobile Evolution" and the analogy between a sphere and the concept of "man-maximum, machine-minimum." Combination gives rise to "systemic knowledge," such as a prototype and new component technologies. The micro-merchandizing program in the Kraft General Foods example is a systemic knowledge, which includes retail management methods as its components. Internalization produces "operational knowledge" about project management, production process, new-product usage, and policy implementation. The bodily experience of working 150 hours a month in the Matsushita case is an operational knowledge of policy implementation.

These contents of knowledge interact with each other in the spiral

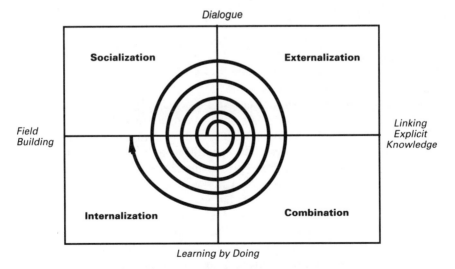

Figure 3-3. Knowledge spiral.

Tacit knowledge   *To*   Explicit knowledge

	Tacit knowledge →	Explicit knowledge →
Tacit knowledge *(From)*	(Socialization) **Sympathized Knowledge**	(Externalization) **Conceptual Knowledge**
Explicit knowledge	(Internalization) **Operational Knowledge**	(Combination) **Systemic Knowledge**

Figure 3-4. Contents of knowledge created by the four modes.

of knowledge creation. For example, sympathized knowledge about consumers' wants may become explicit conceptual knowledge about a new-product concept through socialization and externalization. Such conceptual knowledge becomes a guideline for creating systemic knowledge through combination. For example, a new-product concept steers the combination phase, in which newly developed and existing component technologies are combined to build a prototype. Systemic knowledge (e.g., a simulated production process for the new product) turns into operational knowledge for mass production of the product through internalization. In addition, experience-based operational knowledge often triggers a new cycle of knowledge creation. For example, the users' tacit operational knowledge about a product is often socialized, thereby initiating improvement of an existing product or development of an innovation.

Thus far, we have focused our discussion on the epistemological dimension of organizational knowledge creation. As noted before, however, an organization cannot create knowledge by itself. Tacit knowledge of individuals is the basis of organizational knowledge creation. The organization has to mobilize tacit knowledge created and accumulated at the individual level. The mobilized tacit knowledge is "organizationally" amplified through four modes of knowledge conversion and crystallized at higher ontological levels. We call this the "knowledge spiral," in which the interaction between tacit knowledge and explicit knowledge will become larger in scale as it moves up the ontological levels. Thus, organizational knowledge creation is a spiral process, starting at the individual level and moving up through expanding communities of interaction, that crosses sectional, departmental, divisional, and organizational boundaries (see Figure 3-5).

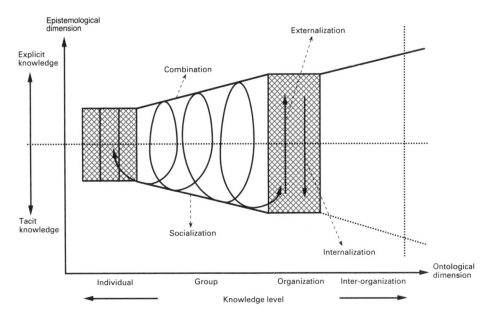

Figure 3-5. Spiral of organizational knowledge creation.

This process is exemplified by product development. Creating a product concept involves a community of interacting individuals with different backgrounds and mental models. While the members from the R&D department focus on technological potential, those from the production and marketing departments are interested in other issues. Only some of those different experiences, mental models, motivations, and intentions can be expressed in explicit language. Thus, the socialization process of sharing tacit knowledge is required. Moreover, both socialization and externalization are necessary for linking individuals' tacit and explicit knowledge. Many Japanese companies have adopted brainstorming camps as a tool for that purpose.

The product created by this collective and cooperative process will then be reviewed for its coherence with mid-range and grand concepts. Even if the newly created product has superior quality, it may conflict with the divisional or organizational goals expressed by the mid-range and grand concepts. What is required is another process at a higher level to maintain the integrity of the whole, which will lead to another cycle of knowledge creation in a larger context.

Enabling Conditions for Organizational Knowledge Creation

The role of the organization in the organizational knowledge-creation process is to provide the proper context for facilitating group activities as well as the creation and accumulation of knowledge at the individual level. In this section we will discuss five conditions required at the organizational level to promote the knowledge spiral.

Intention

The knowledge spiral is driven by organizational intention, which is defined as an organization's aspiration to its goals.[20] Efforts to achieve the intention usually take the form of strategy within a business setting. From the viewpoint of organizational knowledge creation, the essence of strategy lies in developing the organizational capability to acquire, create, accumulate, and exploit knowledge. The most critical element of corporate strategy is to conceptualize a vision about what kind of knowledge should be developed and to operationalize it into a management system for implementation.

For example, NEC viewed technology as a knowledge system when it developed core technology programs at its Central Research Laboratories in 1975. At that time the company was engaged in three main businesses: communications, computers, and semiconductors. Because it was difficult to coordinate R&D of these different areas, it was necessary to grasp technologies at a higher and more abstract level—that is, knowledge. According to Michiyuki Uenohara, former executive vice president, "base technologies" were identified by forecasting product groups for a decade into the future, including the extraction of technologies common to and necessary for them. Synergistically related base technologies were then grouped into "core technologies," such as pattern recognition, image processing, and VLSI. Since 1975, NEC has expanded its core technology programs using autonomous teams; today it has 36 core technology programs in action.

In addition, NEC devised a concept called the "strategic technology domain" (STD) in order to match core technologies with business activities. An STD links several core technologies to create a concept for product development. Thus, an STD represents not only a product domain but also a knowledge domain. At present there are six STDs: (1) functional materials/devices; (2) semiconductors; (3) materials/devices functional machinery; (4) communications systems; (5) knowledge-information systems; and (6) software. Those STDs interact with core technology programs in a matrix, as illustrated in Figure 3-6. By combining core technology programs and the STDs, the knowledge bases at NEC are linked horizontally and vertically. Through this endeavor, NEC has attempted to develop a corporate strategic intention of knowledge creation at every organizational level.

Organizational intention provides the most important criterion for judging the truthfulness of a given piece of knowledge. If not for intention, it would be impossible to judge the value of information or knowledge perceived or created. At the organizational level, intention is often expressed by organizational standards or visions that can be used

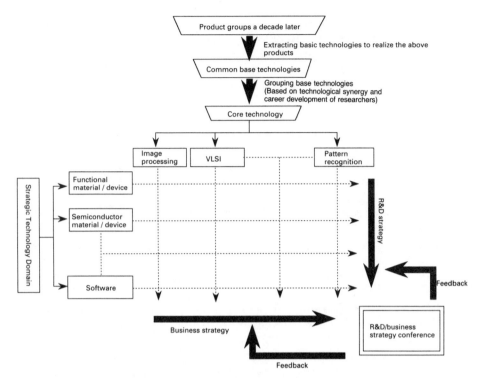

Figure 3-6. NEC's knowledge domain. *Source: NEC*

to evaluate and justify the created knowledge. It is necessarily value-laden.

To create knowledge, business organizations should foster their employees' commitment by formulating an organizational intention and proposing it to them. Top or middle managers can draw organizational attention to the importance of commitment to fundamental values by addressing such fundamental questions as *"What is truth?"* *"What is human being?"* or *"What is life?"* This activity is more organizational than individual. Instead of relying solely on individuals' own thinking and behaviors, the organization can reorient and promote them through collective commitment. As Polanyi (1958) notes, commitment underlies the human knowledge-creating activity.

Autonomy

The second condition for promoting the knowledge spiral is autonomy. At the individual level, all members of an organization should be allowed to act autonomously as far as circumstances permit. By allowing them to act autonomously, the organization may increase the chance of introducing unexpected opportunities. Autonomy also increases the possibility that individuals will motivate themselves to create new knowledge. Moreover, autonomous individuals function as part of the holographic structure, in which the whole and each part share the same information. Original ideas emanate from autonomous individuals, diffuse within the team, and then become organizational ideas. In this respect, the self-organizing individual assumes a position that may be seen as analogous to the core of a series of nested Russian dolls. From the viewpoint of knowledge creation, such an organization is more likely to maintain greater flexibility in acquiring, interpreting, and relating information. It is a system in which the "minimum critical specification" principle (Morgan, 1986) is met as a prerequisite for self-organization, and therefore autonomy is assured as much as possible.[21]

A knowledge-creating organization that secures autonomy may also be depicted as an "autopoietic system" (Maturana and Varela, 1980), which can be explained by the following analogy. Living organic systems are composed of various organs, which are again made up of numerous cells. Relationships between system and organs, and between organ and cells, are neither dominate-subordinate nor whole-part. Each unit, like an autonomous cell, controls all changes occurring continuously within itself. Moreover, each unit determines its boundary through self-reproduction. This self-referential nature is quintessential to the autopoietic system.

Similarly to an autopoietic system, autonomous individuals and groups in knowledge-creating organizations set their task boundaries by themselves to pursue the ultimate goal expressed in the higher intention of the organization. In the business organization, a powerful tool for creating circumstances in which individuals can act autonomously is provided by the self-organizing team.[22] Such a team should be cross-functional, involving members from a broad cross-section of different organizational activities. Project teams with cross-functional diversity are often used by Japanese firms at every phase of innovation. As illustrated in Table 3-3, most innovation project teams consisted of 10 to 30 members with diverse functional backgrounds, such as R&D, planning, production, quality control, sales and marketing, and customer service. In most companies there are 4 to 5 core members, each of whom has had a multiple functional career. For example, the core members who developed Fuji Xerox's FX-3500 have had at least three functional shifts, even though they were only in their 30s at that time (see Table 3-4).

The autonomous team can perform many functions, thereby amplifying and sublimating individual perspectives to higher levels. Honda, for example, organized a cross-functional project team to develop the City model that was composed of people from the sales, development, and production departments. This system was called the "SED system," reflecting the sales, engineering, and development functions. Its initial goal was to manage development activities more systematically by integrating the knowledge and wisdom of "ordinary people" instead

Table 3-3. Functional Backgrounds of Product Development Team Members

Company (Product)	R&D	Production	Sales Marketing	Planning	Service	Quality Control	Other	Total
			Functional Background					
Fuji Xerox (FX-3500)	5	4	1	4	1	1	1	17
Honda (City)	18	6	4	—	1	1	—	30
NEC (PC 8000)	5	—	2	2	2	—	—	11
Epson (EP101)	10	10	8	—	—	—	—	28
Canon (AE-1)	12	10	—	—	—	2	4	28
Canon (Mini-Copier)	8	3	2	1	—	—	1	15
Mazda (New RX-7)	13	6	7	1	1	1	—	29
Matsushita Electric (Automatic Home Bakery)	8	8	1	1	1	1	—	20

Source: Nonaka (1990a)

of relying on a few heroes. Its operation was very flexible. The three functional areas were nominally differentiated and there was a built-in learning process that encouraged invasion into other areas. The members jointly performed the following functions:

- procuring personnel, facilities, and budget for the production plant
- analyzing the automobile market and competition
- setting a market target
- determining a price and a production volume.

Table 3-4. Corporate Careers and Educational Backgrounds of Core Members of the FX-3500 Development Team

Name	Career Path within Fuji Xerox	University Specialization
Hiroshi Yoshino	Technical Service Staff → Personnel → Product Planning → Product Management	Education
Ken'ichiro Fujita	Marketing Staff → Product Planning → Product Management	Commerce
Masao Suzuki	Design → Research → Design	Mechanical Engineering
Mitsutoshi Kitajima	Technical Service Staff → Quality Control → Production	Electrical Engineering

The actual work flow required team members to collaborate with their colleagues. Hiroo Watanabe, the team leader, commented:

> I am always telling the team members that our work is not a relay race in which my work starts here and yours there. Everyone should run all the way from start to finish. Like rugby, all of us should run together, pass the ball left and right, and reach the goal as a united body.[23]

Type C in Figure 3-7 illustrates the rugby approach. Type A shows the relay approach in which each phase of the development process is clearly separated and the baton is passed from one group to another. Type B is called the *"sashimi* system" at Fuji Xerox, because it looks like sliced raw fish (*sashimi*) served on a plate with one piece overlapping another (Imai, Nonaka, and Takeuchi, 1985, p. 351).

Fluctuation and Creative Chaos

The third organizational condition for promoting the knowledge spiral is fluctuation and creative chaos, which stimulate the interaction between the organization and the external environment.[24] Fluctuation is different from complete disorder and characterized by "order without recursiveness." It is an order whose pattern is hard to predict at the beginning (Gleick, 1987). If organizations adopt an open attitude toward environmental signals, they can exploit those signals' ambiguity, redundancy, or noise in order to improve their own knowledge system.

When fluctuation is introduced into an organization, its members face a "breakdown" of routines, habits, or cognitive frameworks. Winograd and Flores (1986) emphasize the importance of such periodic breakdowns in the development of human perception. A breakdown

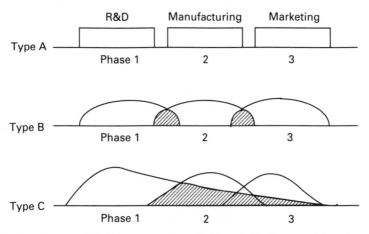

Figure 3-7. Sequential (A) vs. overlapped (B and C) phases of development. *Source: Takeuchi and Nonaka, 1986.*

refers to an interruption of our habitual, comfortable state of being. When we face such a breakdown, we have an opportunity to reconsider our fundamental thinking and perspective. In other words, we begin to question the validity of our basic attitudes toward the world. Such a process requires a deep personal commitment on the part of the individual. A breakdown demands that we turn our attention to dialogue as a means of social interaction, thus helping us to create new concepts.[25] This "continuous" process of questioning and reconsidering existing premises by individual members of the organization fosters organizational knowledge creation. An environmental fluctuation often triggers a breakdown within the organization, out of which new knowledge can be created. Some have called this phenomenon creating "order out of noise" or "order out of chaos."[26]

Chaos is generated naturally when the organization faces a real crisis, such as a rapid decline of performance due to changes in market needs or significant growth of competitors. It can also be generated intentionally when the organization's leaders try to evoke a "sense of crisis" among organizational members by proposing challenging goals. Ryuzaburo Kaku, chairman of Canon, often says, "The role of top management is to give employees a sense of crisis as well as a lofty ideal" (Nonaka, 1985, p. 142). This intentional chaos, which is referred to as "creative chaos," increases tension within the organization and focuses the attention of organizational members on defining the problem and resolving the crisis situation. This approach is in sharp contrast to the information-processing paradigm, in which a problem is simply given and a solution found through a process of combining relevant information based upon a preset algorithm. Such a process ignores the importance of defining the problem to be solved. To attain such definition, problems must be constructed from the knowledge available at a certain point in time and context.

Japanese companies often resort to the purposeful use of ambiguity and "creative chaos." Top management often employs ambiguous visions (or so-called "strategic equivocality") and intentionally creates a fluctuation within the organization. Nissan's CEO, Yutaka Kume, for example, coined the catch phrase "Let's change the flow," by which he tried to promote creativity through an active investigation of alternatives to established procedures. When the philosophy or vision of top management is ambiguous, that ambiguity leads to "interpretative equivocality" at the level of the implementing staff.

It should be noted that the benefits of "creative chaos" can only be realized when organizational members have the ability to reflect upon their actions. Without reflection, fluctuation tends to lead to "destructive" chaos. Schön (1983) captures this key point as follows: "When someone reflects while in action, he becomes a researcher in the practice context. He is not dependent on the categories of established theory and technique, but constructs a new theory of the unique case" (p.

68). The knowledge-creating organization is required to institutional-
ize this "reflection-in-action" in its process to make chaos truly "creative."

Top management's ambiguity with respect to philosophy or vision
can lead to a reflection or questioning of value premises as well as of
factual premises upon which corporate decision making is anchored.
Value premises are subjective in nature and concern preferences; they
make possible a far broader range of choice. Factual premises, on the
other hand, are objective in nature and deal with how the real world
operates; they provide a concrete but limited range of choice.

Chaos is sometimes created independently of top management's philosophy. An individual organizational member can set a high goal in
order to elevate him- or herself or the team to which he or she belongs.
Hiroo Watanabe's pursuit of the "ideal" car, challenging the "reasoning of Detroit," is an example of a goal set high. High goals, whether
set by top management or individual employees, enhance personal
commitment. As Taiyu Kobayashi, the former chairman of Fujitsu,
pointed out, high goals may intensify individual wisdom as well:

> Relaxed in a comfortable place, one can hardly think sharply. Wisdom is
> squeezed out of someone who is standing on the cliff and is struggling to
> survive . . . without such struggles, we would have never been able to
> catch up with IBM. (Kobayashi, 1985, p. 171)

In sum, fluctuation in the organization can trigger creative chaos,
which induces and strengthens the subjective commitment of individuals. In actual day-to-day operation, organizational members do not regularly face such a situation. But the example from Nissan has shown
that top management may intentionally bring about fluctuation and
allow "interpretative equivocality" to emerge at lower levels of the organization. This equivocality acts as a trigger for individual members
to change their fundamental ways of thinking. It also helps to externalize their tacit knowledge.

Redundancy

Redundancy is the fourth condition that enables the knowledge spiral
to take place organizationally. To Western managers who are preoccupied with the idea of efficient information processing or uncertainty
reduction (Galbraith, 1973), the term "redundancy" may sound perni-
cious because of its connotations of unnecessary duplication, waste, or
information overload. What we mean here by redundancy is the existence of information that goes beyond the immediate operational requirements of organizational members. In business organizations, redundancy refers to intentional overlapping of information about
business activities, management responsibilities, and the company as
a whole.

For organizational knowledge creation to take place, a concept created by an individual or group needs to be shared by other individuals who may not need the concept immediately. Sharing redundant information promotes the sharing of tacit knowledge, because individuals can sense what others are trying to articulate. In this sense, redundancy of information speeds up the knowledge-creation process. Redundancy is especially important in the concept development stage, when it is critical to articulate images rooted in tacit knowledge. At this stage, redundant information enables individuals to invade each other's functional boundaries and offer advice or provide new information from different perspectives. In short, redundancy of information brings about "learning by intrusion" into each individual's sphere of perception.

Redundancy of information is also a prerequisite to realization of McCulloch's (1965) "principle of redundancy of potential command"— that is, each part of an entire system carrying the same degree of importance and having a potential of becoming its leader. Even within a strictly hierarchical organization, redundant information helps build unusual communication channels. Thus redundancy of information facilitates the interchange between hierarchy and nonhierarchy.[27]

Sharing extra information also helps individuals understand where they stand in the organization, which in turn functions to control the direction of individual thinking and action. Individuals are not unconnected but loosely coupled with each other, and take meaningful positions in the whole organizational context. Thus redundancy of information provides the organization with a self-control mechanism to keep it heading in a certain direction.

There are several ways to build redundancy into the organization. One is to adopt an overlapping approach, as illustrated by Japanese companies' "rugby-style" product development in which different functional departments work together in a "fuzzy" division of labor (Takeuchi and Nonaka, 1986). Some companies divide the product development team into competing groups that develop different approaches to the same project and then argue over advantages and disadvantages of their proposals. This internal competition encourages the team to look at a project from a variety of perspectives. Under the guidance of a team leader, the team eventually develops a common understanding of the "best" approach.

Another way to build redundancy into the organization is through a "strategic rotation" of personnel, especially between vastly different areas of technology or functions such as R&D and marketing. Such rotation helps organizational members understand its business from multiple perspectives, thereby making organizational knowledge more "fluid" and easier to put into practice. It also enables each employee to diversify her or his skills and information sources. The extra information held by individuals across different functions helps the organization expand its knowledge-creation capacity.

One of the most notable characteristics of Japanese organizations

compared with their Western counterparts is the value placed on redundant information. Leading Japanese firms have institutionalized
redundancy within themselves in order to develop new products and
services swiftly in response to fast-changing markets and technologies.
Japanese firms have also developed many other organizational devices
that increase and maintain redundancy. Among them are frequent
meetings on both regular and irregular bases (e.g., Honda's brainstorming camp or *tama dashi kai*) and formal and informal communication networks (e.g., drinking sessions after working hours). These
devices facilitate the sharing of both tacit and explicit knowledge.

Redundancy of information increases the amount of information to
be processed and can lead to the problem of information overload. It
also increases the cost of knowledge creation, at least in the short run
(e.g., decreased operational efficiency). Therefore, balancing between
creation and processing of information is another important issue. One
way to deal with the possible downside of redundancy is to make clear
where information can be located and where knowledge is stored
within the organization.

Requisite Variety

The fifth condition that helps to advance the knowledge spiral is requisite variety. According to Ashby (1956), an organization's internal diversity must match the variety and complexity of the environment in
order to deal with challenges posed by the environment. Organizational members can cope with many contingencies if they possess requisite variety, which can be enhanced by combining information differently, flexibly, and quickly, and by providing equal access to
information throughout the organization. To maximize variety, everyone in the organization should be assured of the fastest access to the
broadest variety of necessary information, going through the fewest
steps (Numagami, Ohta, and Nonaka, 1989).

When information differentials exist within the organization, organizational members cannot interact on equal terms, which hinders the
search for different interpretations of new information. Kao Corp., Japan's leading maker of household products such as detergents, believes
that all employees should have equal access to corporate information.
Kao has developed a computerized information network for this purpose. It has become the basis for opinion exchanges among various organizational units with different viewpoints.

Kao has also built an organizational structure, shown in Figure 3-
8, that allows the various organizational units and the computerized
information network to be interwoven organically and flexibly. Kao
named this structure a "bio-function-type" of organization. Under this
structure, each organization unit works in unison with other units to
cope with various environmental factors and events, just as a living

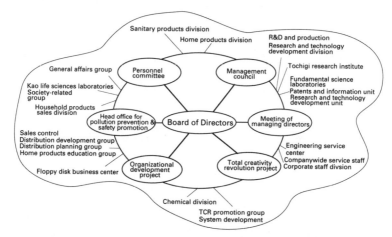

Figure 3-8. Kao's bio-function-type organizational structure.
Source: Kao Corp.

organism would. The human body, for example, reacts instinctively to itching by scratching the part of the body affected. The message relayed from the skin is received by the brain, which orders the hand movement. Lymph glands also go into action if necessary. Kao regards this kind of coordinated chain reaction an ideal way to cope with the external environment. Kao believes this "bio-function-type" structure helps to eliminate hierarchy and foster organizational knowledge creation.

Developing a flat and flexible organizational structure in which the different units are interlinked with an information network is one way to deal with the complexity of the environment. Another way to react quickly to unexpected fluctuations in the environment and maintain internal diversity is to change organizational structure frequently. Matsushita, for example, restructured its divisional system three times in the past decade. In addition, frequent rotation of personnel enables employees to acquire multifunctional knowledge, which helps them to cope with multifaceted problems and unexpected environmental fluctuations. Such a fast-cycle rotation of personnel can be seen at the Ministry of International Trade and Industry (MITI), where the bureaucrats rotate from one job to the next every two years.

Five-Phase Model of the Organizational Knowledge-Creation Process

Thus far we have looked at each of the four modes of knowledge conversion and the five enabling conditions that promote organizational knowledge creation. In this section we present an integrated, five-phase model of the organizational knowledge-creation process, using the basic constructs developed within the theoretical framework and incorporating the time dimension into our theory. The model, which should be interpreted as an ideal example of the process, consists of five phases: (1) sharing tacit knowledge; (2) creating concepts; (3) justifying concepts; (4) building an archetype; and (5) cross-leveling knowledge (see Figure 3-9).

The organizational knowledge-creation process starts with the sharing of tacit knowledge, which corresponds roughly to socialization, since the rich and untapped knowledge that resides in individuals must first be amplified within the organization. In the second phase, tacit knowledge shared by, for example, a self-organizing team is converted to explicit knowledge in the form of a new concept, a process similar to externalization. The created concept has to be justified in the third phase, in which the organization determines if the new concept is truly worthy of pursuit. Receiving the go-ahead, the concepts are converted in the fourth phase into an archetype, which can take the form of a prototype in the case of "hard" product development or an operating mechanism in the case of "soft" innovations, such as a new corporate value, a novel managerial system, or an innovative organizational structure. The last phase extends the knowledge created in, for example, a division to others in the division, across to other divisions, or even to outside constituents in what we term cross-leveling of knowledge. These outside constituents include consumers, affiliated companies, universities, and distributors. A knowledge-creating company does not operate in a closed system but in an open system in

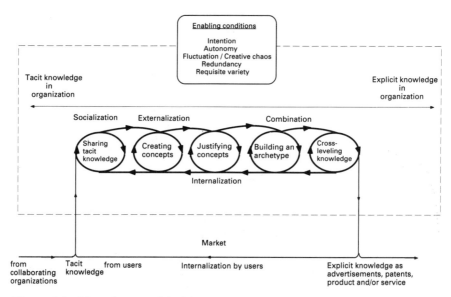

Figure 3-9. Five-phase model of the organizational knowledge-creation process.

which knowledge is constantly exchanged with the outside environment. We shall describe each of the five phases in more detail below.

The First Phase: Sharing Tacit Knowledge

As we have mentioned repeatedly, an organization cannot create knowledge by itself. Since tacit knowledge held by individuals is the basis of organizational knowledge creation, it seems natural to start the process by focusing on tacit knowledge, which is the rich, untapped source of new knowledge. But tacit knowledge cannot be communicated or passed onto others easily, since it is acquired primarily through experience and not easily expressible in words. Thus, the sharing of tacit knowledge among multiple individuals with different backgrounds, perspectives, and motivations becomes the critical step for organizational knowledge creation to take place. The individuals' emotions, feelings, and mental models have to be shared to build mutual trust.

To effect that sharing, we need a "field" in which individuals can interact with each other through face-to-face dialogues. It is here that they share experiences and synchronize their bodily and mental rhythms. The typical field of interaction is a self-organizing team, in which members from various functional departments work together to achieve a common goal. Examples of a self-organizing team include Matsushita's Home Bakery team and the Honda City team. At Matsushita, team members apprenticed themselves to the head baker at the Osaka International Hotel to capture the essence of kneading skill through bodily experience. At Honda, team members shared their mental models and technical skills in discussing what an ideal car should evolve into, often over *sake* and away from the office. These examples show that the first phase of the organizational knowledge-creation process corresponds to socialization.

A self-organizing team facilitates organizational knowledge creation through the requisite variety of the team members, who experience redundancy of information and share their interpretations of organizational intention. Management injects creative chaos by setting challenging goals and endowing team members with a high degree of autonomy. An autonomous team starts to set its own task boundaries and, as a "boundary-spanning unit," begins to interact with the external environment, accumulating both tacit and explicit knowledge.

The Second Phase: Creating Concepts

The most intensive interaction between tacit and explicit knowledge occurs in the second phase. Once a shared mental model is formed in the field of interaction, the self-organizing team then articulates it through further continuous dialogue, in the form of collective reflection. The shared tacit mental model is verbalized into words and phrases, and finally crystallized into explicit concepts. In this sense, this phase corresponds to externalization.

This process of converting tacit knowledge into explicit knowledge is facilitated by the use of multiple reasoning methods such as deduction, induction, and abduction. Particularly useful for this phase is abduction, which employs figurative language such as metaphors and analogies. In developing City, for example, the Honda development team made ample use of figurative language such as "Automobile Evolution," "man-maximum, machine-minimum," and "Tall Boy." The quality of dialogue among team members can also be raised through the use of dialectics, which instills a creative way of thinking into the organization. It is an iterative and spiral process in which contradictions and paradoxes are utilized to synthesize new knowledge.

Concepts are created cooperatively in this phase through dialogue. Autonomy helps team members to diverge their thinking freely, with intention serving as a tool to converge their thinking in one direction. To create concepts, team members have to rethink their existing premises fundamentally. Requisite variety helps the team in this regard by providing different angles or perspectives for looking at a problem. Fluctuation and chaos, either from the outside or inside, also help members to change their way of thinking fundamentally. Redundancy of information enables team members to understand figurative language better and to crystallize their shared mental model.

The Third Phase: Justifying Concepts

In our theory of organizational knowledge creation, knowledge is defined as justified true belief. Therefore, new concepts created by individuals or the team need to be justified at some point in the procedure. Justification involves the process of determining if the newly created concepts are truly worthwhile for the organization and society. It is similar to a screening process. Individuals seem to be justifying or screening information, concepts, or knowledge continuously and unconsciously throughout the entire process. The organization, however, must conduct this justification in a more explicit way to check if the organizational intention is still intact and to ascertain if the concepts being generated meet the needs of society at large. The most appropriate time for the organization to conduct this screening process is right after the concepts have been created.[28]

For business organizations, the normal justification criteria include cost, profit margin, and the degree to which a product can contribute to the firm's growth. But justification criteria can be both quantitative and qualitative. For example, in the Honda City case, the "Tall Boy" concept had to be justified against the vision established by top management—to come up with a product concept fundamentally different from anything the company had done before and to make a car that was inexpensive but not cheap. It also had to be justified against the product-line concept articulated by middle management—to make the car "man-maximum, machine-minimum." More abstract criteria may include value premises such as adventure, romanticism, and aesthetics. Thus justification criteria need not be strictly objective and factual; they can also be judgmental and value-laden.

In a knowledge-creating company, it is primarily the role of top management to formulate the justification criteria in the form of organizational intention, which is expressed in terms of strategy or vision. Middle management can also formulate the justification criteria in the form of mid-range concepts. Although the key justification criteria are set by top management, and to some extent by middle management, this does not preclude other organizational units from having some autonomy in deciding their own subcriteria. For example, a committee comprised of 200 young employees within Matsushita determined that Matsushita employees in the twenty-first century should become "voluntary individuals" to adapt to expected social changes, as will be discussed in more detail in the next chapter. To this extent, a company's justification criteria should be consistent with value systems or needs of the society at large, which should ideally be reflected in organizational intention. To avoid any misunderstanding about the company's intention, redundancy of information helps facilitate the justification process.

The Fourth Phase: Building an Archetype

In this fourth phase, the justified concept is converted into something tangible or concrete, namely, an archetype. An archetype can be thought of as a prototype in the case of a new-product development process. In the case of service or organizational innovation, an archetype could be thought of as a model operating mechanism. In either case, it is built by combining newly created explicit knowledge with existing explicit knowledge. In building a prototype, for example, the explicit knowledge to be combined could take the form of technologies or components. Because justified concepts, which are explicit, are converted into archetypes, which are also explicit, this phase is akin to combination.

Just as an architect builds a mock-up before starting the actual construction, organizational members engage in building a prototype of the real product or a model of the actual system. To build a prototype, they pull together people with differing expertise (e.g., R&D, production, marketing, quality control), develop specifications that meet everyone's approval, and actually manufacture the first full-scale form of a newly created product concept. To build a model, say, of a new organizational structure, people from the affected sections within the organization, as well as experts in different fields (e.g., human resources management, legal, strategic planning), are assembled to draw up a new organizational chart, job description, reporting system, or operating procedure. In a way, their role is similar to that of the architect—they are responsible for developing the blueprint as well as actually building the new form of an organizational concept. Attention to detail is the key to managing this complex process.

Because this phase is complex, dynamic cooperation of various departments within the organization is indispensable. Both requisite variety and redundancy of information facilitate this process. Organizational intention also serves as a useful tool for converging the various kinds of know-how and technologies that reside within the organization, as well as for promoting interpersonal and interdepartmental cooperation. On the other hand, autonomy and fluctuation are generally not that relevant at this stage of the organizational knowledge-creation process.

The Fifth Phase: Cross-Leveling of Knowledge

Organizational knowledge creation is a never-ending process that upgrades itself continuously. It does not end once an archetype has been developed. The new concept, which has been created, justified, and modeled, moves on to a new cycle of knowledge creation at a different ontological level. This interactive and spiral process, which we call cross-leveling of knowledge, takes place both intra-organizationally and inter-organizationally.

Intra-organizationally, knowledge that is made real or that takes form as an archetype can trigger a new cycle of knowledge creation, expanding horizontally and vertically across the organization. An example of horizontal cross-fertilization can be seen within Matsushita, where Home Bakery induced the creation of other "Easy & Rich" product concepts, such as a fully automatic coffee maker within the same division and a new generation of large-screen TV sets from another division. In these cases, cross-fertilization took place across different sections within a division as well as across different divisions. An example of vertical cross-fertilization also comes from Matsushita. The development of Home Bakery inspired Matsushita to adopt "Human Electronics" as the umbrella concept at the corporate level. This umbrella concept opened up a series of soul-searching activities within the company to address what kind of company Matsushita should be in the twenty-first century and how "human" Matsushita employees can be. These activities culminated in the development of MIT'93 (Mind and Management Innovation Toward '93), which was instrumental in reducing the number of annual working hours at the front line to 1,800 hours, thereby freeing up time for people at the front line. In this case, knowledge created in one division led to the adoption of an umbrella concept at the corporate level, which in turn affected the lives of employees at the front line.

Inter-organizationally, knowledge created by the organization can mobilize knowledge of affiliated companies, customers, suppliers, competitors, and others outside the company through dynamic interaction. For example, an innovative new approach to budgetary control developed by one company could bring about changes in an affiliated company's financial control system, which in turn may trigger a new round of innovation. Or a customer's reaction or feedback to a new-product concept may initiate a new cycle of product development. At Apple Computer, for example, when product development engineers come up with ideas for new products, they build a prototype that embodies those ideas and bring it directly to customers to seek their reaction. Depending on the reaction or feedback, a new round of development may be initiated.

For this phase to function effectively, it is essential that each organizational unit have the autonomy to take the knowledge developed somewhere else and apply it freely across different levels and boundaries. Internal fluctuation, such as the frequent rotation of personnel, will facilitate knowledge transfer. So will redundancy of information and requisite variety. And in intra-organizational cross-leveling, organizational intention will act as a control mechanism on whether or not knowledge should be cross-fertilized within the company.

Summary

Recall that we started to develop our theoretical framework in this chapter by pointing out the two dimensions—epistemological and ontological—of organizational knowledge creation (see Figure 3-1). The epistemological dimension, which is graphically represented on the vertical axis, is where knowledge conversion takes place between tacit knowledge and explicit knowledge. Four modes of this conversion—socialization, externalization, combination, and internalization—were discussed. These modes are not independent of each other, but their interactions produce a spiral when time is introduced as the third dimension. We introduced five organizational conditions—intention, fluctuation/chaos, autonomy, redundancy, and requisite variety—that enable (thus the term "enabling conditions") the four modes to be transformed into a knowledge spiral.

The ontological dimension, which is represented in the horizontal axis, is where knowledge created by individuals is transformed into knowledge at the group and organizational levels. These levels are not independent of each other, but interact with each other iteratively and continuously. Again we introduced time as the third dimension to develop the five-phase process of organizational knowledge creation—sharing tacit knowledge, creating concepts, justifying concepts, building an archetype, and cross-leveling knowledge. Another spiral takes place at the ontological dimension, when knowledge developed at, for example, the project-team level is transformed into knowledge at the divisional level, and eventually at the corporate or inter-organizational level. The five enabling conditions promote the entire process and facilitate the spiral.

The transformation process within these two knowledge spirals is the key to understanding our theory. If we had a three-dimensional chart, we could show that the knowledge spiral at the epistemological level rises upward, whereas the knowledge spiral at the ontological level moves from left to right and back again to the left in a cyclical motion. And, of course, the truly dynamic nature of our theory can be depicted as the interaction of the two knowledge spirals over time. Innovation emerges out of these spirals.

Notes

1. Shannon later commented: "I think perhaps the word "information" is causing more trouble . . . than it is worth, except that it is difficult to find another word that is anywhere near right. It should be kept solidly in mind that [information] is only a measure of the difficulty in transmitting the sequence produced by some information source" (quoted by Roszack, 1986, p. 12). Boulding (1983) notes that Shannon's assessment was analogous to a telephone bill, which is calculated on the basis of time and distance but gives no insight into the content of information, and called it Bell Telephone (BT) information. Dretske (1981) argues that a genuine theory of information would be a theory about the content of our messages, not a theory about the form in which this content is embodied.

2. The importance of the knowledge-action relationship has been recognized in the area of artificial intelligence. For example, Gruber (1989) examined experts' "strategic knowledge" that guides their actions and has attempted to develop tools for acquiring such knowledge.

3. Brown and Duguid's (1991) work on "evolving communities of practice" shows how individuals' actual ways of working and learning might be very different from relatively rigid, official practices specified by the organization. In reality, informal groups evolve among individuals seeking to solve a particular problem or pursuing other commonly held objectives. Membership in these groups is decided by individuals' abilities to trade practically valuable information. Orr (1990) argues that members exchange ideas and share narratives or "war stories," thereby building a shared understanding out of conflicting and confusing information. Thus knowledge creation includes not only innovation but also learning that can shape and develop approaches to daily work.

4. For example, we recognize our neighbor's face without being able to explain how to do so in words. Moreover, we sense others' feelings from their

facial expressions, but explaining them in words is more difficult. Put another way, while it is virtually impossible to articulate the feelings we get from our neighbor's face, we are still aware of the overall impression. For further discussion on tacit knowledge, see Polanyi (1958) and Gelwick (1977).

5. We did not include Polanyi in Chapter 2, because he is still considered minor in Western philosophy because of his view and background. Michael Polanyi was born in Hungary and was the brother of Karl Polanyi, an economist, who may be better known as the author of *The Great Transformation*. Michael Polanyi himself was a renowned chemist and rumored to be very close to the Nobel prize until he turned to philosophy at the age of 50. Polanyi's philosophy has implicit or explicit agreements with those of "later" Wittgenstein and Merleau-Ponty in terms of their emphases on action, body, and tacit knowledge. For a discussion on an affinity between Polanyi and later Wittgenstein with regard to tacit knowledge, see Gill (1974).

6. Brown (1992) argues that "The organizations of the future will be 'knowledge refineries' in which employees will synthesize understanding and interpretations from the sea of information that threatens to flood them from all sides (p. 3)." In a knowledge refinery, he continues, workers need to collaborate with both the past and the present. While collaboration with the present is about sharing tacit knowledge, collaboration with the past draws on experiences gained from previous ways of doing things.

7. According to Maturana and Varela (1980), "The linguistic domain as a domain of orienting behavior requires at least two interacting organisms with comparable domains of interactions, so that a cooperative system of consensual interactions may be developed in which the emerging conduct of the two organisms is relevant for both. . . . The central feature of human existence is its occurrence in a linguistic cognitive domain. This domain is constitutively social" (pp. xxiv, 41).

8. The ACT model is consonant with Ryle's (1949) categorization of knowledge into knowing that something "exists" and knowing "how" it operates. Also, Squire (1987) listed contending taxonomies with more than a dozen labels, such as "implicit" vs. "explicit" and "skill memory" vs. "fact memory." Most of these distinctions separate properties to be grouped under "procedural" from those to be classified "declarative."

9. A survey of 105 Japanese middle managers was conducted to test the hypothesis that the knowledge creation construct is comprised of four knowledge conversion processes—socialization, externalization, combination, and internalization. Factor loadings from first-order and second-order factor analyses empirically validated the existence of these four conversion processes. For details, see Nonaka, Byosiere, Borucki, and Konno (1994).

10. For a limited analysis of externalization from a viewpoint of information creation, see Nonaka (1987).

11. Cannon-Bowers, Salas, and Converse (1993) define "shared mental models" as "knowledge structures held by members of a team that enable them to form accurate explanations and expectations for the task, and in turn, to coordinate their actions and adapt their behavior to demands of the task and other team members" (p. 228), based upon their extensive review of the literature on the shared mental model and their research on team decision making. To understand how a shared mental model is created, the German philosopher

Hans-Georg Gadamer's concept of "fusion of horizons" is helpful. The concept was developed for philosophical hermeneutics or the study of methodology for interpreting historical texts. Gadamer (1989) argues that a true understanding of a text is a "fusion" of the interpreter's and the author's horizons. He defines the horizon as "the range of vision that includes everything that can be seen from a particular vantage point" (p. 302). Applying this concept to our context, we can argue that socialization is a "fusion" of participants' tacit knowledge into a shared mental model.

12. Proposing the concept of "field epistemology," Scheflen (1982) emphasizes the importance of "interaction rhythms" in forming a field for common understanding, and contends that communication is the simultaneous sharing of information existing in the situation. Similarly, Condon (1976) argues that communication is a simultaneous and contextual phenomenon in which people feel a change occurring, share the same sense of change, and are moved to take action. In other words, he says, communication is like a wave that passes through people's bodies and culminates when everyone synchronizes with the wave. From a social psychological perspective, Hogg and Abrams (1993) observe that "group behavior might be motivated by a search for meaning and a coherent self-concept" (p. 189).

13. Graumann (1990) views dialogue as multiperspective cognition. As noted before, language is inherently related to action, as suggested by the term "speech act" (Austin, 1962; Searle, 1969). Dialogue, therefore, may be seen as a collective action. Moreover, according to Kant, the world is created by language, and creating concepts is creating the world.

14. Interviewed on January 25, 1984.

15. These authors emphasize the importance of creating shared meaning for organized action, arguing that "equifinal meanings" for joint experience need to be developed to create shared meaning in the organization. Metaphor is one of four mechanisms to develop equifinal meanings that they found through their discourse analyses. For more discussion about metaphor and the other three mechanisms—logical argument, affect modulation, and linguistic indirection—see Donnellon, Gray, and Bougon (1986). Moreover, metaphor can be seen as an economical cognitive tool. According to Rosch (1973), we understand things not through their attributes but through better examples of them, or what she called "prototypes." As a prototype for birds, a robin is better than a seagull, which is better than a penguin. The best prototype provides maximum information with minimum cognitive energy.

16. The following famous episode illustrates the process. F. A. Kekule, a German chemist, discovered the chemical structure of benzene—a hexagonal ring of carbon atoms—through a dream of a snake gripping its own tail. In this case, the snake pattern was a metaphor, and possible combinations of the pattern became analogies of other organic chemical compounds. Thus, Kekule developed the structural model of organic chemistry.

17. According to Lakoff and Johnson (1980), "metaphor is pervasive in everyday life, not just in language but in thought and action" (p. 3).

18. Information and communications technologies used for this purpose include VAN (Value-Added Network), LAN (Local Area Network), E-Mail (Electronic Mail), POS (Point-Of-Sales) system, "Groupware" for CSCW (Computer Supported Cooperative Work), and CAD/CAM (Computer-Aided Design/Manufacturing).

19. In the triad database system, data from the Market Metrics' Supermarket Solutions system, which integrates POS data from supermarkets nationwide, is hooked to customized data on shopping behaviors provided by Information Resources, and lifestyle data from the Equifax Marketing Decision System's Microvision database. For more information, see "Micro-Merchandizing with KGF," *Food and Beverage Marketing,* 10, no. 6 (1991); "Dawn of Brand Analysis," *Food and Beverage Marketing,* 10, no. 10 (1991); and "Partnering," *Supermarket Business,* 46, no. 5 (1991).

20. Neisser (1976) argues that cognition as knowing and understanding occurs only in the context of purposeful activity. From an organization theory perspective, moreover, Weick (1979) contends that an organization's interpretation of environmental information has an element of self-fulfilling prophecy, because the organization has a strong will to self-actualize what it wants to become. He calls this phenomenon the "enactment" of environment.

21. Seen from the Simonian viewpoint of "bounded rationality" and the viewpoint that the goal of the organization is to process information efficiently, autonomy is merely a source of "noise" and therefore not desirable. The notion of cognitive limit is indeed a commonsensical one that is difficult to beat. If, however, we approach the same problem from the viewpoint that human beings have an unlimited capability to obtain and create knowledge, it appears that human beings know no boundary in experiencing and accumulating tacit knowledge. Underlying that accumulation of tacit knowledge is the sense of purpose and autonomy. Human beings often create noise intentionally, thereby overcoming themselves.

22. The team should be established with due consideration of the principles of self-organization such as learning to learn, requisite variety, minimum critical specification, and redundancy of functions (Morgan, 1986). Requisite variety will be discussed later.

23. In our *Harvard Business Review* article entitled "The New New Product Development Game" (Takeuchi and Nonaka, 1986), we argued that in today's fast-paced and fiercely competitive world, this overlapping, rugby-style approach has tremendous merit in terms of speed and flexibility.

24. Gibson (1979) hypothesizes that knowledge lies in the environment itself, contrary to the traditional epistemological view that it exists inside the human brain. According to him, we perceive "affordance" or what things in our environment afford us as we interact with them. Some information on a chair, for example, can be perceived only when we actually sit on the chair. Norman (1988) argues that knowledge exists not only inside the brain but also in the external world in the forms of things, others, and situations.

25. Piaget (1974) notes the importance of the role of contradiction in the interaction between subject and environment. The root of contradiction, he argues, lies in the coordination between the positive and negative sides of specific perception or behavior, which in turn is indispensable for creating new concepts.

26. According to the principle of "order out of noise" proposed by von Foerster (1984), the self-organizing system can increase its ability to survive by purposefully introducing such noise into itself. Order in the natural world includes not only the static and crystallized order in which entropy is zero but also the "unstable" order in which new structures are formed by the working of matter and energy. The latter is what Prigogine and Stengers (1984) call

"order out of chaos" in their theory of dissipative structure. In an evolutionary planning perspective, moreover, Jantsch (1980) argues: "In contrast to widely held belief, planning in an evolutionary spirit therefore does not result in the reduction of uncertainty and complexity, but in their increases. Uncertainty increases because the spectrum of options is deliberately widened; imagination comes into play" (p. 267). Researchers who have developed the chaos theory have found the creative nature of chaos. See, for example, Gleick (1987) and Waldrop (1992). For applications of the chaos theory to management, see Nonaka (1988a) and Zimmerman (1993).

27. Using the term "heterarchy" which means "non-hierarchy," Hedlund (1986) explains the role of redundant information as a vehicle for problem formulation and knowledge creation on the basis of procedures different from those officially specified by the organization.

28. The final justification of created concepts and their realized forms, i.e., products and/or services, occurs in the marketplace.

4

Creating Knowledge
in Practice

This chapter uses the Matsushita Electric Industrial Co., Ltd., to illustrate the theoretical framework of organizational knowledge creation presented in Chapter 3. Although a variety of references have been used to illustrate each component of the theoretical framework, this chapter will illustrate the entire process of knowledge creation within a single Japanese company. The Matsushita case is divided into two parts. The first part explains the development by Matsushita of a bread-making appliance, known as "Home Bakery," and its subsequent effect throughout the company. In the second part, we analyze the continuous process of knowledge creation at the corporate level of Matsushita.

Matsushita's Home Bakery is the first fully automatic bread-making machine for home use, introduced to the Japanese market in 1987. It transforms raw ingredients into freshly baked bread, doing everything from kneading and fermenting the dough to actually baking bread of a quality that compares favorably with what a professional baker would produce. All that is required is the mixing of flour, butter, salt, water, and yeast. For even further convenience, a premeasured bread-mix package can be used to save the trouble of measuring out the required ingredients. The machine is remarkable in that it embodies the skills of a master baker in a device that can be operated easily by people with no knowledge of bread making. It captures the skills of a baker in such a way that the critical dough-kneading process, which previously depended on the baker's tacit knowledge, can be reproduced consistently using electromechanical technology.

The Home Bakery's development story supports our theory presented in the previous chapter in two ways. First, it illustrates the four modes of knowledge conversion—socialization, externalization, combination, and internalization. It is especially suited to show how tacit knowledge is mobilized in the pursuit of creative innovation. Second, it illustrates enabling conditions as well as the five phases of knowledge creation—sharing tacit knowledge, creating concepts, justification, building archetypes, and cross-leveling of knowledge. We will discover that knowledge creation is not a linear process, but rather a cyclical and iterative process. As evidence of this, the development of Home Bakery required knowledge creation to move along the five phases a total of three times or cycles.

The second half of the case shows how the knowledge created through the development of Home Bakery was elaborated within Matsushita, resulting in a broader spiral of knowledge creation. The developments that took place in the Cooking Appliances Division eventually triggered changes in other parts of the company and strongly affected corporate strategy. The case also highlights the importance of an organization's ability (1) to identify the type of knowledge required by the changing competitive environment, and (2) to enhance the enabling conditions continuously. With knowledge being perishable, organizations cannot become complacent with today's knowledge, as different types of knowledge will be required as the competitive environment changes. And as we have already seen, it is this ability to create new knowledge continuously that becomes the source of competitiveness in the knowledge society.

Corporate Background

We start the case by describing the corporate background leading to the development of Home Bakery. As the Japanese household appliances market matured in the 1970s, Matsushita's operational profitability diminished in the face of strong price competition. By 1977, 95.4 percent of Japanese households already owned color television sets, 94.5 percent owned vacuum cleaners, 98.4 percent owned refrigerators, 98.5 percent owned washing machines, and 94.3 percent owned irons. In addition, rivals from newly industrialized countries had been improving their position as low-cost competitors.

A three-year corporate plan called "ACTION 61" was announced in May 1983. ACTION was an acronym that stood for "Action, Cost reduction, Topical products, Initiative in marketing, Organizational reactivation, and New management strength." The number 61 stood for the sixty-first year of Emperor Hirohito's era, or 1986. The objectives of this plan were twofold: (1) to improve Matsushita's competitiveness in its core businesses through careful attention to cost and marketing, and (2) to assemble the resources necessary to enter new markets historically dominated by competitors such as IBM, Hitachi, NEC, and Fujitsu. These two objectives were expressed in a slogan that came to be known as "Beyond Household Appliances." Naoki Wakabayashi, then chief of the Strategy Planning Section, recalls the sentiment in those days:

> Looking at market share, we were losing share in TV sets and in radios. The whole market was for replacements and not growing. That's why we needed to move into the industrial market. We felt that we might not be able to survive without moving into a new world. . . . Of course, the household appliances were our core business and we were not going to retreat from them. . . . [We wanted to move] beyond but not out of household appliances. (Yanagida, 1986, p. 31)

Creative chaos was brought into the Household Appliances Group in 1983 as the company shifted its strategic focus from household appliances to high-tech and industrial products. This strategic shift led to the restructuring of the core business and also led to the integration of three divisions into the Cooking Appliances Division, as we shall see below. This integration brought further *chaos* and *requisite variety* into the newly formed division and put pressure on the Household Appliances Group to develop innovative products. Improving competitiveness and assuring survival were the name of the game.

Integration of the Three Problem Children

In May 1984, three divisions were integrated into the Cooking Appliances Division as part of ACTION 61. The intent was twofold: to improve organizational efficiency by eliminating the duplication of resources and to restore the growth track by combining the technology and know-how of the three divisions. The three divisions were the Rice-Cooker Division, which made microcomputer-controlled rice cookers; the Heating Appliances Division, which made hot plates, oven-toasters, and coffee makers using induction heater technology; and the Rotation Division, which made motorized products such as food processors.

All of these products faced market maturity (see Figure 4-1). The market for rice cookers was no longer growing, with the only growth coming from microcomputer-controlled rice cookers replacing conventional types. The oven-toaster market was not growing as well, while the demand was shrinking for food processors because consumers felt the setup and cleaning after use were inconvenient.

The benefits of the integration were not initially apparent (see Fig-

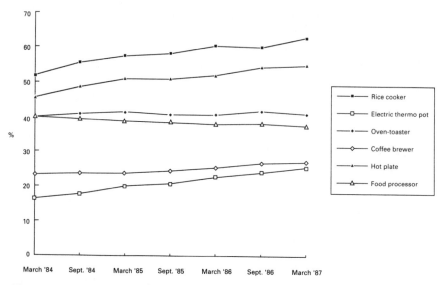

Figure 4-1. Market penetration rates of the main products. *Source: Matsushita Electric Industrial Co., Ltd.*

ure 4-2). In the two years immediately following the integration, the new division's profitability improved from 7.2 percent in 1984 to 9.0 percent as a result of eliminating excess capacity. However, the division still suffered declining sales, from 62.7 billion yen in 1984 to 60.4 billion yen in 1986. Consequently, people in the division as well as in other parts of the company started to question the benefits of the integration. Ikuji Masumura, the Strategy Planning Section chief, said:

> It was apparent that sales had been slowing after the integration. Many discussions took place on the benefits of integration on sales. We thought it was not enough to combine existing businesses, reduce fixed costs, and survive. There was a sentiment that something new had to be started, utilizing the characteristics of the three divisions.[1]

Enabling Conditions at Matsushita

The company's strategic shift and the integration of the three divisions introduced a sense of crisis into the Cooking Appliances Division. The resulting *creative chaos* inspired individual *intention* and commitment throughout the division. These employees, who had pride in the traditional core business, felt that unless they could develop a home-run product, a completely new product based on a unique technology that combined the knowledge of the three divisions, their ability to improve competitiveness would be questioned.

The integration also brought in *requisite variety*. The three divisions

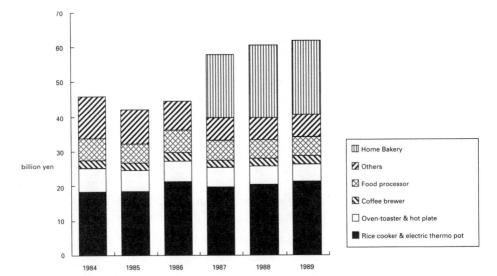

Figure 4-2. Sales of the Cooking Appliances Division. *Source: Matsushita Electric Industrial Co., Ltd.*

contained a total of 1,400 employees coming from completely different divisional cultures. It was apparent that they had different backgrounds and different ways of doing business. It almost seemed as though they spoke different languages.

Following the introduction of *creative chaos,* communications had to be improved in order to foster the *redundancy* of information. The fact that the three divisions had totally different cultures, ways of doing things, and even languages made it very difficult for communication to flow with any ease. To deal with this problem, the new division sent 13 middle managers from various sections to a three-day retreat to discuss the division's present situation and future direction, which was an attempt to mobilize and share their tacit knowledge. To diffuse explicit knowledge within the division, the personnel department published a newspaper called "Hot-Line" for factory workers. Keimei Sano, the Cooking Appliances Division chief, commented on the importance of communication as follows:

> Speaking a common language and having discussions can assemble the power of the group. This is a vital point, even though it takes time to develop a common language.[2]

The final enabling condition was the development of organizational *intention,* which was to guide a group of diverse individuals toward one goal, one direction. To find clues and suggestions about what that direction might be for the division, a planning team was sent to the United States in 1984 to observe trends in the daily lives of Americans.

What they observed there were "more working women, increasingly simplified home cooking, and poorer diets," according to Masumura. Recognizing that the same trends were evident in Japan, the team came to the conclusion that cooking appliances should make meals simple to prepare but at the same time make them tasty and rich in nutrition. As a result, the division came up with an overall concept that came to be known as "Easy & Rich." The team believed that an appliance that could produce delicious and nutritious food easily would respond to the needs of working women and gourmet aficionados.

The First Knowledge-Creation Spiral Around the Development of Home Bakery

It was not long after the return of the planning team to Japan that a rough design for an automatic home bakery machine was proposed by Hoshiden Electronics Co., Ltd.[3] From this development, Matsushita's team immediately saw that "Easy & Rich" could be associated with an automatic bread-making machine. The idea of a fully automatic bread-making machine also embodied many qualities that were appropriate to the division's new objectives. It was completely new, and it involved multiple technologies, such as computer-controlled heating systems from rice cookers, motors from food processors, and heating devices from hot plates.

The idea of an automatic bakery was not entirely new to Matsushita. Some development work had been done at Kyushu Matsushita, its subsidiary, in 1977, but it was suspended in 1980 because of technological difficulties and the prediction of a small anticipated demand. The former Heating Appliances Division also developed and marketed an electric oven in 1973 to ferment and bake bread, but attempts to develop an oven that kneaded dough had failed. This experience was instrumental in Matsushita's decision to reject Hoshiden's proposal for joint product development. Nevertheless, Matsushita was still attracted to the idea of an automated bread maker and elected to develop its own machine in-house.

Given this background, we are now ready to look in greater depth into the specifics of the product development process for Home Bakery. We will observe three cycles of the knowledge-creation process. Each cycle starts with the sharing of experiences among the team members. From these shared experiences, concepts and/or archetypes are created. These concepts and/or archetypes are justified against the organizational *intention*. The next cycle starts either to improve upon the outcome or to overcome the shortcomings of the previous cycle.

The first cycle started with the sharing of experiences by the members of the pilot team. They then externalized the product concept into specific product features and assembled a prototype. However, the original prototype could not produce bread tasty enough to be justified against the concept of "Rich." As a result, the process went into the second cycle.

The second cycle started with a software developer, Ikuko Tanaka, sharing experience with a master baker to learn how to knead bread dough properly. To put this difficult know-how into a machine, Tanaka created the mental image of a "twisting stretch" motion to explain kneading. The skill of kneading was then materialized into specific mechanics such as the movement of the propeller, which kneaded dough, and the design of the special ribs. Because the new prototype succeeded in producing tasty bread, the development moved into the third cycle with the new challenge of meeting cost requirements.

The third cycle began with sharing of tacit knowledge among members of the commercialization team. New members from the manufacturing and marketing sections were added to the team. An innovative way to control fermentation, known as "Chumen" in Japanese, was developed by the team. This innovation, which added yeast during the kneading process, produced even better bread at lower cost. The resulting bread was justified against cost and quality requirements set when the product concept was originally developed. The perfected Home Bakery machine differentiated itself from competing brands that eventually entered the market and became a hit product. The success of Home Bakery led to the cross-leveling of knowledge at the corporate level.

The First Cycle of the Home Bakery Spiral

Keimei Sano, who headed the Cooking Appliances Division, initiated the development work on Home Bakery in April 1984. He formed a pilot team, bringing together employees from the Household Appliances Laboratory, an R&D lab for four divisions including the Cooking Appliances Division, with a mechanical designer and a software developer, both of whom were familiar with bread making. This ad hoc team conducted several discussions to develop the product concept that would realize "Easy & Rich." Masao Torikoshi, who was with the Household Appliances Laboratory, served as the leader. He developed the following product specifications himself in order to avoid any compromises:

1. The machine must knead, ferment, and bake bread automatically once the ingredients are put into the machine.
2. It should not need a special mix of ingredients.
3. A built-in timer must allow the user to prepare the ingredients at night and have bread ready to serve in the morning.
4. Bread making must not be affected by room temperature.
5. The bread should have a good shape.

6. It should taste better than a mass-produced and mass-marketed one.
7. The retail price should be between 30,000 yen and 40,000 yen.

Since these specifications were defined in terms of ideals rather than technological feasibility, many hurdles still had to be cleared.

In January 1985 the project was formally approved by the company, and an official team was formed jointly between the Lab. and the Cooking Appliances Division. But the 11-member team was drawn from several sections, with Torikoshi serving as the project leader. One member came from product planning, three from machines, two from control systems, and three from software development. They came into the project from completely different cultures, having been assembled into one division as the result of the integration that had occurred the previous year.

Because the machine itself was new to the company, everything had to be developed in-house. Several activities—such as developing the taste-measurement system and recipes for the automatic bakery, learning bread-kneading and baking skills, and developing the body of the machine, machinery, and control system—were conducted simultaneously (see Figure 4-3).

The first prototype produced something that could hardly be described as bread, since it had an overcooked crust but was raw inside. Several problems had to be resolved. The very shape of the dough case presented the initial problem. Because English bread was square, the case had to be square. However, kneading would be much easier if the case were round. The difference in electric cycles presented another problem. The eastern and western parts of Japan had different electric cycles, which affected the motor's rotation and therefore required an adjustment in the control system. The team also discovered that temperature had a significant effect on the fermenting and baking process. The ideal temperature for fermentation was 27 to 28 degrees centigrade, yet the variation in summer temperatures in the different re-

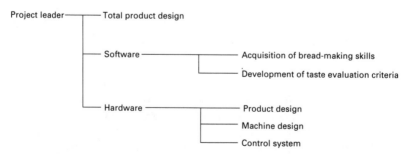

Figure 4-3. Product development tasks for Home Bakery. *Source: Matsushita Electric Industrial Co., Ltd.*

gions of Japan ranged between 5 and 35 degrees centigrade. At too high a temperature, the bread overfermented and became sour. At temperatures too low, the bread did not ferment enough and the dough did not rise. In addition, different brands and kinds of flour and yeast further complicated the control system. The system had to be robust enough to produce tasty bread under any circumstances.

In the first cycle of knowledge creation, we can observe the five enabling conditions at work. First, the pilot team was given full *autonomy*. Second, *requisite variety* existed because each member of the pilot team came into the project with a unique knowledge base. Third, there was *redundancy* of information because members with diverse knowledge bases had basically the same job description. Fourth, *creative chaos* was introduced after the three divisions were integrated. Finally, the concept of "Easy & Rich" was the organizational *intention* that served to coordinate and direct the activities of the Cooking Appliances Division employees.

On the pilot team, many discussions took place about what exactly Home Bakery should be. The overall divisional concept of "Easy & Rich" served as a guideline for discussion *(sharing tacit knowledge)*. It was general enough to accommodate ideas that reflected each member's tacit knowledge. At the same time, the concept was specific enough to clarify the critical requirements of all product development in the Cooking Appliances Division, namely ease of use and the realization of genuine quality.

In realizing ease of use, the tacit knowledge of each team member and the wants of consumers were *externalized* into product features that specified that "the machine must knead, ferment, and bake bread automatically once the ingredients set" and "a built-in timer must allow the user to prepare the ingredients at night and have bread ready to serve in the morning." A concrete product *concept* was *created* after sharing tacit knowledge. This product concept was then *justified* against the organizational intention. In this case, the specific product features were justified against "Easy & Rich" and accepted. Once the concept was justified, an *archetype* was *built* by combining explicit knowledge. In other words, a prototype of Home Bakery was built by *combining* existing technology. However, this prototype, which overcooked the crust while leaving the dough raw inside, was *not justified* against the original product concept. As a result, the knowledge-creation process moved back to the beginning of the second cycle (see Figure 4-4).

The Second Cycle of the Home Bakery Spiral

The second cycle began with a software developer, Ikuko Tanaka, sharing the tacit knowledge of a master baker in order to learn his kneading skill. A master baker learns the art of kneading, a critical step in

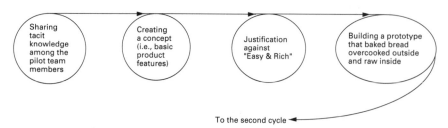

Figure 4-4. First cycle of the Home Bakery spiral.

bread making, following years of experience. However, such expertise is difficult to articulate in words. To capture this tacit knowledge, which usually takes a lot of imitation and practice to master, Tanaka proposed a creative solution. Why not train with the head baker at Osaka International Hotel, which had a reputation for making the best bread in Osaka, to study the kneading techniques? Tanaka learned her kneading skills through observation, imitation, and practice. She recalled:

> At first, everything was a surprise. After repeated failures, I began to ask where the master and I differed. I don't think one can understand or learn this skill without actually doing it. His bread and mine [came out] quite different even though we used the same materials. I asked why our products were so different and tried to reflect the difference in our skill of kneading.[4]

Even at this stage, neither the head baker nor Tanaka was able to articulate knowledge in any systematic fashion. Because their tacit knowledge never became explicit, others within Matsushita were left puzzled. Consequently, engineers were also brought to the hotel and allowed to knead and bake bread to improve their understanding of the process. Sano, the division chief, noted, "If the craftsmen cannot explain their skills, then the engineers should become craftsmen."[5]

Not being an engineer, Tanaka could not devise mechanical specifications. However, she was able to transfer her knowledge to the engineers by using the phrase "twisting stretch" to provide a rough image of kneading, and by suggesting the strength and speed of the propeller to be used in kneading. She would simply say, "Make the propeller move stronger," or "Move it faster." Then the engineers would adjust the machine specifications. Such a trial-and-error process continued for several months.

Her request for a "twisting stretch" movement was interpreted by the engineers and resulted in the addition inside the case of special ribs that held back the dough when the propeller turned so that the dough could be stretched. After a year of trial and error and working closely with other engineers, the team came up with product specifications that successfully reproduced the head baker's stretching technique and the quality of bread Tanaka had learned to make at the hotel. The team then materialized this concept, putting it together into a manual, and embodied it in the product.

In November 1985, the team succeeded in developing a machine that could make tasty bread. As illustrated in Figure 4-5, the product had a kneading mechanism with a motor, a dough case, and a yeast case that held the yeast until exactly the right moment. A microcomputer controlled the heater and yeast case by way of a timer and temperature sensor.

The prototype was now ready for trial. Members of the project team as well as the heads of the cooking appliances sales department, the technology department, and the division all took the prototype home for trial. Their spouses and children made bread with the prototype and provided feedback. Their comments proved that the goal of producing homemade, quality bread was finally achieved.

In the second cycle, the team had to resolve the problem of getting the machine to knead dough correctly. (See Figure 4-6.) To solve the kneading problem, Ikuko Tanaka apprenticed herself with the head baker of the Osaka International Hotel. There she learned the skill through *socialization,* observing and imitating the head baker, rather than through reading memos or manuals. She then translated the kneading skill into explicit knowledge. The knowledge was *externalized* by *creating the concept* of "twisting stretch." In addition, she *externalized* this knowledge by expressing the movements required for the

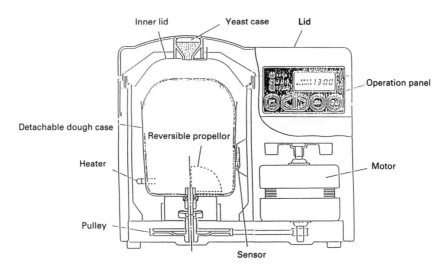

Figure 4-5. Schematic of Home Bakery. *Source: Matsushita Electric Industrial Co., Ltd.*

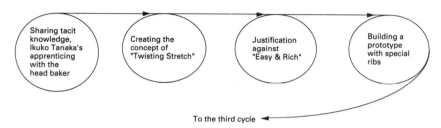

Figure 4-6. Second cycle of the Home Bakery spiral.

kneading propeller, using phrases like "more slowly" or "more strongly." For those who had never touched dough before, understanding the kneading skill was so difficult that engineers had to *share experiences* by spending hours at the baker to experience the touch of the dough. Tacit knowledge was *externalized* by lining special ribs inside the dough case. *Combination* took place when the "twisting stretch" concept and the technological knowledge of the engineers came together to produce a prototype of Home Bakery. Once the prototype was *justified* against the concept of "Rich," the development moved into the third cycle.

The Third Cycle of the Home Bakery Spiral

Seeing the success of the new prototype, Sano moved the project from technological development to the commercialization stage, and transferred the project from the lab to the division. The design staff was expanded, and members from the marketing and manufacturing departments were added at this time. The project team had to deal with industrial design, quality stabilization, and cost reduction as the main issues at this stage.

Although the project leader switched from Torikoshi to Yuzuru Arao, head of the division's planning department, Torikoshi continued to attend major meetings so that his tacit knowledge could be utilized. The other ten original members also remained on the team. Even though the tacit knowledge of bread making had been captured in the prototype, the tacit knowledge of the original members was still needed. In the commercialization stage, several changes were expected in order to meet the cost requirement. The original members' tacit knowledge of bread making was considered to be indispensable in finding a way to make these changes without harming the quality of bread.

The biggest challenge in the commercialization stage was to reduce the overall cost so that the retail price would become less than 40,000 yen. The major cost concern was over the cooler, which kept the yeast-laden dough from overfermenting in high temperatures. Chief Engineer Tsuneo Shibata recalls, "We were behind schedule and did not have a machine that could make tasty bread within the cost requirement. Everybody was very nervous."[6] A major advance came when someone on the team discovered that it was possible to mix the other ingredients and then add the yeast at a later stage in the process, a process known as "Chumen" in Japanese. It was the way people had made bread in the past, when means to control the temperature were not available. Matsushita obtained a patent on this technology, which subsequently proved to be an important factor in enabling the company to maintain its technological edge over rival companies that entered the market later.

The process of bread making using an automatic machine is shown in Figure 4-7. In total, the development process involved the baking of more than 5,000 loaves of bread using 1.5 tons of flour, 66 kilograms of butter, and 100 kilograms of sugar.

The only problem with the new process was that it required design changes—such as developing a new yeast case controlled by a timer, as well as taking out the coolant—that would postpone market introduction by at least four months. Home Bakery had been enthusiastically welcomed at a distributors meeting in February 1986, and its market introduction in November 1986 was much anticipated. It was also rumored that competitors were trying to develop automatic breadmaking machines of their own. In a hard choice between quality and market-introduction timing, an important factor in the competitive Japanese market, Sano's commitment to "Easy & Rich" won out, and the changes were made.

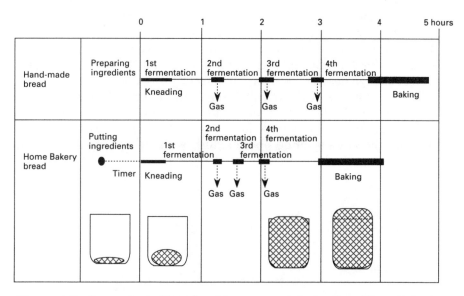

Figure 4-7. Comparison of bread-making processes by hand vs. Home Bakery. *Source: Matsushita Electric Industrial Co., Ltd.*

Matsushita's Home Bakery was introduced to the market in February 1987 at 36,000 yen and sold a record-setting 536,000 units in its first year. It hit the top of the list of Mother's Day gifts. Its success was so extraordinary and rare in the mature cooking appliances market that *Fortune* magazine featured the machine in its October 26, 1987, issue. Six months after market introduction in Japan, Matsushita began exporting Home Bakery to the United States, West Germany, and Hong Kong. Shipments were later expanded to Sweden, Thailand, Australia, and New Zealand. Though prices were set much higher than in the domestic market, Home Bakery has been selling well worldwide beyond the expectations of the manufacturing plan. In the United States, according to Matsushita, the entire market for an automatic bread-maker expanded to as much as one million units, as new competitors entered the market.

Justification played a critical role in the third cycle. (See Figure 4-8.) During the commercialization stage, the team faced the problem of having to reduce the cost of the machine significantly while maintaining the initial quality requirement. The team dealt with this problem by coming up with an innovative solution that did away with a costly yeast cooler. The solution was to put in yeast at a later stage of the dough-kneading process, instead of mixing it with the other ingredients at the very beginning. This improved quality and lowered cost at the same time. This method, referred to as "Chumen," was the result of the *socialization* and *externalization* of the team members' tacit knowledge.

However, a change in the design required the postponement of market introduction, which was a major dilemma, since market-introduction timing is considered crucial for a product's success in the Japanese market. Sano's commitment to the *organizational intention* of "Easy & Rich" allowed him to *justify* the decision to incorporate the design change despite the delay in market introduction.

The three cycles of the five-phase process are presented in Figure 4-9. As shown, the first cycle passes through four of the five phases of knowledge creation, then repeats the cycle two more times before moving into the cross-leveling phase, which we shall discuss in the next

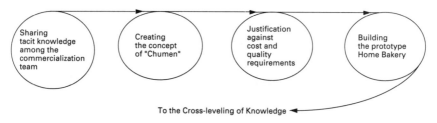

Figure 4-8. Third cycle of the Home Bakery spiral.

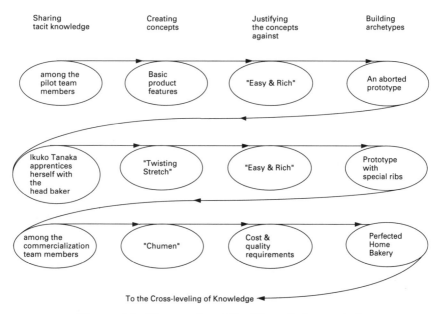

Figure 4-9. Three cycles of the Home Bakery spiral.

section. This figure clearly shows how knowledge is created through an iterative and spiral process, not through a one-time linear process.

Cross-Leveling of Knowledge Within the Division

The success of Home Bakery is especially remarkable in light of the fact that Matsushita's previous image was as a price-based competitor for relatively standard products in mature markets. Its corporate culture had become conservative and status quo-oriented. Thus the emergence of a "new" product and a "new" process was a sharp break with past tradition. This case provides insight into how established organizational procedures can be revitalized to support the generation of creative approaches that foster innovation.

The experience of developing Home Bakery dissolved the rigid boundaries within the organization through the initiation of interdepartmental project teams, which provided a forum for debate covering a wide cross-section of organizational activities. Home Bakery also brought the users' voices close to the engineers, which seemed like a breath of fresh air to the Cooking Appliances Division. Having previously dealt with mature products, the process brought a sense of enlightenment to the engineers. Comments like the following were heard:

"It was so shocking that I laughed with joy."

"I almost shouted, 'unbelievable'! Thank you for developing this."

The success of Home Bakery changed the engineers' attitudes toward new projects. Their experience brought confidence and a desire among Matsushita employees to develop another innovative product. Prior to Home Bakery, engineers developed products to compete within the company. After its introduction, the focus shifted to creating products with genuine quality that met real consumer needs. In addition, engineers started to investigate the desires of consumers when developing concepts. Sano said, "By asking what dreams people have in their daily lives and how they realize them, we can get to the next breakthrough."[7]

Inspired by the Home Bakery's success, products intended to enhance the "quality of life" of consumers began to follow. One such product was an automatic coffee brewer that came equipped with an integrated coffee mill, the first in Japan, introduced in the autumn of 1987. It ground beans and brewed coffee automatically, so that users could enjoy fresh, delicious coffee, like that served at coffee shops or restaurants, at home. The mill-integrated coffee brewer was extremely successful, and this category now accounts for half of Matsushita's unit sales of coffee makers in Japan.

Another product that followed in Home Bakery's footsteps was the "Induction Heating (IH) Rice Cooker," which cooked rice in a manner similar to the traditional *kamado* (Japanese steam oven) with an automatic electronic system. Introduced in 1988, this new rice cooker has an induction heating system that achieved higher temperatures and allowed for more accurate control. Though priced at 59,000 yen (about $480), which was nearly twice the price of a conventional electric rice cooker, it sold well and now accounts for more than 40 percent of rice cooker sales within Matsushita. Thanks to the IH rice cooker, Matsushita rice cooker sales increased overall by 50 percent and its market share rose by 7 percent since the market introduction in 1988.

The new knowledge created by developing Home Bakery spilled over beyond the product development team. It showed that an innovative product could be developed through cooperation rather than through internal competition. It also showed that consumers would respond positively to products that fulfilled "Easy & Rich." Furthermore, it demonstrated the value of asking people what kinds of dreams they had in their daily lives and of *creating* a product *concept* that met those needs.

The success story of Home Bakery spread throughout Matsushita by word of mouth and in-house publications. As mentioned above, the newly created knowledge was transferred among division members beyond the development team, which we refer to as *cross-leveling of knowledge*. It radically changed employee perspectives about the potential of home appliances and inspired other people within the organization to develop other innovative products similar to Home Bakery.

The fully automatic coffee maker with an integrated mill and a new generation of rice cookers followed the example of Home Bakery, but all these products were based on the same concept of "Easy & Rich" (organizational *intention*) (see Figure 4-10).

Cross-Leveling of Knowledge Between Divisions

The development of Home Bakery inspired Akio Tanii, the CEO, to adopt "Human Electronics" as the umbrella or grand concept for Matsushita at large in January 1986. Under "Human Electronics," Matsushita was going to develop more "human" products utilizing high technology (electronics). A "human" product, to Tanii, was a product that could free and elevate the human spirit through ease of use. Electronics would enhance the satisfaction and happiness of consumers by providing "genuine" quality. Matsushita's managing director, Hiroyuki Mizuno, said, "Household appliances is the very place where electronics technology will have a big bang at last" (Shiozawa, 1989, p. 196).

Home Bakery provided a good fit with "Human Electronics" since it (1) allowed people to have fresh-from-the-oven bread every morning at home, freeing and elevating the human spirit through ease of use and genuine quality, and (2) was realized as a result of the application of microcomputers, sensors, and other electronics. Home Bakery stimulated a new spiral of knowledge creation that had far-reaching effects on organizational procedures. The new tacit knowledge gained can be expressed as follows: Have engineers develop a product by interfacing directly with consumers and by pursuing genuine quality without any constraint. This knowledge was informally conveyed to other Matsu-

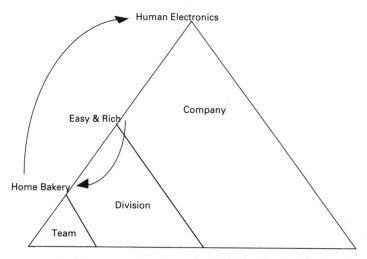

Figure 4-10. Cross-leveling of knowledge within Matsushita.

shita employees, who used it to develop new products with equivalent quality standards for TV sets, kitchen appliances, audiovisual equipment, and others (see Figure 4-11).

One example of a new product that embodied "Human Electronics" was "Gaoh" (named "The One" in the United States), a series of large-screen TV sets introduced in October 1990. Gaoh owed its success to the pursuit of genuine quality and consumers' wishes for TV sets. As Toshihaya Yamawaki, director and TV department chief, said, "Gaoh was developed after a re-examination of the function and design of existing TV sets from every aspect" (Kohno, 1992, p. 79).

Matsushita started the development of Gaoh in 1987, just when the large-screen TV market was taking off and competitors were racing to introduce new products. With the knowledge gained from Home Bakery, namely that the pursuit of genuine quality should take precedence no matter what technological difficulties came up, Matsushita's development team tried to surmount all the shortcomings of existing large-screen TVs. Ultimately, the Gaoh development team came to the conclusion that producing a television that offered genuine quality would

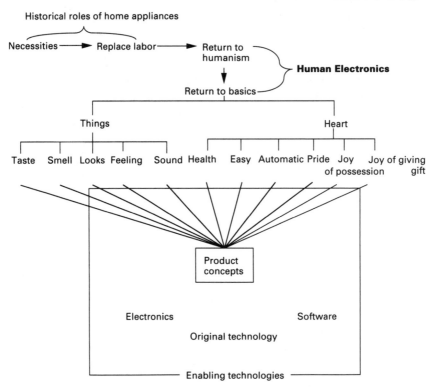

Figure 4-11. The impact of Human Electronics and "Things and Heart" on product conception. *Source: Matsushita Electric Industrial Co., Ltd.*

make consumers happy. In other words, if consumers can have genuine quality in terms of sharp image, high-fidelity sound, beautiful design (including hidden speakers), and easy usage, their spirits would be elevated; TV sets, in fact, could be "tender to humans."

Development of a new TV set usually takes six months and few technological changes are undertaken. However, it took the TV division at Matsushita two years to release Gaoh, which contained a number of major technological breakthroughs. As one development team member recalled:

> Technological development was tough and required changes up until four or five months before market introduction. We were under enormous pressure. . . . We had a sense of crisis . . . that the TV division may not survive.[8]

Gaoh sold more than one million units within 14 months of its introduction, which was equivalent to more than 10 percent of all domestic TV-set sales in Japan. With sales of 16 billion yen a month on average, Gaoh was ranked third among the "Top 20 Hit Products of 1991" (measured in terms of sales volume by Mitsubishi Research Institute), following the Honda Civic Ferio and the Sony camcorder. It was remarkable that a mature household appliance like TV was ranked in the top 20.

To summarize, the success of Home Bakery validated the idea behind "Easy & Rich" that genuine quality and ease of use will create successful products. To *cross-level* this *knowledge* beyond the divisional boundaries, Matsushita developed an umbrella concept called "Human Electronics," which inspired such products as Gaoh (see Figure 4-10).

The Second Knowledge-Creation Spiral
at the Corporate Level

In the previous section we presented a detailed description of the first spiral of knowledge creation. It started with Tanaka's apprenticeship, continued onward to the success of Home Bakery, and ended with the diffusion of knowledge beyond the original development team and the Cooking Appliances Division, resulting in other successful products such as Gaoh.

In this section we will analyze Matsushita's efforts to create knowledge continuously at the corporate level. The output of knowledge creation in the first spiral took the form of a product such as Home Bakery or Gaoh. But products are not the only output of knowledge creation. New knowledge can also be created with respect to ways of doing business, operating a division, developing new products, or managing people. In the second spiral, we focus our attention on the "soft" side of knowledge creation, as opposed to the "hard" side, which focused on product development. The "soft" side deals with less tangible outcomes—such as management systems, operational mechanisms, or human resource management programs—which are equally as important in creating innovation within a company and, in turn, gaining sustainable competitive advantage in the marketplace.

The second spiral takes us through a search for the "ideal" of what Matsushita should be in the twenty-first century and a discussion of what Matsushita people should be like under that umbrella concept. This process is termed the first cycle of knowledge creation at the corporate level. Having decided what kind of a company Matsushita should be and what kind of individuals Matsushita employees should be, the next cycle of the knowledge-creation process takes us through the development of managerial and operational systems that can accommodate the "new" ideal.

The First Cycle of the Corporate Spiral

Matsushita began the process of establishing its corporate vision for the twenty-first century in 1989. Top managers questioned where the company was heading and what kind of company they would like it to be. While the whole nation was caught up in the economic bubble euphoria, Matsushita's top management was quite skeptical about the company's position. Thus they decided to evaluate the company critically (Hirata, 1993).

Realizing that the young people of today would be the leaders of the company in the future, Matsushita asked 200 employees in their 20s and 30s to formulate the company's corporate vision for the twenty-first century. Originally, the task for developing the corporate vision was entrusted to the Human 21 Committee, composed of upper-middle managers with heavy responsibilities. Since original and stimulating ideas rarely emerged from these managers, Matsushita decided to form another group composed of younger employees, most of whom were between 25 and 32 years old. Called the Human 200-People Committee, it started out with 200 "stars" selected from a large pool of applicants.

The Human 200-People Committee was organized in each of the 12 companies in the Matsushita Group. Approximately 20 teams were formed, and the members, who would be the company's leading forces in the twenty-first century, discussed their visions for the coming century and wrote reports on their discussions. The Human 21 Committee then played the ombudsman's role by examining the reports and deciding if the company should adopt their suggestions.

Meetings were held every other weekend in either Tokyo or Osaka. One of the questions that the group tried to answer was: "What type of a group should Matsushita employees form?" The concept of "a group of voluntary individuals" emerged from their discussions. The younger employees felt that people's value systems would change in the future.

More specifically, people in the twenty-first century would pursue not only material affluence but also spiritual contentment. In such a society, each member of the corporation should be what Matsushita called "voluntary individuals," who embraced values such as volunteerism, ambition, creativity, and mental productivity. Each employee of Matsushita should thoroughly rethink work and management, and try to be not only a good businessperson but also a good citizen, family member, and individual. Such efforts will lead to "a group of voluntary individuals." This idea was the fruit of the project members' reflections on how the corporation could be truly spontaneous, ambitious, and creative.

The idea of "a group of voluntary individuals" became the basis for the Human 21 Committee to develop a "possibility-searching company" as Matsushita's corporate vision. In such a company, a group of voluntary individuals with rich and diversified individual knowledge bases would share similar ideals and values. In short, Matsushita envisioned itself as becoming a knowledge-creating company. But because the idea of becoming a knowledge-creating company was radical and new, it was not surprising that some senior managers of the company were reluctant to accept this vision. However, the enthusiasm of the younger employees eventually won over top management.

In April 1990, Matsushita officially announced to the outside world its corporate vision of becoming "a possibility-searching company." Under this vision, Matsushita set forth the following four objectives in the areas of business, technology, people, and globalization:

1. "Human innovation business": business that creates new lifestyles based on creativity, comfort, and joy in addition to efficiency and convenience.
2. "Humanware technology": technology based on human studies such as artificial intelligence, fuzzy logic, and neuro-computers as well as on chip systems and networking technology, all necessary for the "human innovation" business.
3. "Active heterogeneous group": a corporate culture based on individuality and diversity.
4. "Multilocal and global networking management": a corporate structure that enables both localization and global synergy.

Notice that the first two objectives are derived directly from the umbrella concept of "Human Electronics," with a heavy emphasis on customers and high technology. The third objective corresponds to one of our enabling conditions, *requisite variety*. Matsushita knew that knowledge creation would not be possible without the diversity of individual experiences. The fourth objective points out the importance of transcending the dichotomy between localization and globalization.

The first cycle of knowledge creation at the corporate level started out with 200 people *sharing their experiences* and carrying on a dialogue in the Human 200-People Committee. The dialogue was centered on what society would be in the future and what that would mean for Matsushita. The *concept* of "voluntary individuals" emerged as a result, which was *justified* by the Human 21 Committee. The five-phase model is not fully represented, but the first cycle of the knowledge-creation process takes us through three of the phases (see Figure 4-12).

We can also observe the five enabling conditions at work here. Through the Human 21 program, top management cast its doubt on the status quo and developed a new ideal or organizational *intention* regarding what Matsushita should be like. This redefinition brought about a chain reaction, heightening the anxiety among employees *(fluctuation/chaos)*, which in turn induced young employees' commitment to the Human 200-People Committee. The committee was composed of 200 people from various divisions and group companies *(requisite variety)*. This diversity was vital when the committee was trying to deal with an uncertain future, since uncertainty (of the environment) is often reduced or absorbed by uncertainty itself (i.e., uncertainty of membership). The fact that 200 people shared their tacit knowledge resulted in *redundancy* of information, which provided a common knowledge base for all the members. This committee of 200 young employees was given full *autonomy* by the Human 21 Committee to come up with innovation.

In addition, we can clearly observe two of the four modes of knowledge conversion in the first cycle of the knowledge-creation process. *Socialization* took place among the Human 200-People Committee members as they shared their experiences. *Externalization* took place when their discussion of what type of individuals Matsushita would need in the future was articulated explicitly as "voluntary individuals."

The Second Cycle of the Corporate Spiral

In the second cycle, the concept of "voluntary individuals," which was created in the first cycle, was operationalized. The objectives of "voluntary individuals" were to have Matsushita employees become volun-

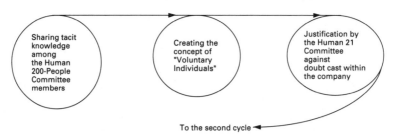

Figure 4-12. First cycle of the corporate spiral.

tary, ambitious, creative, and mentally productive, and also become not only good businesspersons but good citizens, family members, and individuals. One of the operational means of achieving these objectives was the reduction of working hours. By eliminating or reducing time spent on routine jobs (e.g., information processing), employees would be able to be more mentally productive, ambitious, and creative. By increasing private time, their personal lives as citizens or family members would be enriched.

Matsushita discovered that inefficiencies at work were blocking the creativity of its employees and taking away their personal time. People in the staff organization were suffering from low productivity, while productivity of line activities had reached a plateau, which led to routinized overtime work. Matsushita's average yearly working hours in 1990 were 2,131 hours for staff people and 1,903 hours for line people, for an average of 2,036 hours for the company.

To solve this problem, Matsushita set a goal in 1991 to reduce its annual working hours to 1,800 hours under the program called MIT'93 (Mind and Management Innovation Toward 1993). Osamu Tanaka, general manager of the MIT'93 Promotion Office, emphasized that the purpose of the program was to enhance employee creativity rather than to simply reduce working hours or costs:

> We do not need MIT if we only want to reduce working hours. We can just tell employees that the company will not pay for any overtime work. Layoffs might be another alternative during a recession like this. But we must remember the purpose of MIT. It is not a simple reduction in working hours. We have wanted to improve the productivity of our staff organization through this project. . . . The company wants to give time back to individuals for their creativity. How can anyone be creative if he works until twelve midnight everyday? People's sense of value is rapidly changing. You cannot make original products just by looking at plans at the office every night.[9]

To enhance creativity, Matsushita felt that innovation had to take place both in people's mindset and in the management system, hence the name of the program. The 1,800-hour project was considered a symbol of Matsushita's innovation with respect to management and operational systems.

The MIT'93 Promotion Office asked every division of Matsushita to develop new managerial and operational systems that would enable annual working hours to be reduced to 1,800 hours. Three committees were established—in labor-management relations, personnel, and general accounting—in order to coordinate that effort. But the actual development of new managerial and operational systems to reduce working hours was left up to self-organizing teams within each division. No specific details on how to go about reducing working hours were provided. The only guidelines that the MIT'93 Promotion Office provided were: (1) to analyze existing working hours and business processes; (2) to uncover causes of inefficiencies; and (3) to make people actually experience a 150-hours-a-month schedule (equivalent to 1,800 hours a year).

The analysis of existing working hours and business processes in the staff organizations led to the following findings:

- 45 percent of working hours in the R&D sections were spent on non-developmental work, which consisted of follow-up work necessitated by additional design changes that took place after product designs were handed over to the production division.

- 40 percent of working hours in the materials management sections were spent on follow-up work caused by changes in product designs or production plans.

- 20 percent of working hours in R&D were spent on internal meetings, contacts with visitors, and interviews unassociated with development work.

- Less than 20 percent of the sales staff's working hours were spent talking with customers.

These findings revealed ample opportunities to improve current operating systems. Team members in the R&D sections and materials management sections discovered that the inefficiencies were largely due to the shortcomings of the Japanese-style product development process. Matsushita's product development was conducted using the rugby style, in which several functional areas—such as engineering, manufacturing, planning, and marketing—worked together in a multifunctional team, exchanging information and sharing tacit knowledge through dialogue held in meetings or camps. This system had some advantages, such as allowing coordination to take place more easily, enabling development to be completed in a shorter period of time, and ensuring that the resulting new products met customer needs. But it also led to the disadvantage of having the original designs and specifications changed constantly. The rugby-style development had the tendency of overreliance on the socialization mode, which led to inefficiencies as the number of people involved in the project increased and the number of suggestions for change multiplied.

Having employees actually experience a 150-hours-a-month schedule, for example, helped those involved in product development realize the pitfalls of rugby-style product development. They had first-hand experience of what can and cannot be done within a shorter working schedule. Their bodily experience convinced them that a lot of design changes cannot be accommodated and certain unnecessary work had to be eliminated. This experience led to the tacit knowledge of what it meant to work 1,800 hours a year.

This experience also resulted in the development of an innovative product development process called "concurrent engineering," which could set all the specifications at an early stage of development and consequently reduce design changes at later stages. The experience of working 150 hours a month led people to realize that they could not have as many face-to-face meetings as before, and that communication using computer networks had to be more fully employed. By relying on concurrent engineering, specifications of product features were documented in detail at the early stage of product development through the use of electronic media, such as CAD/CAM. Front-loading explicit information helps product engineering (upstream) "to do it right the first time" and affords process engineering (downstream) earlier exposure to product design specifications, which reduces problem-solving lead time. CAD/CAM assures more accuracy in communicating information and reduces the length of the communication chain.

In the second cycle of the corporate spiral, a new operational system was created to give employees more time so that they could become creative (see Figure 4-13). For this purpose, Matsushita established a self-organizing team in every division and group company. The knowledge-creation process started when members of each team *shared tacit knowledge* on what types of work employees at Matsushita should do and shouldn't do to utilize their creativity fully. The teams also analyzed existing work patterns and uncovered causes of inefficiencies. For instance, they felt that R&D people should be spending most of their time on actual research and development, and not on follow-up work for additional design changes. The *concept* of "Mind and Management Innovation Toward 1993" was *created* to enhance creativity and reduce working hours. This concept was *justified* against the objective of fostering "voluntary individuals," allowing it to be developed into an operational system *(archetype)* that combined elements of concurrent engineering into existing operational systems. The objective has been achieved, and Matsushita dissolved the MIT'93 Promotion Office in March 1994.

In this cycle, we can also observe the five enabling conditions at work. Matsushita's challenging goal to reduce annual working hours

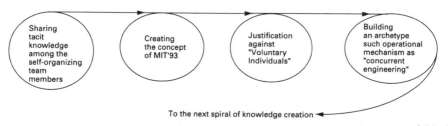

Figure 4-13. Second cycle of the corporate spiral.

to 1,800 brought *fluctuation/chaos* into the organization. A sense of crisis took hold, inducing people's commitment to search for the causes of inefficiencies. Matsushita's organizational *intention* to produce "voluntary individuals" reoriented people's commitment to one direction. Teams, consisting of people with different backgrounds, were set up in all the divisions and group companies, and given full *autonomy* to develop ideas for improvement. *Redundancy* of information prevailed within these teams in the form of common knowledge held about the rugby style of product development process, for example. This redundancy helped members of the teams by providing a common language with which to share their tacit knowledge. *Requisite variety* was enhanced by involving people whose working environments differed from division to division.

Among the four modes of knowledge conversion, *internalization* played an important role. Being forced to experience shorter working hours (150 hours a month) experimentally, people actually felt *(internalized)* how short such a curtailed schedule was and how much work had to be eliminated. They engaged in "learning by doing." In addition, team members exchanged their own tacit understandings of what it meant to limit their working hours to 150 *(socialization)*, and came up with a new development system called concurrent engineering *(externalization)*. This mechanism was combined with existing operational systems and other explicit knowledge to form a new operational system *(combination)*.

Enhancing Enabling Conditions for Knowledge Creation

Thus far, we have seen two spirals of the knowledge-creation process within Matsushita. The first was around Home Bakery, a product, and the second around MIT'93, an operating system. But in both spirals, enabling conditions played a key role in stimulating and promoting the knowledge-creation process. Matsushita's case illustrates that for knowledge creation to continue, enabling conditions should be enhanced or upgraded continuously as well. Next, we shall briefly describe the company's ongoing efforts to continuously upgrade the enabling conditions.

Matsushita recently enhanced one of the enabling conditions, *redundancy* of information, by improving its communication infrastructure. Matsushita installed a new communication infrastructure called Market-Oriented Total Management System (MTM) in 1991. By connecting R&D organizations, factories, and retail stores on line, Matsushita was able to eliminate excess inventory and avoid out-of-stock situations for popular items. But its greatest impact, from a knowledge-creation perspective, resides in the free flow and sharing of information among different functional groups. Under this system, the sales and the manufacturing departments shared the same explicit knowledge (i.e., sales information at retail stores). This common knowledge, which represents *redundancy* of information, helped the sales and manufacturing groups exchange their mental models and gut feelings about the future. In this sense, MTM has facilitated the coordination of production plans between the two departments and, as a result, improved overall efficiency.

MTM allowed product development teams to obtain instant feedback on how well a particular product or model sold at retail. This detailed market information, as opposed to warehouse shipment data, was *internalized* by the development people, bringing variety into their knowledge base *(requisite variety)*. Development people could develop a variety of "what if" solutions more precisely in anticipation of customer reactions. In this sense, MTM paved the way for joint knowledge creation between customers and development teams. Vice president Shoji Sakuma stressed the importance of retail-based information as follows:

> If I told my staff members, "Go to the front lines because they are very important," they would all rush to the front line of the manufacturing sector. But if you really care about consumers, you would soon know there is another important front line, the store fronts of retailers, where you could have contact with consumers. Matsushita, however, has tended to isolate itself from consumers, clinging to the manufacturing sector.[10]

Another effort on the part of Matsushita to enhance *autonomy,* one of the enabling conditions, can be seen in the change it initiated in 1993 to terminate its business group system, which was a layer created above the divisional layer to coordinate interdivisional activities. The predecessor of this business group system was the sector system, introduced in 1984, to coordinate activities such as joint product development or joint marketing across the divisions. But after nine years, Matsushita realized that the extra umbrella layer (business group system) was inhibiting the divisions' *autonomy* and commitment to innovation. Elimination of the group layer led the divisions to take more initiative in coordinating activities across the divisions through a more flexible and ad hoc system, such as an interdivisional project team.

Matsushita also enhanced *intention* and *fluctuation/chaos* by setting extremely challenging goals. On January 10, 1994, Matsushita announced "The Revival Plan," which stipulated that by fiscal 1996 profitability would be increased to 5 percent return on sales (ordinary income-to-sales ratio) from 1.4 percent in 1993. In order to achieve this profitability level, Matsushita identified the necessity to shift its strategic domain to multimedia, an emerging industry in which the company could capitalize on its capabilities in hardware equipment (e.g., audiovisual, television), computers and communication equipment, and software (e.g., entertainment). At the same time, the company decided to increase the productivity of its staff organization by 30 percent. This challenging goal introduced *creative chaos* throughout the company, which forced its employees to relinquish the status quo and seek brand new solutions. "The Revival Plan" also upgraded organizational *intention,* which had the effect of reorienting the employees toward one ambitious goal.

Summary and Implications

We used the Matsushita case to illustrate the actual process by which organizational knowledge is created within a company. Several implications can be drawn from the case on how a successful organizational knowledge-creation process can be implemented. The case points out the importance of: (1) leveraging the tacit knowledge base of an individual and making use of *socialization* to transfer it throughout the organization; (2) amplifying knowledge creation across different levels of the organization, i.e., *cross-leveling;* (3) enhancing the enabling conditions; and (4) continuing to create new knowledge constantly. Each implication is elaborated below.

First, Home Bakery's development process emphasizes the importance of tapping into an individual's tacit knowledge, which in this case was represented by the head baker's kneading skill. By its very nature, tacit knowledge is hard to formalize and communicate. But this skill was critical in making the machine knead the dough correctly. The Home Bakery example also shows the importance of *socialization* as a means to share tacit knowledge between individuals. Ikuko Tanaka apprenticed herself to the head baker and learned the skill by observation and imitation. Engineers had to experience the actual bread-making process to learn that skill.

Second, the success of Home Bakery led to the creation of "Human Electronics" and a series of successful products that embodied that concept. In order to make knowledge creation truly dynamic, knowledge created at one level needs to be amplified across different levels of the organization. Only by *cross-leveling* can companies obtain the true benefits of organizational knowledge creation. In Matsushita's case, we saw how the knowledge created in developing Home Bakery spiraled itself to create new knowledge at the corporate level. Umbrella concepts such as "Easy & Rich" and "Human Electronics" played a significant role in connecting one knowledge creation to another.

Third, Matsushita's knowledge-creation process highlights the importance of enhancing organizational enabling conditions, which promote the four modes of knowledge conversion as well as the five-phase process. We saw how Matsushita tried to (1) increase *redundancy* and *requisite variety* by providing the R&D people with up-to-date sales information; (2) bring *autonomy* back to the divisions by restructuring organization; and (3) instill *intension* and *creative chaos* into the organization by setting challenging goals, represented by the shift to multimedia or the improvement of productivity by 30 percent.

Fourth, the case illustrates that organizational knowledge creation is a never-ending process that requires continuous innovation. Because the competitive environment and customer preferences change constantly, existing knowledge becomes obsolete quickly. We saw how the rugby style of product development, which had provided a source of competitive advantage for Japanese companies in the past, was already becoming obsolete as their competitors in the West began utilizing the same style and as the recession rekindled the search for eliminating inefficiencies. The continuous upgrading of organizational *intention* or values is important, since new knowledge must be constantly *justified* against the latest *intention*.

We presented the essential elements of our theory in Chapter 3 and their practical application within a firm in this chapter. We now proceed to discuss the managerial style and the organizational structure most conducive to organizational knowledge creation, "middle-up-down" and "hypertext," respectively, in the next two chapters. As we shall see, in order for the new paradigm to be effective, it cannot be housed in an old setting, such as top-down or bottom-up management styles or a traditional hierarchical structure. A new setting or context is in order.

Notes

1. Interviewed on April 1, 1988.
2. Interviewed on April 1, 1988.
3. Hoshiden Electronics Co., Ltd., is a manufacturer of electronic parts and devices, and not affiliated with Matsushita.
4. Interviewed on July 19, 1988.
5. Interviewed on April 1, 1988.
6. Interviewed on April 1, 1988.
7. Interviewed on April 1, 1988.
8. Interviewed on December 2, 1993.
9. Interviewed on December 2, 1993.
10. Interviewed on July 2, 1991.

5

Middle-up-down
Management Process
for Knowledge Creation

The preceding chapters presented our theoretical model of organizational knowledge creation and its practical application within Japanese firms. We shift our focus in the next two chapters to consider the most appropriate setting under which organizational knowledge creation will flourish. In this chapter we focus our attention on a management process that can best facilitate the creation of organizational knowledge. Since organizational knowledge creation calls for a radically different setting than that which exists today, we will turn our attention in the next chapter to the most appropriate organizational structure.

We start this chapter by examining two dominant models of the management process, the top-down model and the bottom-up model, both of which fall short of fostering the dynamic interaction necessary to create organizational knowledge. We propose a new model, which we call middle-up-down, and explain why it is superior for knowledge-creation management than the more traditional models. The new model puts the middle manager at the very center of knowledge management and redefines the role of top management as well as of frontline employees. We will draw on the product development case of the Mini-Copier at Canon to describe the expected roles of the key players in the middle-up-down model.

Top-down and Bottom-up Management

Sooner or later, any organization ends up creating new knowledge. But in most organizations this process is haphazard, serendipitous, and therefore impossible to predict. What distinguishes the knowledge-creating company is that it systematically manages the knowledge-creation process. And the experience of the Japanese companies we have been studying suggests that the management process best suited to creating organizational knowledge is substantially different from the traditional managerial models with which most executives are familiar, namely the top-down and bottom-up management models.

Top-down management is basically the classic hierarchical model. It has its roots in Max Weber and Frederick Taylor and reaches its culmination in Herbert Simon. The top-down model conceives of knowledge creation within the confines of the information-processing perspective. Simple and selected information is passed up the pyramid to top executives, who then use it to create plans and orders, which are eventually passed down the hierarchy. Information is processed using division of labor, with top management creating the basic concepts so that lower members can implement them. Top-management concepts become the operational conditions for middle managers, who will decide on the means to realize them. The middle managers' decisions, in turn, constitute the operational conditions for front-line employees, who will implement the decisions. At the front-line level, execution becomes largely routine. As a consequence, the organization as a whole executes a huge amount of work and information.

A top-down organization is shaped like a pyramid, if we visualize the dyadic relations between top vs. middle managers and middle vs. front-line employees. An implicit assumption behind this traditional model of organization is that only top managers are able and allowed to create knowledge. Moreover, knowledge created by top managers exists only to be processed or implemented, therefore it is only a means, not an end. The concepts that top management generates should be void of any ambiguity or equivocality. In other words, the concepts are anchored in the premise that they have a singular meaning. As such, the concepts are strictly functional and pragmatic. It is this deductive transformation that enables workers with limited information-processing capacity to deal with a mass of information.

Bottom-up management is basically a mirror image of top-down management. As our review of the managerial literature in Chapter 2 made clear, there have been critics of top-down management, which is closely linked to the scientific management tradition of Taylor, from the very beginning. These critics, who belonged to the humanistic camp, devised an alternative model of management process that eventually came to be known as bottom-up management. Instead of hierarchy and division of labor, there is autonomy. Instead of knowledge being created at and controlled from the top, it is created at and, to a large extent, controlled by the bottom.

A bottom-up organization has a flat and horizontal shape. With hierarchy and division of labor eliminated, the organization might have only three or four layers of management between the top and the front line. Few orders and instructions are given by the top managers, who serve as sponsors of entrepreneurially minded front-line employees. Knowledge is created by these employees, who operate as independent and separate actors, preferring to work on their own. There is little direct dialogue with other members of the organization, either vertically or horizontally. Autonomy, not interaction, is the key operating principle. Certain individuals, not a group of individuals interacting with each other, create knowledge.

These two traditional models may seem like alternatives to each other, but neither is adequate as a process for managing knowledge creation. The top-down model is suited for dealing with explicit knowledge. But in controlling knowledge creation from the top, it neglects the development of tacit knowledge that can take place on the front line of an organization. Bottom-up, on the other hand, is good at dealing with tacit knowledge. But its very emphasis on autonomy means that such knowledge is extremely difficult to disseminate and share within the organization.

Put another way, both managerial processes are not very good at knowledge conversion. The top-down model provides only partial conversion focused on combination (explicit to explicit) and internalization (explicit to tacit). Similarly, the bottom-up model carries out only partial conversion focused on socialization (tacit to tacit) and externalization (tacit to explicit).

As we have seen in Chapter 3, the core process for creating organizational knowledge takes place intensively at the group level. Successive rounds of direct and meaningful dialogue within the group, for example, trigger externalization. Through these dialogues, team members articulate their own thinking, sometimes through the use of metaphors or analogies, revealing hidden tacit knowledge that is otherwise hard to communicate. This kind of intense interaction hardly takes place in the military-like hierarchy of the top-down model or among the autonomy-driven individuals of the bottom-up model. Furthermore, notions such as noise, fluctuation, and chaos are fundamentally not permitted in the top-down model and are incarnated only within individuals in the bottom-up model.

The fact that knowledge is formed primarily in the minds of individuals and not amplified or refined through interaction creates another potential problem. In the case of the top-down model, there is a danger of the alignment of the fate of a few top managers with the fate of the firm. In the case of the bottom-up model, the preeminence and autonomy given to an individual make knowledge creation much more time-consuming, since the pace with which creation takes place is dependent on the patience and talent of the particular individual.

Another obvious, but major, limitation of the two models is the lack of recognition and relevance given to middle managers. They seem almost to have been neglected by the two models. In top-down management, the knowledge creator is top management. Middle managers process a lot of information in a typical top-down organization, but play at most a minimal role in creating knowledge. In a hierarchy, middle managers are often responsible for submitting reports to top managers, analyzing business problems and opportunities, or transmitting commands and orders from above to those below them, but nothing more relevant. In bottom-up management, the knowledge creator is the entrepreneur-like individual lower in the organization. Given the small headquarters, a flat organizational structure, the propensity for top managers to serve as direct sponsors, and the autonomy provided to individuals, middle managers do not even seem to have a place within a typical bottom-up model.

Middle-up-down Management

The Japanese companies we have been studying suggest a third way to manage knowledge creation. It is neither top-down nor bottom-up, but "middle-up-down." As strange as this term may sound, it best communicates the continuous iterative process by which knowledge is created. Simply put, knowledge is created by middle managers, who are often leaders of a team or task force, through a spiral conversion process involving both the top and the front-line employees (i.e., bottom). The process puts middle managers at the very center of knowledge management, positioning them at the intersection of the vertical and horizontal flows of information within the company.

The fact that middle-up-down management emphasizes the dynamic role of the middle manager sharply distinguishes our theory from the conventional managerial wisdom. In the West, where companies are laying off middle managers by the thousands, the very term "middle manager" has become almost a term of contempt, synonymous with "backwardness," "stagnation," and "resistance to change." Yet we are arguing that middle managers are the key to continuous innovation.

We disagree with the assessment of some of the leading management thinkers in the West. Not long ago, Tom Peters (1987) stated, "I, like many others, have repeatedly attacked middle managers. And we do indeed have too many layers, too much staff" (p. 367). Rosabeth Kanter flatly declared in 1989 that tomorrow's winning firms will have almost no middle managers and that the era of the linear career has ended (Peters, 1992). James Quinn (1992) sees them as an obstacle:

> Problems typically lie not at the top or the bottom of the organization, but in middle management. Just as Gorbachev could change the top level of the

USSR and establish grassroots support for change quickly—but not move the middle layers of his bureaucracy—Western middle managers resist radical changes endlessly. Jan Carlson found it easy to change the top and motivate point people at SAS, but devilishly difficult to move the huge midlevel bureaucracies that past practices had built up. Few middle managers want to change from the style and skills they have so painstakingly learned. Their old predictable progress ladder is suddenly gone. And they wonder: How can one go up, when the organization is flat and there is no up. (p. 377)

Middle managers usually have been portrayed in recent literature as frustrated, disillusioned, stuck in the middle of a hierarchy in dreary jobs (Johnson and Frohman, 1989) with little hope of career progression, and increasingly subject to being replaced by technological advancements (Dopson and Stewart, 1990).[1] Doomsayers argue, according to Borucki and Byosiere (1991), that the traditional role of middle managers as strategy implementers is disappearing as a result of new management philosophies and notions such as total employee involvement, the self-designing organization, and sociotechnical systems and autonomous work teams. These arguments give the impression that perhaps middle managers may be in the business of going out of business.

But a handful of researchers have portrayed the fate of middle management with much more optimism, arguing that they are indeed "enlightened" or "empowered."[2] Being among the leading protagonists, we see middle managers playing a key role in facilitating the process of organizational knowledge creation. They serve as the strategic "knot" that binds top management with front-line managers. They work as a "bridge" between the visionary ideals of the top and the often chaotic realities of business confronted by front-line workers. As we shall see later, they are the true "knowledge engineers" of the knowledge-creating company.

To repeat what we said at the outset of this book, front-line employees are immersed in the day-to-day details of particular technologies, products, and markets. No one is more expert in the realities of a company's business than they are. But while these employees are deluged with highly specific information, they often find it extremely difficult to turn that information into useful knowledge. For one thing, signals from the marketplace can be vague and ambiguous. For another, these front-line employees can become so caught up in their own narrow perspective that they lose sight of the broader context. Moreover, even when they do develop meaningful ideas and insights, it can still be difficult to communicate the importance of that information to others. People don't just receive new knowledge passively; they interpret it actively to fit their own situation and perspectives. Thus what makes sense in one context can change or even lose its meaning when communicated to people in a different context. The main job of middle managers in middle-up-down management is to orient this chaotic situation toward purposeful knowledge creation. Middle managers do this by providing their subordinates with a conceptual framework that helps them make sense of their own experience.

But the conceptual framework that middle management develops is quite distinct from that of top management, which provides a sense of direction regarding where the company should be headed. In the middle-up-down model, top management creates a vision or a dream, while middle management develops more concrete concepts that front-line employees can understand and implement. Middle managers try to solve the contradiction between what top management hopes to create and what actually exists in the real world. In other words, top management's role is to create a grand theory, while middle management tries to create a mid-range theory that it can test empirically within the company with the help of front-line employees (see Figure 5-1).

In the Honda City example from Chapter 1, top management dreamed of creating "something different from the existing concept" and began the City project with the slogan, "Let's gamble." Hiroo Watanabe, a middle manager who was 35 years old at the time, developed more concrete concepts—"Automobile Evolution," "man-maximum, machine-minimum," and "Tall Boy"—that front-line employees could understand and implement. One of these front-line employees recalled, "I feel, however illogical it may sound, that the success of this project owes a lot to the very wide gap between the ideal and the actual. A revolutionary reformulation was necessary, and, in order to achieve this, new technologies and concepts were generated one after another."

Table 5-1 compares and contrasts the relevant features of the three

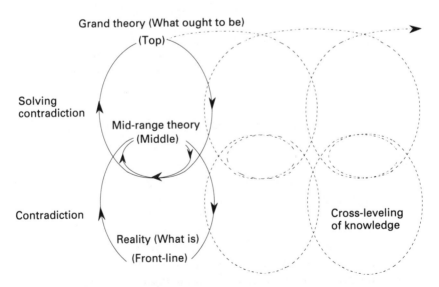

Figure 5-1. Middle-up-down knowledge-creation process.

Table 5-1. Comparison of the Three Management Models Regarding Knowledge Creation

		Top-down	Bottom-up	Middle-up-down
Who	Agent of knowledge creation	Top management	Entrepreneurial individual	Team (with middle managers as knowledge engineers)
	Top management role	Commander	Sponsor/mentor	Catalyst
	Middle management role	Information processor	Autonomous intrapreneur	Team leader
What	Accumulated knowledge	Explicit	Tacit	Explicit and tacit
	Knowledge conversion	Partial conversion focused on combination/internalization	Partial conversion focused on socialization/externalization	Spiral conversion of internalization/externalization/combination/socialization
Where	Knowledge storage	Computerized database/manuals	Incarnated in individuals	Organizational knowledge base
How	Organization	Hierarchy	Project team and informal network	Hierarchy and task force (hypertext)
	Communication	Orders/instructions	Self-organizing principle	Dialogue and use of metaphor/analogy
	Tolerance for ambiguity	Chaos/fluctuation not allowed	Chaos/fluctuation premised	Create and amplify chaos/fluctuation
	Weakness	High dependency on top management	Time-consuming Cost of coordinating individuals	Human exhaustion Cost of redundancy

models discussed above. As we will discover in the following section of this chapter, the middle-up-down management model is by far the most comprehensive in terms of *who* gets involved; the most all-inclusive in terms of *what* kind of knowledge is created; the broadest in terms of *where* knowledge is stored; and the most flexible in terms of *how* knowledge is created. We will discuss this table in more detail at the end of the next section.

Case Studies of the Three Management Models

In this section we present three case studies that illustrate the three management models discussed above. General Electric (GE) under Jack Welch is offered as an example of top-down, 3M as an example of bottom-up, and the Mini-Copier development process at Canon as an example of middle-up-down management. In the GE case, Jack Welch develops concepts that become the operating conditions for people throughout the organization. At 3M, top management serves as a mentor to "individuals with initiative" who appear almost obsessed with developing new ideas. The Canon Mini-Copier case shows the crucially important role middle managers played within the product development task force in creating a breakthrough concept.

Top-down Management: General Electric under Jack Welch

What Jack Welch inherited in 1981, when he became CEO of GE, was a bureaucracy. Since then, he has implemented a number of actions aimed at getting rid of the bureaucracy and hierarchy. But the manner in which he proceeded to bring about the necessary changes was top-down in nature. The top-down nature of Welch's management style can be seen in the role he played as a concept maker and a deal maker. We shall look at each of these roles below.[3]

Concept Making

On December 8, 1981, Jack Welch articulated to an audience of Wall Street security analysts a vision that became a hallmark of his early tenure as CEO. The vision called for GE to become "No. 1 or No. 2" in every market it served. He predicted that there would be no room for the mediocre supplier of products and services in the 1980s. The winners would be those who insisted upon being number one or number two in every business they were in already. He asked his GE managers a very straightforward question:

> Can you be number one or number two in the game you're going to play, in the war you're going to wage, in the skirmish you're going to be in? Can you clearly go to war, go to the skirmish, with good equipment, good arms, good troops, with anything else you want to use as a metaphor? Can you play in that arena as a number one or number two player?

Welch did not leave much unanswered. He warned that any business that could not become No. 1 or No. 2, for whatever reason, would not be part of GE:

> Where we are not number one or number two, and don't have or can't see a route to a technological edge, we have got to ask ourselves Peter Drucker's very tough question: "If you weren't in the business, would you enter it today?" The managements and companies in the 80s that don't do this, . . . won't be around in 1990. (Slater, 1991, p. 74)

The vision that Welch articulated made little impact on the security analysts who gathered to hear his first explanation of what he was trying to do. The same vision was a "big yawn" to a lot GE executives who believed the company was already a No. 1 player. It was unpopular or a "crazy idea" to GE, who didn't want Welch to rock the boat. But Jack Welch pursued his vision relentlessly, helping GE to become one of the most competitive enterprises in the world a decade later.

Jack Welch kept trying to explain his vision whenever he had a chance, although his early efforts often failed to convey what he had in mind. But early in 1982 he scribbled three interlocking circles on the back of an envelope to illustrate what the company was, as well as what it was not. This sketch, which came to be known as the "three-circles concept," helped GE visualize Welch's grand design in no ambiguous terms (see Figure 5-2). One circle contained GE's core businesses, the second had high-technology businesses, and the third consisted of service businesses, for a total of 15 businesses. Only No. 1 or No. 2 businesses were allowed inside the circles. Businesses outside the circles that did not meet the No. 1 or No. 2 criterion had to come up with a strategy to get in the circles or be divested. Being placed outside the circles did not mean being put on hold. These businesses were given the choice to "fix, sell, or close." The message was clear. The three-circles diagram clarified Welch's thinking and, more important, helped communicate his vision more effectively within the organization.

Concepts such as "No. 1 or No. 2," "three circles," or "fix, sell, or

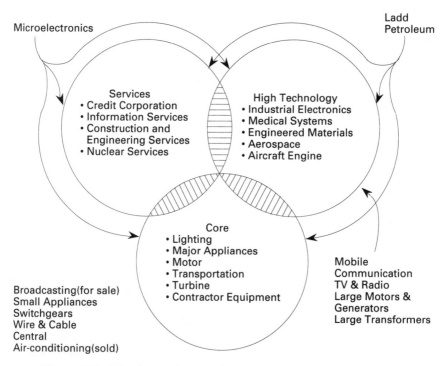

Figure 5-2. The shape of new GE. *Source: Forbes, March 26, 1984.*

close" were strategic in nature. They sent a clear message about the strategic direction of the company. But Welch also relied on the power of his ideas to build operational concepts, which enabled him to drive the process of fundamental change, or "revolution," as he called it, within the organization. In the late 1980s, for example, he developed "speed, simplicity, and self-confidence" as an operational concept for driving change within the organization, and embarked on Work-Out, a program that gives front-line employees within a team the authority to recommend solutions to business problems. More recently, he came up with the concept of "integrated diversity," which was built on the conviction that GE's varied businesses could maintain their operating independence while working closely together as a team. Another recent Welch concept is "boundarylessness," which signals the breakdown of internal barriers such as hierarchy, geography, and function, while trying to integrate all the constituencies outside the company.

What is unique about GE is the fact that the CEO himself drove the entire process—coming up with the concepts (both strategic and operational), refining them, communicating them in an understandable manner through the use of metaphors and analogies, and reiterating them repeatedly. Take the concept of "boundarylessness" as an example. It is a prototype that many people have trouble understanding. To explain his thinking, Welch uses a house as an analogy for three kinds of barriers that exist within an organization. They consist of: (1) the walls that serve as a horizontal barrier; (2) the floors and the ceilings that become a vertical barrier; and (3) the outside walls that constitute an external barrier. His message is clear: (1) break down functional boundaries, product division boundaries, and geographic boundaries that serve as walls; (2) blow up the layers—the floors and ceilings—that come with hierarchy; and (3) build close relationships with customers, suppliers, and venture partners on the outside. Welch believes that boundarylessness will become a substitute for bureaucracy.

Welch's dislike of bureaucracy was quite evident when he took office in 1981. He is still preoccupied with removing bureaucracy from GE. In the 1991 annual report, he wrote the following:

We've been trumpeting the removal of bureaucracy and the layers at GE for several years now—and we did take out "sectors," "groups," and other superstructure—but much more remains. Unfortunately, it is still possible to find documents around GE businesses that look like something out of the National Archives, with five, ten or even more signatures necessary before action can be taken. In some businesses you might still encounter many layers of management in small areas: boiler operators reporting to the supervisor of boilers, who reports to the utility manager, who reports to the manager of plant services, who reports to the plant manager, and so on. Layers insulate. They slow things down. They garble. Leaders in highly layered organizations are like people who wear several sweaters outside on a freezing winter day. They remain warm and comfortable but are blissfully ignorant of the realities of their environment. They couldn't be further from what's going on.

Welch keeps on repeating his message. He is still the key driving force fighting bureaucracy, the top-down structure that he so abhors. What is evident to us today is that the boundaries at GE are starting to break down primarily due to the "head, heart, and guts" of the man at the top and his style of management.[4]

Deal Making

Jack Welch is also known as a consummate deal maker. During his first four years in office, Welch sold off 125 businesses. One of these divestitures was the sale of the housewares division to Black & Decker. This division, which produced irons, toasters, and other small appliances, had been considered an essential part of GE's identity since its establishment in the early 1900s. Another divestiture that raised eyebrows was Utah International, a highly profitable coal property in Australia. Sale of this unit, which was considered a sector by itself, brought in $2.4 billion for GE. Welch had placed both of these businesses—housewares and Utah International—outside the circles. So it was no big surprise that they were sold off.

But two deals in the following two years put Welch's creativity as a deal maker to the test. The first was the $6.3 billion cash purchase of RCA. Welch explained the rationale for this bold deal, the biggest non-oil acquisition to date, as follows:

> RCA, with its strong array of domestic businesses—defense, services, and the NBC network—will provide General Electric with a strong domestic earnings base to fuel many of our businesses that must win in the global marketplace. . . . Our defense businesses should be able to develop synergies that will benefit the nation as well as the company. The services and technology assets go together very well. . . . The television network, NBC, is a particularly attractive property, number one in an exciting services industry. (Slater, 1991, pp. 122–123)

The fit seemed ideal, probably in part because GE and RCA had been one company until 1933, when GE sold RCA under threat of antitrust litigation. Thus, they still seemed to belong together, 52 years later. But Welch did not purchase RCA simply to reunite with an old ally for the sake of becoming bigger. The deal, more than anything else, fit Welch's grand design.

The RCA deal was struck between Welch and Thornton Bradshaw, chairman of RCA, in Bradshaw's apartment near the Rockefeller Center. Welch took the initiative and called Bradshaw. At this meeting, Welch offered to buy RCA for $61 per share in cash, a 30 percent premium over RCA's $47 market price. They had a deal in less than a week.

The second deal was a swap that was conceived during a short conversation in France between Welch and Alain Gomez, chairman of Thomson S.A., the largest French electronics company. A deal was struck between the two to swap GE's consumer electronics business for Thomson's medical diagnostics business plus $800 million in cash. Thomson acquired all the TV, video, and audio products that carried the RCA and GE labels, while GE acquired x-ray and other diagnostic machines sold in Europe. As Welch recalls, it was very much a top-down decision:

> We didn't need to go back to headquarters for a strategic analysis and a bunch of reports. Conceptually, it took us about 30 minutes to decide that the deal made sense. (Slater, 1991, p. 195)

Both of these deals took the public and the press by surprise. In fact, the RCA deal was probably the riskiest thing Welch ever did. But in both cases, the CEO was in full control. It was his acumen as a deal maker that enabled Welch to pull off these two "home-runs," to use one of Welch's favorite expressions.

Welch's ability to strike a deal with a handshake "justifies" the vision that he created. In fact, he does not have to rely on others to provide the justification; he can justify his vision and action on his own. This kind of power becomes particularly effective in promoting combination (conversion of knowledge from explicit to explicit) within the company as well as across companies. Strong leadership fosters the inter-organizational mixing of knowledge across company boundaries.

Bottom-up Management: 3M

At Minnesota Mining and Manufacturing Company (3M), top management is not the focus of attention. The names of successive CEOs are relatively unknown, and what they say or do appears to be of little relevance to 3M employees. Instead, individual inventors and entrepreneurs are more the focus of attention and, quite possibly, better known than the CEO to the outside world. The stories of how a lab technician named Dick Drew created masking tape and Scotch tape or how a sales manager named John Borden created a dispenser with a built-in blade for Scotch tape have become legend. More recently, the story of how Art Fry created those ubiquitous little stick-on yellow note pads known as Post-it Notes has been heard over and over again in and out of the company.

In many respects, 3M represents an antithesis to the top-down management style at GE. The guiding principles at 3M are autonomy and entrepreneurship, which get translated into practices such as the following:

- absence of overplanning
- brevity of paperwork
- acceptance of mistakes as normal
- regular crossing of boundaries
- encouragement of initiative taking
- flow of ideas from below
- minimum interference from above
- inability of top to kill an idea
- maintenance of a small and flat organizational structure

In our opinion, 3M exemplifies the bottom-up model of management better than any of the large companies we know of today.

3M's origin may have something to do with its management style. Several local Minnesota investors bought a mine in 1902, thinking it contained the very valuable and hard mineral corundum, which was used in high-grade abrasives. But the mine contained only low-grade mineral. The disappointed investors concluded that the only way to redeem themselves was to come up with offshoot products that had high value. Says Lew Lehr, the CEO from 1979 to 1986:

> The salesmen would go from smokestack to smokestack knocking on doors. But they didn't stop at the purchasing agent's office. They went into the back shop to talk to the boys and see what was needed that nobody was making.[5]

A company of practical problem solvers, be they salesmen or technical people, was born as a result.

The bottom-up approach seems to have become entrenched within the company early in its history. An accountant and the third CEO, William McKnight, describes how 3M was managed in its formative years:

> As our business grows, it becomes increasingly necessary for those in managerial positions to delegate responsibility and to encourage men to whom responsibility is delegated to exercise their own initiative. This requires considerable tolerance. Those men to whom we delegate authority and responsibility, if they are good men, are going to have ideas of their own and are going to want to do their jobs in their own way. It seems to me these are characteristics we want in men and [they] should be encouraged as long as their way conforms to our business policies and our general pattern of operation. Mistakes will be made, but if the man is essentially right himself, I think the mistakes he makes are not so serious in the long run as the mistakes management makes if it is dictatorial and undertakes to tell men under its authority to whom responsibility is delegated, exactly how they must do their job. If management is intolerant and destructively critical when mistakes are made I think it kills initiative and it is essential that we have many men with initiative if we are to continue to grow. (Huck, 1955, p. 239)

Individuals with Initiative

3M has been blessed over the years with a large number of what McKnight called "individuals with initiative." Peters and Waterman (1982) referred to them as "heroes" and Gifford Pinchot (1985) as "intrapreneurs." Whatever they may be called, we need to focus on specific individuals if we are to understand the essence of bottom-up management at 3M. We shall highlight the stories of two individuals—Dick Drew and Art Fry.[6]

Dick Drew

When Dick Drew was selling sandpaper, he noticed the difficulty his customers in the automobile industry were having painting two-tone cars. One day he promised a painter to make a tape that could solve his problem. Since neither Drew nor 3M had ever worked on tape before, the early attempts all failed. After a number of successive failures, McKnight, the president, for fear of damaging 3M's reputation with auto industry customers, told Drew's boss to take him off the tape project and put him back on sandpaper.

Drew was assigned to work on a flexible crepe-paper backing for sandpaper. Still obsessed with solving the problem of the painting of two-tone cars, Drew came up with the idea of crepe with adhesives. As he was about to test his idea in the lab, Drew bumped into McKnight, who asked Drew if he knew he had been ordered to stop working on tape and to go back to sandpaper. Drew admitted that he knew but explained with conviction how his idea was going to work and how it was going to help his customers. McKnight allowed him to continue and, after hundreds of failures, the crepe-paper backing worked. A masking tape, the first tape 3M ever made, was born. Five years later, Drew went on to invent Scotch tape.

Art Fry

Fry sang in the church choir and noticed that the slips of paper he inserted to mark selected hymns would fall out. He decided to create a marker that would stick to the page but would peel off without damaging it. He made use of a peelable adhesive that Spence Silver at the Central Research Lab had developed four years previously, and made himself some prototypes of the self-attaching sheets of paper.

Sensing a market beyond just hymnal markers, Fry got permission to use a pilot plant and started working nights to develop a process for coating Silver's adhesive on paper. When he was told that the machine he designed could take six months to make and cost a small fortune, he singlehandedly built a crude version in his own basement overnight and brought it to work the next morning. The machine worked. But the marketing people did some surveys with potential customers, who said they didn't see the need for paper with a weak adhesive. Fry said, "Even though I felt that there would be demand for the product, I didn't know how to explain it in words. Even if I found the words to explain, no one would understand. . . ." Instead, Fry distributed samples within 3M and asked people to try them out. The rest was history. Post-it Notes became a sensation, thanks to Art Fry's entrepreneurial dedication and dogged persistence.[7]

Stories like these are heard over and over again within 3M. The company treasures these stories and keeps them alive. Each story centers around a hero and a legend. Each story also has a moral to tell, but a common theme runs through all of them: "Pursue your dream with freedom." Pursue your dream despite opposition or interference from above. Pursue your dream no matter how long a raw idea may take to make it in the marketplace. Pursue your dream using informal channels. Pursue your dream even if you fail.

It is important to note that individuals with initiative will not be able to pursue their dreams unless the company gives them the freedom and the funding to do so. At 3M, researchers can spend up to 15 percent of their on-the-job time pursuing their own dreams. This "15 percent rule" means that researchers are free to do whatever they want roughly one day out of the week. 3M also provides those pursuing their dreams with access to company resources. Art Fry took advantage of this access by using bottles of Spence Silver's adhesive that were lying around the lab to make himself some self-sticking hymnal markers. He also used the equipment of other divisions—different kinds of coasters and paper handles—to try out his ideas. Al Boese, another 3M individual with initiative, and his group received funding to explore new uses for nonwoven material in order to produce successful products beyond lens wipers.

Top Management as Mentor

The idea of a "boss" does not sit well at 3M. Entrepreneurs like to believe they are in control of their own destinies. An episode from the 1950s illustrates how 3M tries to deny the concept of hierarchy:

> Ames Smithers, a *Wall Street Journal* reporter calling in the late 1950s to write an article about the 3M company, interviewed President Buetow. The newsman mentioned at one point that his understanding of 3M would be enhanced considerably if he could see an organization chart. Buetow changed the subject, almost as though he had not heard. The visitor repeated his request several times. Still no direct response from Buetow.
>
> Finally, in growing exasperation, the reporter interjected, "From your reluctance to talk about or show me an organization chart, may I assume you don't even have one?" "Oh, we have one all right," Buetow replied, reaching sheepishly into his desk drawer. "But we don't like to wave it

around. There are some great people here who might get upset if they found out who their bosses are." (Pinchot, 1985, p. 208)

In this kind of a setting, rarely does a boss give an order or a command. McKnight once did, if you recall. He became concerned that 3M's reputation with auto industry customers would be damaged by Dick Drew's frequent failures as he tested his tape, and ordered Drew's boss to remove him from the tape project. We all know what became of that order. It was ignored. An order or a command has little meaning in a company that encourages meritorious disobedience.

At 3M, senior managers act as mentor, coach, and sponsor. They are there to keep a sharp eye out for individuals who believe passionately in something and to empower them to follow their intuitions. They are there to protect people below from premature interference and to push them out of the nest when the time is right. The following homily is often used within 3M to describe their role: "The captain bites his tongue until it bleeds." It's a naval expression concerning the patience the captain has to endure when watching a junior officer bring a big ship alongside the dock for the first time. Lew Lehr explains as follows:

> "The captain bites his tongue until it bleeds" means that, once a sponsor has bet on someone, he doesn't speak out against the project represented. The qualities that a sponsor needs are (1) belief, (2) patience, and (3) the vision to differentiate between one-time and mortal failure.[8]

As befits a company that was founded on a mistake, 3M has prided itself on having continued to accept failure as a normal part of running a business. Lehr admits that every one of his colleagues in senior management has backed a few losers along the way. On the other hand, Desi DeSimone, the current CEO, admits the mistake of opposing what turned out to be a very successful product:

> Actually, when Thinsulate was being developed, I stood on the side that wanted to kill the project, saying, "Enough already, stop this thing." Even so, I left open a loophole to permit its continued autonomous development. In other words, at a suitable stage, one "closes one's eyes" to process.[9]

In addition to biting its tongue, management at 3M has to "close its eyes and just grit its teeth," to use DeSimone's words.

Obsession with New-Product Ideas

Very few things are considered sacred within 3M, but the development of new-product ideas is certainly one of them. Individuals are set free to pursue their dream while management bites its tongue and grits its teeth to foster the development of new-product ideas. There is even a commandment that serves as a behavioral guide. Known as the "eleventh commandment" within 3M, it says, "Thou shall not kill ideas for new products." If someone wants to stop a project aimed at the development of a new product, the burden of proof is on the person who wants to stop the project, not the person proposing it. "When you switch the burden from proving that the idea is good to the burden of proving that the idea is not good, you do an awful lot for changing the environment within the company with respect to the sponsorship of entrepreneurial people," says one 3M employee. (Peters and Waterman, 1982, pp. 227–228)

More formally, each division has to comply with a corporate requirement that at least 25 percent of its sales must be derived from products that did not exist five years ago. This requirement, which is uniquely 3M's, serves as the positive driving force behind the company's financial structure. It also forces each divisional manager to pursue new products, especially since compensation at senior levels is linked to the percentage of sales that come from new products. According to DeSimone, that percentage has exceeded 30 percent on a companywide basis in recent years.

This kind of requirement drives the "15 percent rule" and the "eleventh commandment" inside the company and fosters close contacts with customers and users outside the company. To facilitate new-product development, the company provides funding for virtually any idea and makes pilot testing facilities accessible to anyone. See Figure 5-3 for the various organizational characteristics supporting the continuous innovation process at 3M.

Middle-up-down Management: Canon

At the end of the 1970s, the top management at Canon feared that the demand for plain paper copiers targeted toward the office market would eventually level off. Canon had entered the plain copier business in 1970, with its introduction of the NP1100, which sold for 880,000 yen.

In early 1979, Canon's top management asked researchers in their mid-30s to develop a radically new copier. "We insisted on developing a small multi-feature product that could be used by anyone and produced at minimum cost," said Hiroshi Tanaka, a senior managing director and a director of the Imaging Business Machines Development Center, who headed this development effort at the time.[10]

The new product would target small offices, owners of small businesses, professionals such as doctors or lawyers, salesmen or writers working out of their homes, and even families—in short, people who would buy a plain paper copier for personal use. To appeal to this market, the new product had to be small, light, inexpensive, and easy to use, but without a compromise on quality. "Top management expressed a strong hope, not a command, to realize the dream of developing a '$1,000 copier' based on a totally new concept," said Teruo Yamanouchi, director of the Corporate Technical Planning and Operations Center (Yamanouchi, 1991, pp. 344–345).

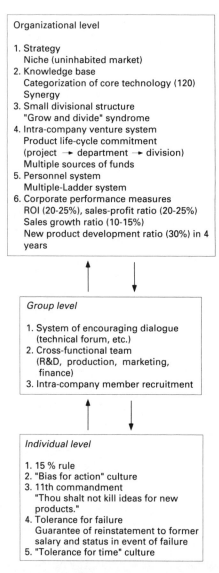

Figure 5-3. Organizational characteristics for continuous innovation at 3M.

After a number of informal discussions, a rough image began to emerge for a personal copier that met the broad guidelines set by top management. That image was expressed in terms of the following five goals. First, the copier must produce clear and stable copies constantly. Second, it should be the world's smallest and lightest (less than 20 kg or 50 lbs.). Third, it should have a market price about half that of the smallest plain paper copier on the market, or below 200,000 yen or $1,000 in the United States. Fourth, it should be as close to maintenance-free as possible, without the need for parts replacement or regular servicing. Fifth, it should be creative and contain an element of fun (e.g., use of colors or different paper sizes). "When these goals were established, there were no technological solutions nor were there any signs this would work," Yamanouchi (1991, p. 346) added.

Feasibility Study Team

A feasibility study team was formed to examine what it would take to realize the project. The 14-member team, headed by Hiroshi Nitanda, consisted of 8 people from R&D, 3 from production, 2 from marketing, and 1 from product design. The average age of this team was 28. The team began with a technical analysis. The important questions were crystal clear. Why are plain paper copiers so expensive? And why do they need so much servicing?

The feasibility study team members faced a big challenge. They had to resolve what appeared to be a contradiction between reliability and cost. Normally, production costs would increase in order to improve reliability, and service requirements could increase when cost was reduced. How could both reliability and cost be improved simultaneously? To resolve this challenge, members from different disciplines had to abandon their conventional wisdom and create a totally new concept of how a copier operated. Internally, this challenge was referred to as the creation of a "Canon Revolution."

The feasibility study team discovered that the two questions they raised had a common source. Most plain paper copiers used a complicated, delicate imaging mechanism that needed regular servicing. Apart from paper jams, the researchers found that 97 to 98 percent of copier service problems were related to the drum and its surrounding mechanisms. Since this servicing was very costly, any reduction in periodic maintenance meant that a copier could be sold for much less. Or better still, maintenance could be eliminated altogether.

Members of the feasibility team engaged in outspoken arguments at several impromptu *gasshuku,* or camp sessions, which were overnight brainstorming seminars held outside the workplace. Team members not only debated among themselves, but also invited people from other areas of Canon to discuss how the problem could be solved. As Kei Saito, a key member of the feasibility team, pointed out, managing the different "rhythms" that existed within the team became the key to achieving a creative solution during a camp session:

> To solve a fundamental question like the "seesaw" between cost and reliability requires a reorientation of the mind. First, one needs to ask, "What is the essence?" Then, the available approaches to deal with it are enumerated and diffused. I think the diverging mind is different from the converging mind, which figures out what sort of technology is used for making products. When these are mixed up, what comes out is something which is

shrunken. Often, conflicts occur when people have rhythms that do not agree with each other. Attempts to bring them together don't succeed when they are diverging. If the rhythms are in unison from the beginning, we can hardly have good result. Only one major proposition is given, and later people are divided into groups which will do complete divergence to make them compete. Because there are several groups, instead of just one, which work in parallel, naturally there is waste, and we are aware of it as we do it. Creating the rhythms of divergence and convergence is the trick of conducting a successful camp session.[11]

Camp sessions were an ideal forum for bringing together people with different rhythms, having conflicts emerge as a result, and eventually synchronizing them to find a creative solution.

Disposable Cartridge

After much debate (or "seesaw"), one of the emerging ideas began to make sense to everyone. What if the troublesome part of the copier— the drum and its surrounding mechanism—could be made disposable, so that the user simply discarded the entire module after making a certain number of copies and inserted a fresh unit as a replacement? With this idea, the copier would be essentially maintenance-free. Whereas the drum in a conventional copier was a component with an open-ended operating life, which meant that it would certainly fail at some point in time and then would have to be repaired, the feasibility team came up with an entirely new way of thinking about the drum. It was reconceptualized as a cartridge with a limited but known life expectancy. All the major parts of the copier mechanism—photosensitive drum, toner, and development assembly—would be fitted into a disposable cartridge. Thus a totally new concept was born, using an imaging cartridge that eliminated the need for regular maintenance service. Hiroshi Tanaka reflected on this breakthrough in 1982:

> Up until now, copier maintenance and service calls have been inseparable from the copier business because the copier's circuitry and developer as well as the charging units are sophisticated and therefore susceptible to the least environmental change. To aggravate the problem, some geographic regions lack sufficient qualified service engineers. We decided that a way around service-related obstacles would be to put the heart of the copier mechanism in a protective cartridge that could be changed after a certain number of copies were taken, putting an end to the need for maintenance calls by service engineers. And we set the life of a cartridge at 2,000 copies.[12]

The disposable cartridge provided a conceptual breakthrough that triggered other benefits. Nitanda explained the ripple effect as follows:

> The idea of packaging the drum and surrounding components as a cartridge revealed a great number of things to us. First of all, as everything is brought together, the structure can be simplified and only a very small

number of essential parts are needed. So, high precision design becomes possible by combination in design. The product becomes less messy. Also, the key module becomes quite compact as the release mechanisms between units are no longer needed. So, low cost as well as high reliability will be achieved at the same time. Moreover, with a cartridge, the toner seal is opened only after reaching the customer. This meant the plant was required to develop a production process without imaging inspection. This led to better efficiency.[13]

The feasibility study team organized two additional "camp" sessions—one at a sea resort near Tokyo, the other at a small business hotel in Tokyo—to analyze the cost structure of what came to be called the Mini-Copier. Naturally, the photosensitive drum, which was by far the most costly component, became the focus of the cost-cutting discussion. When many of the feasibility study team members expressed doubts that a cost-down of one figure could be achieved, Hiroshi Tanaka had someone go out and buy some beer. As the team discussed design problems over their drinks, Tanaka held one of the beer cans and wondered aloud, "How much does it cost to manufacture this can?" The question led the team to speculate whether the same process for manufacturing an aluminum can could be applied to the production of an aluminum copier drum. By exploring how the drum is like and unlike a beer can, the Mini-Copier feasibility study team was able to come up with the process technology that could manufacture the disposable cartridge at an appropriately low price.

The disposable cartridge provided the conceptual breakthrough that moved the entire product development forward by leaps and bounds. By reversing their thinking—that is, from treating the entire imaging mechanism as consisting of life-long components to reconceptualizing it as made up of fixed-life components that could be thrown away—the feasibility study team members were able to convert a rough image into something practical and doable. The "reverse concept," as it is known within Canon, is depicted in Figure 5-4.

Mini-Copier Task Force

Having made a conceptual breakthrough, and being satisfied with the results of the cost analysis, Canon decided to go ahead with full-scale product development of the Mini-Copier. A formal task force headed by Hiroshi Tanaka was launched in September 1980. The Mini-Copier task force started with 130 members and eventually involved nearly 200 scientists, engineers, and marketing specialists covering pure research, product development, production engineering, and consumer research. Ryuzaburo Kaku, the company president, attended the kick-off meeting and gave a pep talk about the importance of the project and the need for Canon to win through technology. No specifics were mentioned by Kaku.

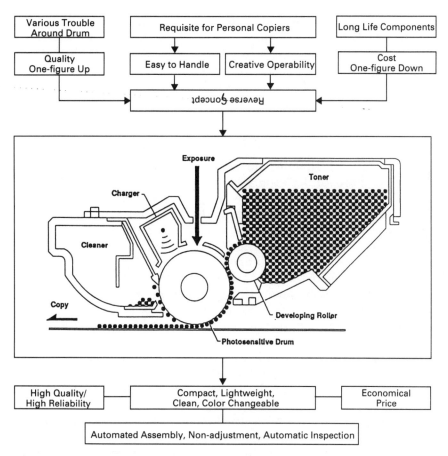

Figure 5-4. Reverse concept: Creation of the disposable cartridge. *Source: Canon.*

Although the Mini-Copier task force was the first to be created within the Reproductive Products Group, it was the second for Canon. The first task force was formed to develop the AE-1 camera, a single-lens reflex camera with a built-in microprocessor, introduced in 1976. The AE-1 was considered the company's greatest product development success.

As with the Mini-Copier, the AE-1 task force came up with new ideas to meet the challenging parameters set forth by top management. Task-force members were asked to develop a high-quality, automatic exposure camera that had to be compact, lightweight, easy to use, and priced 30 percent lower than the prevailing price of single-lens cameras. To reach this ambitious target, the project team achieved several "firsts" in camera design and production: an electronic brain consisting of integrated circuits custom-made by Texas Instruments;

modularized production, which made automation and mass production possible; and reduction in the number of parts by 30 to 40 percent. "It was a struggle because we had to deny our traditional way of thinking," recalled the head of the AE-1 task force.

As the newly appointed head of the Mini-Copier task force, Tanaka saw a lot of similarities with the AE-1 project. Both started with a specific price point and features in mind. Both set ambitious goals that would only be accomplished through a shedding of the traditional way of thinking. Thus, it was natural for Tanaka to try to transfer much of the know-how accumulated during the AE-1 development project to the Mini-Copier project. He even adopted "Let's make the AE-1 of copiers" as the slogan for the Mini-Copier project. The hope, obviously, was to replicate the market success of AE-1. But equally as important, he wanted to rally all the departments within the company behind the Mini-Copier. In particular, Tanaka knew from the AE-1 experience that a joint effort of the R&D and production engineering departments was indispensable to the success of the development process. But at the time, the focus of the production engineering group was directed entirely toward cameras. The slogan, "Let's make the AE-1 of copiers," was created partly to draw the camera-oriented production engineering group into the copier project.

Tanaka organized the task force with two group leaders, one from R&D and the other from production engineering. As shown in Figure 5-5, the R&D group is at the bottom right and the production engineering group at the bottom left. The task force also included two assessment groups. The first was the Product Quality Assessment Group, which stipulated that the copier should aim at achieving the repair-frequency level of TV sets used in the home. The group collected exhaustive information related to TV repair frequencies and set all quality standards for the copier based on that information. The second was the Product Cost Assessment Group, which analyzed the cost and quality standards necessary to achieve a retail price of under 200,000 yen. Two additional groups were created within the task force. The first was the Marketing Group, which invited copier sales representatives from around the world to present marketing ideas. The second was the Sales Software Group, which examined software options such as the use of color.

The multidisciplinary nature of the task force brought about some long-term benefits for its members. As one member, who joined the Mini-Copier task force at age 24, a year and a half after joining Canon, recalls:

Through the task force, I realized how important it was to join hands with other departments. I reaped a big benefit from simply knowing what to ask whom. The personal network that I built then is still a precious asset for me now. (Magami, 1990, p. 85)

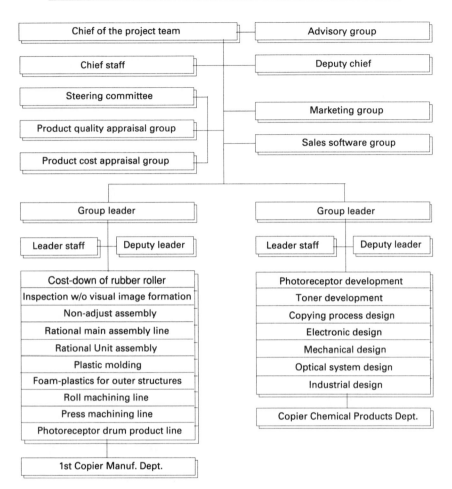

Figure 5-5. Organization of the Mini-Copier task force. *Source: Canon.*

As a rule, representatives from the R&D group and the production engineering group met once a week and often engaged in heated debate over cost and reliability. By their very nature, the two groups had different thought processes. As one project member aptly put it, "If someone from development thinks that 1 out of 100 is good, that's a clear sign for going ahead. But if someone from production thinks that 1 out of 100 is not good, we've got to start all over. This gap in perception creates conflict." But at the same time, these weekly sessions helped to create a synergistic effect. Kei Saito, who was deputy manager of an R&D center at that time, observed the following:

> In any company, good products are created when production engineering and design come together. Working together with Production Engineering, we can propose uniform parts design, or assembly in one direction, how

something should be assembled and in what sequence, or that one should do this or that if possible, when attempting to automate production, for example. If we (in product design) are by ourselves, it is easy to prepare drawings, and do what we like without thinking that far ahead. So, our discussions with the production engineering people and our subsequent effort to accommodate their various requests in our own ways resulted in both tangible and intangible cost reductions.[14]

Hiroshi Nitanda, who was appointed deputy leader of the R&D group within the Mini-Copier task force, attributed the success of the project to the frank and open discussion among members of the team from different functional groups and across different ages and titles. He and other middle managers who were involved in the feasibility study team played a key integrative role along several fronts. One obvious integration was across the various groups within the task force. Nitanda cited the following example as a case in point:

We had people from R&D, production engineering, and the Product Cost Assessment Group working to assign target costs to the various components since we knew that the target retail price was 200,000 yen in Japan or $1,000 in the U.S. We decided what the target costs were for the paper feeder, the optical parts, the drum, the charger, etc. Every group pitched in to make the assigned target costs a reality. We would have an infinite number of discussions. If a problem arose, we'd go back to the specification and conduct a thorough value engineering analysis to realize the target.[15]

Another integration Nitanda conducted was with the very young engineers assigned to the seven subgroups within the R&D group. Each subgroup was made up of from 2 to 10 engineers in their early 20s who had worked for Canon for only two or three years. The only exception was the Copying Process Design subgroup, whose members were in their late 20s. Experience was a key consideration for this subgroup, as the members had to master several diverse fields of technology.

The young engineers on the task force were not at all bashful about expressing their views or contradicting their seniors. Their aggressiveness and autonomy were very much a part of the culture revered within Canon. One of the company's key corporate philosophies has long been the so-called "three-self spirit," in which everyone is encouraged "to proceed in the spirit of self-motivation, self-knowledge, and self-government." According to the director of the Central Laboratory, where these three words were engraved in the three pillars at the entrance:

The three-self spirit enables us to operate in a bottom-up manner. Basically, you can do whatever you please here. There are no fine rules. And from the past, you don't get yelled at even if you attempt something new and fail. (Iwabuchi, 1992, pp. 162–163)

One of the young engineers reflected on his experience within the task force and commented, "We would devote all our energy towards product development, but we realized that our immediate superiors were hard at work trying to manage people above them" (Magami, 1990, p. 85). In fact, the third integration Nitanda and his peers worked on was with senior management. Informally, these middle managers were in constant communication with the heads of the various internal organizations, including Hajime Mitarai, managing director for R&D, Kazuo Naito, director of the Production Engineering Research Center, and Teruo Yamanouchi, director of the Corporate Technical Planning and Operations Center. A formal meeting with the Steering Committee (see Figure 5-5) was organized once every two months. Nitanda explained the rationale for this meeting as follows:

> It was important for everyone to be at the same level, since the task force was large. A Steering Committee consisting of a board of directors was formed for that reason. Tanaka chaired that committee, which met once every two months. We checked how the project was progressing schedule-wise and discussed what breakthroughs were needed when we ran into problems. Budget issues were also discussed in that committee. (Iwabuchi, 1992, p. 126)

Nitanda also involved the top managers at the very end of the project through a product quality assessment program called the "In My House Test," in which they actually tested the Mini-Copier in their homes. He recalls:

> It was in 1982 that we delivered the copiers to the homes of Kaku, Yamaji [vice president], and others and had them actually use the new machines. We also set them up at different offices, but heard no reports of failures. Consequently, none of them was ever returned to us. (Iwabuchi, 1992, p. 124)

At that point, Nitanda, Saito, and other members of the Mini-Copier task force knew that they had a winner on their hands. Canon introduced two versions of the Mini-Copier—the PC-10 and the PC-20—in late 1982. The machines generated 470 patents, 340 for the new cartridge system alone, for Canon.

The knowledge created by the Mini-Copier development project has subsequently been utilized within the company in a number of important areas. First, the product knowledge generated by the Mini-Copier, especially with respect to the disposable cartridge, has been adopted in other successful office-automation equipment introduced by Canon. Such equipment includes laser-beam printers, in which Canon holds 80 percent of the world market share, as well as facsimiles and microfilm reader-printers. Second, the manufacturing process knowledge gained through the Mini-Copier project (such as reduction in the number of parts by one-third, a tenfold improvement in parts-processing precision, and introduction of the automated image inspection system) paved the way for copier production to be automated. This shift was instrumental in boosting sales of copiers and business machines, which today account for over three-quarters of Canon's sales. Third, the organizational knowledge gained from the Mini-Copier, especially with respect to the critical role played by middle managers and the importance of working jointly across functional specializations, is reflected in the way Canon is managed today. Middle managers can be seen in the roles of creators and converters of organizational knowledge, process facilitators, and agents of change. They foster direct dialogue and locate themselves at the center of interaction within the organization. As Nitanda reflects today, "After the Mini-Copier experience, I made sure that the younger people have ample opportunity to voice their opinion. For example, I have them say whatever is on their mind for 30 minutes every morning during the *chorei* [morning gathering], write it up as a memo, and distribute topics before noon" (Magami, 1990, p. 85).

Comparison of the Three Management Models

The three cases presented above help to identify the differences in the prevailing management styles within GE (top-down), 3M (bottom-up), and Canon (middle-up-down). Using Table 5-1 as a frame of reference, we can see the difference in *who* is the agent of knowledge creation in each of these cases. It was clearly Jack Welch, the CEO, in the case of GE; Dick Drew, Art Fry, and other entrepreneurial individuals within 3M; and middle managers—Hiroshi Nitanda and Kei Saito—at Canon. Although Jack Welch acted as the "commander" within GE, creating concepts and justifying them himself, top management at 3M acted more like a sponsor and mentor. As with Kawamoto in the Honda City example, Hiroshi Tanaka at Canon served more as a catalyst, leaving the actual knowledge-creation process to the middle managers he appointed. Thus, it was Nitanda and Saito who were responsible for carrying out the five phases of the process—sharing tacit knowledge, creating concepts, justifying concepts, building archetypes, and cross-leveling knowledge—by involving both the top as well as the front line. The different roles that the top, middle, and front line play within middle-up-down management are discussed in further detail in the next section of this chapter.

Turning to the *what* section of Table 5-1, we notice that the types of knowledge accumulated differ across the three models. As mentioned earlier, the top-down model deals primarily with explicit knowledge, the bottom-up with tacit knowledge, while middle-up-down covers both types of knowledge. Furthermore, the middle-up-down model provides a more appropriate setting for realizing all four modes of knowledge conversion, while the two traditional models are limited to converting only two of the modes.

The *where* and *how* sections of Table 5-1 will be treated in more depth in Chapter 6, which proposes a new organizational structure more conducive to knowledge creation. But we were able to see the difference in how communication takes place within the three models. The concepts created by Jack Welch, such as "No. 1 or No. 2" and "speed, simplicity, and self-confidence," are passed down the organization almost as an order or instruction to be followed. In the case of 3M, the communication of ideas generated by individuals with initiative is left up to the individuals involved, who work on a self-organizing basis. In contrast, companies like Canon and Honda rely more on two-way communications such as dialogue, camp sessions, and drinking sessions (in fact, some companies use the word "nommunication," which is a hybrid created by combining a Japanese word for drinking, "nomu," with "communication," to describe this kind of session) and make frequent use of metaphors and analogies.

Knowledge-Creating Crew

Creating new knowledge in the knowledge-creating company requires the participation of front-line employees, middle managers, and top managers. Everyone in a knowledge-creating company is a knowledge creator. Indeed, the value of any one person's contribution is determined less by his or her location in the organizational hierarchy than by the importance of the information she or he provides to the entire knowledge-creating system. But, this is not to say that there is no differentiation among roles and responsibilities in the knowledge-creating company. In fact, creating new knowledge is the product of dynamic interaction among the following three players: (1) knowledge practitioners, (2) knowledge engineers, and (3) knowledge officers.

Until now, we have referred to the three key players in organizational knowledge creation as front-line employees, middle managers, and top managers. But in hindsight, these are titles inherited from a traditional hierarchical organizational structure in which the dominant management process is top-down. In an organizational structure that can take advantage of both a hierarchy and a task force (a topic covered in depth in the next chapter), we need to develop a more appropriate set of titles. We shall use the term "knowledge-creating crew" to refer to all the individuals engaged in knowledge creation within the company. The knowledge-creating crew is made up of knowledge practitioners, knowledge engineers, and knowledge officers. These three players correspond roughly to the three titles we have been using thus far (see Table 5-2).

Table 5-2. Knowledge-Creating Crew

Knowledge practitioners	Front-line employees and line managers
Knowledge engineers	Middle managers
Knowledge officers	Top managers

Knowledge practitioners are responsible for accumulating and generating both tacit and explicit knowledge. They consist of "knowledge operators," who interface with tacit knowledge for the most part, and "knowledge specialists," who interface primarily with explicit knowledge. Knowledge engineers are responsible for converting tacit knowledge into explicit and vice versa, thereby facilitating the four modes of knowledge conversion. Knowledge officers are responsible for managing the total organizational knowledge-creation process at the corporate level.

These crew members should be distinguished from what Peter Drucker calls "knowledge workers." According to Drucker (1993, p. 8), just as capitalists "owned" the means of production (e.g., capital, land, or labor) in the capitalist society, knowledge workers "own" their knowledge and take it with them wherever they go in the post-capitalist society. Knowledge is viewed as a "resource" by Drucker, whose key concern is with the productivity of knowledge work and the knowledge worker. We view knowledge both as a resource and an "output" and are more concerned with the creation of knowledge by the knowledge-creating crew. Our definition of a knowledge crew member also differs from that of a "symbolic analyst," a term coined by Reich (1991, p. 177) that has been applied generically to people who use their heads instead of their hands. As we shall find out below, included in a knowledge-creating crew are people who use their heads as well as their hands.

Knowledge Practitioners

The basic role of knowledge practitioners is the embodiment of knowledge. They accumulate, generate, and update both tacit and explicit knowledge, acting almost as "walking archives," on a day-to-day basis. Since most of them work at the front lines of business, which means that they are constantly in direct touch with the outside world, they can obtain access to the latest information on developments in the market, technology, or competition. The quality of knowledge that they accumulate and generate is determined by the quality of their direct experiences at the front lines of day-to-day business. Thus, knowledge officers and knowledge engineers need to give them tasks that are as challenging and exploratory as possible.

As mentioned above, knowledge practitioners are made up of two complementary groups—"knowledge operators" and "knowledge specialists." Knowledge operators accumulate and generate rich tacit knowledge in the form of experience-based embodied skills. In most cases, they are front-line employees or line managers who are located closest to the realities of the business. Included in this group are members of the selling organization who interact with customers in the marketplace, skilled workers and supervisors on the production line, skilled craftspersons, line managers, and others engaged in the operational side of the business. They constantly interface with the realities of the various fields and accumulate tacit knowledge through bodily experience.

Knowledge operators generally use their heads and their hands. Members of the Yazaki Group at Nissan Motor, who are test drivers, exemplify the role that knowledge operators play in the knowledge-creating process. These test drivers often live in a specific country for a year or so to get the feel of local driving conditions and driving styles, as well as to learn local lifestyles, habits, customs, and values. Their personal experience and know-how become valuable when designers and planners working on a new-product development project ask their opinion on how the model being developed is likely to perform in that particular country, relative to competitors. Members of the Yazaki Group provide feedback on the potential problems of the new model based on their in-depth knowledge of the local environment and competing models. They sometimes take the design engineers on a test drive to let the designers actually feel the problems.

A similar bodily experience becomes the basis for new knowledge among front-line salespeople. For example, leading apparel companies in Japan, such as Onward-Kashiyama, Renown, or Sanyo, send their own salespeople to the selling floor of major department stores and encourage them to carry on a dialogue with customers. Since most of the customers' needs are tacit, they cannot tell exactly and explicitly what they really need or want. Asked "What do you need or want?," most customers tend to answer with their limited explicit knowledge of what they acquired in the past. By engaging in a meaningful dialogue with customers, these salespeople can mobilize the customers' tacit knowledge base. This knowledge enhances the ability of the apparel companies to discern what the fickle customers are thinking and to make future plans accordingly.

Knowledge specialists, the other group of knowledge practitioners, also accumulate, generate, and update knowledge, but of a different kind from that which interests knowledge operators. Knowledge specialists mobilize well-structured explicit knowledge in the form of technical, scientific, and other quantifiable data, the kind of knowledge that could be transmitted and stored in a computer. Included in this group are scientists in R&D, design engineers, software engineers, sales engineers, strategic planners, and specialists working in staff positions such as finance, personnel, legal, and marketing research. They would be close to what Reich called symbolic analysts, those who primarily use their heads.

Several examples of knowledge specialists come to mind. The younger members of the Honda City development team, Matsushita's Home Bakery development team, and Canon's Mini-Copier development team, for example, qualify as knowledge specialists. System engineers at Kraft General Foods, who developed the micro-merchandising program that provides supermarkets with timely and precise recommendations on optimal merchandise mix and sales promotion (see Chapter 3 for more details), also fall into this group. Researchers at Sharp's corporate R&D group function as knowledge specialists as well. They collect information on the R&D needs of each business group, share the results of the research with the research laboratories of the respective business groups, and develop prototypes for the business groups as well. Another example of knowledge specialists would be marketing researchers who conduct interviews and administer questionnaires and then analyze their responses using sophisticated quantitative methodologies.

Ideally, knowledge practitioners should have the following qualifications: (1) they need to have high intellectual standards; (2) they need to have a strong sense of commitment to re-create the world according to their own perspective; (3) they need to have a wide variety of experiences, both inside and outside the company; (4) they need to be skilled in carrying on a dialogue with customers as well as with colleagues within the company; and (5) they need to be open to carrying out candid discussions as well as debates with others.

Knowledge Engineers

We have pointed out repeatedly that middle managers are the knowledge engineers of a knowledge-creating company. They serve as a bridge between the visionary ideals of the top and the often chaotic market reality of those on the front line of business. By creating mid-level business and product concepts, they mediate between "what is" and "what should be." They remake reality—or, to put it differently, engineer new knowledge—according to the company's vision.

Hiroo Watanabe of Honda Motor, Hiroshi Nitanda of Canon, and Ikuko Tanaka of Matsushita come immediately to mind as middle managers personifying the role of knowledge engineers. At Honda, top management's decision to try something completely new took concrete form at the level of Hiroo Watanabe's product development team through the "Tall Boy" concept. At Canon, the company's aspiration—making an excellent company by transcending the camera business—became a reality when Hiroshi Nitanda and his task force developed the "easy maintenance" concept, which eventually gave birth to the Mini-Copier. And at Matsushita, the company's grand concept, "Human Electronics," came to life through the efforts of Ikuko Tanaka and others who developed the mid-range concept of "Easy & Rich" and embodied it in the automatic bread-making machine.

In remaking reality, knowledge engineers take the lead in converting knowledge. They facilitate all four modes of knowledge conversion, although they make their most significant mark in converting tacit images and perspectives into explicit concepts (i.e., externalization). They synthesize the tacit knowledge of both front-line employees' and senior executives, make it explicit, and incorporate it into new technologies, products, or systems. Of course, this is not to say that they are not adept at "engineering" the three other modes of knowledge conversion—socialization, combination, and internalization.

In addition to knowledge conversion, knowledge engineers play two other key roles, both of which involve the creation of a knowledge spiral. The first is their role in facilitating a knowledge spiral along the epistemological dimension, across the different modes of knowledge conversion. Knowledge created in the socialization mode can trigger knowledge creation in the other three other modes of knowledge conversion, creating a spiral that we presented visually in Figure 3-3. The second is their role in facilitating another spiral along the ontological dimension, across different organization levels. Knowledge created at the individual level can move up to the group level, then to the organizational level, and sometimes up to the inter-organizational level. We shall return to the three knowledge engineers mentioned above to see how they engineered these two spirals.

We start with Ikuko Tanaka, who mobilized others in the Home Bakery development team to create knowledge not only for the team but for the company at large. She facilitated knowledge conversion and the knowledge spiral in the following ways: (1) tacit to tacit (socialization): she learned the tacit secrets of the head baker at Osaka International Hotel; (2) tacit to explicit (externalization): she translated these secrets into explicit knowledge so that the know-how could be communicated and transmitted to her team members as well as to others at Matsushita; (3) explicit to explicit (combination): the team standardized this knowledge, putting it together into a manual or workbook and embodying it in a product; and (4) explicit to tacit (internalization): Ikuko and her team members enriched their own tacit knowledge base through the experience of creating an innovative new product. The new tacit insight about providing genuine quality, which was gained from developing Home Bakery, was conveyed to others within Matsushita, who used it to formulate equivalent quality standards for kitchen appliances, TV sets, and white goods. In this way Ikuko induced a spiral of knowledge for the company at large.

Similarly, Hiroo Watanabe and Hiroshi Nitanda engineered knowledge spirals within Honda and Canon, respectively. Watanabe's image of a sphere and his metaphor of "Automobile Evolution" eventually led to the development of the "Tall Boy" concept, which was used to develop the City model in the early 1980s. Nitanda was one of the project leaders who developed the "easy maintenance" concept, which eventually led to development of the disposable cartridge used in the Mini-Copier introduced in the early 1980s. The tacit knowledge associated with "Tall Boy" was utilized a decade later in developing two 1994 Honda models (Ascot and Rafarga), whose selling approach focuses on their height. Similarly, the tacit knowledge associated with "easy maintenance" was utilized in the late 1980s to develop Canon's laser printer, which also uses a disposable cartridge.

A number of qualifications must be met for middle managers to become effective knowledge engineers: (1) they must be equipped with topnotch capabilities of project coordination and management; (2) they need to be skilled at coming up with hypotheses in order to create new concepts; (3) they need to have the ability to integrate various methodologies for knowledge creation; (4) they need the communication skills to encourage dialogue among team members; (5) they should be proficient at employing metaphors in order to help others generate and articulate imagination; (6) they should engender trust among team members; and (7) they should have the ability to envision the future course of action based on an understanding of the past.

Knowledge Officers

The basic role of knowledge officers, who are top or senior managers of a company, is the management of the total organizational knowledge-creation process at the corporate level. Knowledge officers produce and control the process on a hands-on basis, sometimes resorting to "management by wandering around." At other times they manage the process somewhat more removed from the day-to-day operation, deciding which projects to create and fund. Knowledge officers give a company's knowledge-creating activities a sense of direction by: (1) articulating grand concepts on what the company ought to be; (2) establishing a knowledge vision in the form of a corporate vision or policy statement; and (3) setting the standards for justifying the value of the knowledge that is being created.

If the job of knowledge practitioners is to know "what is," then the job of knowledge officers is to know "what ought to be." Knowledge officers are responsible for articulating the company's "conceptual umbrella," the grand concepts that in highly universal and abstract terms identify the common features linking seemingly disparate activities or businesses into a coherent whole. At NEC, top management has categorized the company's knowledge base in terms of several core technologies and then developed the metaphor "C&C," for computers and communications. At Kao, the umbrella concept is "surface science," referring to technologies for coating the surface area of materials. This concept has guided the company's diversification into products ranging from detergents to cosmetics to floppy disks, all of which are natural derivatives of Kao's core knowledge base.

Another key role of knowledge officers is the establishment of a knowledge vision that defines the value system of the company. It is this value system that evaluates, justifies, and determines the quality of knowledge the company creates. Knowledge officers should be aware that their aspirations and ideals determine the quality of knowledge the company creates. While the ideals of top management are important, on their own they are not enough; they need to foster a high degree of personal commitment by other members of the knowledge-creating crew. To do so, an open-ended and equivocal vision, which is susceptible to a variety of interpretations, is preferable. A more equivocal vision gives members of the self-organizing team the freedom and autonomy to set their own goals, making them more committed to figuring out what the ideals of the top really mean. Thus at Honda, a slogan as vague as "Let's gamble" and an extremely broad mission statement led the Honda City team to set its own goals and develop innovative new concepts.

Knowledge officers are also responsible for justifying the value of knowledge that is constantly being developed by the crew. They need to decide strategically which efforts to support and develop. We have found that qualitative criteria, such as truthfulness, beauty, or goodness, are equally as important as quantitative criteria, such as efficiency, cost, or return on investment.

A classic example of the more qualitative kind of justification can be seen in Mazda's decision to continue developing the rotary engine. Back in 1974, the product development team working on the new engine was facing heavy pressure within the company to abandon the project. The rotary engine was seen as a "gas guzzler" and critics contended that it would never succeed in the marketplace. But Kenichi Yamamoto, who headed the development team and is now chairman of Mazda, argued that stopping the project would mean giving up the company's dream of revolutionizing the combustion engine. "Let's think of it this way," Yamamoto proposed. "We are making history, and it is our fate to deal with this challenge." Yamamoto invoked the fundamental aspiration of the company—what he termed "dedication to uncompromised value"—and the strategy of technological leadership that top management had articulated in order to show how the rotary engine project expressed the organization's commitment to its vision. The decision to continue the project led eventually to the development of a successful rotary engine sports car, the Savanna RX-7.

We have seen several senior managers who personify the role of knowledge officers. The first is Hiroshi Tanaka of Canon, who was senior managing director at the time of the Mini-Copier development. Tanaka managed the entire Mini-Copier development process—setting up an initial feasibility study team, organizing camp sessions, using beer cans as a metaphor for the photosensitive drum, adopting "Let's make the AE-1 of copiers" as the slogan for the Mini-Copier task force, and encouraging a middle-up-down type of management style. The second is Nobuhiko Kawamoto, who was vice president at the time of the City development and is now president of Honda. Kawamoto appointed Hiroo Watanabe to be the team leader of the City project, handed him a challenging goal to "create something different from the existing concept," and rejected the team's proposal repeatedly by telling Watanabe to start all over from the very beginning, but gave the young project team considerable autonomy and authority throughout the development process.

A senior or top manager should ideally have the following characteristics to qualify as a knowledge officer: (1) ability to articulate a knowledge vision in order to give a company's knowledge-creating activities a sense of direction; (2) capability to communicate the vision, as well as the corporate culture on which it is based, to project team members; (3) capability to justify the quality of the created knowledge based on organizational criteria or standards; (4) uncanny talent for selecting the right project leader; (5) willingness to create chaos within the project team by, for example, setting inordinately challenging goals; (6) skillfulness in interacting with team members on a hands-on basis and soliciting commitment from them; and (7) capability to direct and manage the total process of organizational knowledge creation.

In this chapter, we have proposed a new model of management process, which we call middle-up-down management. It provides the best setting in which organizational knowledge creation can take place. Middle-up-down management synthesizes the best that the two traditional models—top-down and bottom-up—have to offer. But for a knowledge-creating company to make the most of this new management model, it has to rethink the roles of its key players. We suggested the establishment of a knowledge-creating crew, made up of knowledge practitioners, knowledge engineers, and knowledge officers, to facilitate the knowledge-creation process. In addition, a knowledge-creating company has to establish a new organizational structure that provides institutional support for these knowledge-crew members. This new knowledge-based organizational structure is proposed in the next chapter.

Notes

1. In the recent literature on the roles and responsibilities of middle managers, see, e.g., Guth and Macmillan (1986), Westley (1990), Wooldridge and Floyd (1990), Kaplan (1984), Conger and Kanungo (1988), Kraut et al. (1989), and Block (1987). For past research on middle management, see, e.g., Stewart (1967), Campbell et al. (1970); and Mintzberg (1973).

2. See, e.g., Nonaka (1988b), Dopson and Stewart (1990), Borucki and Byosiere (1991), and Nonaka, Amikura, Kanai, and Kawamura (1992).

3. Based on an interview on March 25, 1986, at GE headquarters, and on other published materials.

4. Although we have depicted Jack Welch's style as top-down, he has undergone a transformation of his own, evolving from being the "toughest boss in America" or "Neutron Jack" in the early 1980s to cultivating a more wholesome attitude in the late 1980s. Noel Tichy, who has worked closely with Jack

Welch since the early 1980s, says, "Having started out as the man with the bullhorn, in effect yelling at subordinates who couldn't keep pace, he evolved into a coach, willing to pause . . . to help others along" (Tichy and Stratford, 1993, pp. 209–210). A GE insider also noticed a similar change: "You know, I've watched the rebirth of Welch, or the renaissance of Welch, or whatever has happened to him. I don't know all the elements that went into his being born again, and I don't even care what they are. But I'm sure glad it's happened. He's a different man than he was in 1981" (p. 210). Some say that this transformation coincided with the roll-out of Work-Out, which is very much a bottom-up process involving front-line employees empowered to provide solutions to day-to-day business problems. But the adoption of Work-Out does not mean that Jack Welch has made a full swing to either the bottom-up model or the middle-up-down model. Teams are much more prevalent today within GE, but they still do not function in a self-organizing manner. Middle managers no longer "kick the dog," but neither are they the leader of the pack.

5. Interviewed on November 14, 1985, at 3M headquarters.

6. The stories in this section have been adapted primarily from Minnesota Mining and Manufacturing Company (1977) and Huck (1955).

7. Interviewed on November 12, 1985.

8. Interviewed on November 14, 1985.

9. Interviewed on November 12, 1985.

10. Titles used here are those that Canon employees had at that time.

11. Interviewed on November 28, 1984.

12. Interviewed on September 4, 1984.

13. Interviewed on November 28, 1984.

14. Interviewed on November 28, 1984.

15. Interviewed on November 28, 1984.

6

A New
Organizational Structure

The previous chapter introduced middle-up-down as the management style most conducive to organizational knowledge creation.
But for middle-up-down management to work effectively, we
need an organizational structure that supports the management process. Knowledge creation has implications not only for the management process; it also has profound implications for organizational
structure. This chapter develops the theoretical and practical bases of
a new organizational structure, referred to as a "hypertext" organization, that enables an organization to create knowledge efficiently and
continuously.

As knowledge and innovation become more central to competitive
success, it should come as no surprise that there has been growing
dissatisfaction with traditional organizational structures. For most of
this century, organizational structure has oscillated between two basic
types: bureaucracy and task force. But when it comes to knowledge
creation, neither of these structures is adequate. What is necessary is
some combination or synthesis of the two.

We discover in this chapter that there is a surprising model for such
a synthesis. It is the U.S. military, which is bureaucratic in peacetime
but highly task force-oriented in wartime. We view the U.S. victory
against Japan in World War II as an "organizational" victory of the
synthesized structure (U.S. military) over a purely bureaucratic structure (Japanese military).

The military case is a prelude to two case studies of Japanese companies attempting to carry out the synthesis of bureaucracy and task force. We introduce Kao as an "in transition" model of the new synthesized structure and Sharp as a "more perfected" model. But before we move on to describe this new organizational structure, which we refer to as "hypertext," a quick look is in order at the two traditional structures—bureaucracy and task force—that form the basis of the new structure.

Critique of Traditional Organizational Structures

The oscillation between bureaucracy and task force goes back to the nineteenth century, when Max Weber asserted that the most rational and efficient organizations in modern society have bureaucratic characteristics (Gerth and Mills, 1972, pp. 196–198).[1] A bureaucratic structure works well when conditions are stable, since it emphasizes control and predictability of specific functions. Bureaucratic structure, which is highly formalized, specialized, centralized, and largely dependent on the standardization of work processes for organizational coordination, is suitable for conducting routine work efficiently on a large scale. It is common in stable and mature industries with mostly rationalized, repetitive type of work.

However, bureaucratic control can come at the cost of hobbling individual initiative and can be extremely dysfunctional in periods of uncertain and rapid change.[2] Bureaucracy can generate other dysfunctional characteristics, such as intra-organizational resistance, red tape, tension, shirking of responsibility, means becoming objectives, and sectionalism (Merton, 1940; Selznik, 1949; Gouldner, 1954). It can also hinder the motivation of organizational members. Many social psychologists have argued that a participation-oriented and organic organizational structure can be more effective than bureaucracy in impelling motivation (McGregor, 1960; Likert, 1961; Argyris, 1964).

The task force is an organizational structure designed precisely to address the weakness of bureaucracy. It is flexible, adaptable, dynamic, and participative. In business organizations, the task force is an institutionalized form of team or group that brings together representatives from a number of different units on an intensive and flexible basis, in many cases to deal with a temporary issue.[3] People in a task force work within a certain time frame, and focus their energy and effort on achieving a certain goal. In this way, the task-force organization often succeeds in making quantum leaps in fields such as new-product development.

However, the task-force model has its limits as well. Because of its temporary nature, new knowledge or know-how created in the task-force teams is not easily transferred to other organizational members after the project is completed. The task force is therefore not appropriate for exploiting and transferring knowledge continuously and widely throughout entire organizations. When composed of many different small-scaled task forces, the organization becomes incapable of setting and achieving its goals or vision at the corporate level.

In recent years, a myriad of new organizational models, basically versions of the task-force model, have been proposed. These include an "adhocracy," an "infinitely flat organization," a "spider's web (network)," an "inverted pyramid," a "starburst (satellite)," and an "internal market."[4] Proponents of these models argue that the bureaucratic structure is too sluggish in responding to uncertain environments. When properly conceptualized, these new models can focus attention away from authority in order to eliminate costly administrative structures and support the rapid execution of strategies. These organizational forms have forced a complete rethinking of the relationships among top executives, middle management, and the lower level.

All of these new organizational concepts share certain common characteristics. These new organizations: (1) tend to be flatter than their hierarchical predecessors; (2) assume a constant dynamic rather than a static structure; (3) support the empowerment of people in building intimacy vis-à-vis customers; (4) emphasize the importance of competencies—unique technologies and skills; and (5) recognize intellect and knowledge as one of the most leverageable assets of a company.

Although these new organizational models have often been touted as cures for almost any management ill, they are not a panacea. Each model is useful in certain situations, but not in others. Each requires a carefully developed infrastructure—culture, style, and reward system—to support it. When configured properly, these disaggregated organizations can be effective in harnessing intellectual resources for a given purpose. When configured improperly, they can be less effective than the old-fashioned bureaucracy.

In fact, these newly developed managerial models merely recapitulate a very old and by now somewhat stale debate over the dichotomy between bureaucracy and task force. But from the viewpoint of knowledge creation, this debate may represent a false dichotomy. Indeed, one might argue that it is a product of some peculiarly Western tendency toward dichotomous thinking. We should consider the traditional bureaucracy and the task force as complementary rather than mutually exclusive approaches to organizations.

A business organization should be equipped with the strategic capability to exploit, accumulate, share, and create new knowledge continuously and repeatedly in a dynamic and spiral process. From that point of view, bureaucracy is effective in bringing about combination and internalization, while the task force is suitable for socialization and externalization. In other words, the former is the more appropriate structure for the exploitation and accumulation of knowledge, while the latter is effective for the sharing and creation of knowledge. The business organization should pursue both the efficiency of a bureaucracy and the flexibility of a task-force organization; some combination or synthesis of the two is needed to provide a solid base for knowledge creation.

An Attempt at Synthesis—Case of the Military Organization

Before describing such a synthesis within the business organization, we take a look at military structures of the United States and Japan during World War II. Although the Japanese military stuck to bureaucracy, the U.S. military made a clear-cut attempt to synthesize bureaucracy and the task force. We contend that the Japanese military over-adapted itself to past successes that were achieved under bureaucracy. In contrast, the U.S. military evolved into a more flexible structure with a focus on the task-force organization, and eventually won the war.

While organizational theory has often addressed the dichotomy between bureaucracy and task force, military organizations have historically been concerned with the task of how a bureaucracy could be maintained in a dynamic and flexible manner. Military organizations certainly maintain a typical bureaucratic structure in peacetime. However, in wartime, they must also demonstrate mobility. A look at the confrontation of the Japanese and U.S. militaries during World War II provides a unique case study of the synthesis we have been discussing.

Bureaucracy under the Japanese Imperial Military

The central feature of the Japanese military organization was its strict conformity to bureaucracy. The Japanese Imperial Army and Navy were set up as organizationally separate entities under the direct control of the Emperor, as shown in Figure 6-1. The rigid bureaucracy of

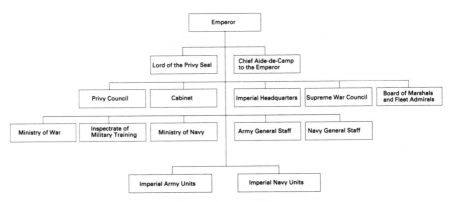

Figure 6-1. The Japanese Imperial Army and Navy: Organizational structure.

the Japanese military became a major obstacle during World War II, when it was confronted with a totally new and dynamic environment. Structure directed strategy in the case of the Japanese military.

The strategies of both the Japanese Army and Navy were strongly dominated by paradigms that were formed from successful experiences during the Russo-Japanese War and the China Incident. These experiences and subsequent successes eventually ingrained certain paradigms or models of operation that became treated almost as "sacred" within the Japanese military. The paradigm prevalent within the Imperial Army, for example, revolved around the concept of hand-to-hand fighting. The key to victory on the battlefield, according to the Imperial Army, was thought to be the last great bayonet charge and the resulting hand-to-hand combat. This paradigm was articulated in the "Basics of Training for Warfare," issued by the Imperial Army Training Headquarters in 1908. The technique proved to be more than adequate for defeating the Chinese and the British-Indian Army in a number of battles during the war in Asia.

The Imperial Navy's model of operation was to focus on a battle of cannon fire with enemy warships. Victory was to be decided by the great salvos between giant battleships. This paradigm was formed during the Battle of Tsushima in the Russo-Japanese War. The victory of the Imperial Navy over the Russian Baltic Fleet on May 27 and 28, 1905, was the first complete triumph in world naval history, and had a strong influence on the Imperial Navy's strategic thinking. From that point forward, the Japanese Navy believed that the result of a battle between opposing fleets would have a great influence on the eventual outcome of the war.

The Japanese military's organizational characteristics reinforced these models or paradigms. Its structure, control system, promotion system, and leadership style were designed to conform to its paradigms. Table 6-1 shows the pattern of environmental adaptation of the Japanese military. Note that the organizational characteristics under the "hand-to-hand battle" paradigm of the Army and the "battle between warships" paradigm of the Navy were internally consistent. The heroes who eventually emerged and the technology employed were consistent with the respective paradigms as well.

The rigid paradigms worked well within a particular environment. The Army's paradigm of the bayonet charge and the resulting hand-to-hand battle was actually a great success, at least in battles in East Asia. From Manchuria and China to Hong Kong and Singapore, successes based on the existing paradigm gave the military confidence in their model, and led to the elevation of this pattern of success to the level of a behavioral norm for the organization.

However, it became difficult to abandon what had worked well in the past even when the environment changed. Not long after their general success, the Japanese military confronted the American military at

Table 6-1. Organizational Characteristics of the Japanese Imperial Forces

Characteristics	Army	Navy
Paradigm	Hand-to-hand battle	Battle between warships
Resource priority	Priority on the number of forces	Priority on individual warships
Organizational structure	Separation of soldiers from artillery	Fleet-dominant structure
Promotion system	Biased in favor of infantry	Biased in favor of gunnery
Leadership	Embodied in hand-to-hand combat	Embodied in battle between fleets
Heroes	Maresuke Nogi	Heihachiro Togo
Technology	Light and medium tanks to follow infantry	Big battleships, e.g., Musashi and Yamato

Source: Tobe et al. (1984).

Guadalcanal Island. They faced the U.S. Marines, who had developed a new fighting technique combining ground, sea, and air warfare. Against the U.S. Marines, the Japanese Army made three attempts to attack at night, on each occasion using a bayonet charge. This strategy resulted in heavy losses.

Despite recognizing the importance of firepower after the Battle of Guadalcanal, the Imperial Army was unable to break away from the main concept of hand-to-hand battle, epitomized by the bayonet charge. And although the Imperial Navy attempted to strengthen its aircraft carriers, it believed up to the very end that the destructive force of the 46-cm guns of the Yamato and the Musashi—which were embodiments of the principle of the big gun—would be the key to naval success.

The theory of organizational evolution points out that "adaptation precludes adaptability." In other words, there is a danger of overadaptation to past success. The dinosaur is a case in point. At one point, this animal was both physiologically and morphologically suited to a particular environment. But it overadapted itself to that environment and could not adjust to eventual changes in the climate and food supply. The Japanese bureaucratic military fell into the same trap. It overadapted itself to past success and failed to "unlearn" those success factors within a new and changing environment.

A Synthesis under the U.S. Marines

Unlike the Japanese military, the U.S. military developed a flexible organizational structure in addition to a bureaucracy during World War II.[5] Among its various organizational innovations, we look at its introduction of the task-force organization, with particular attention paid to amphibious (combining both land and sea) operations.[6] The

U.S. military developed an amphibious operation through actual landings on 18 Pacific islands during the war against Japan. The landing on the island of Guadalcanal was the first U.S. offensive, as well as the first actual use of an amphibious operation by the U.S. Marines.

While an amphibious operation had some characteristics in common with the usual land or sea battle, it required the simultaneous integration of many activities that were usually conducted separately by ground, sea, and air forces. Under an amphibious operation, soldiers traveled on battleships for a long distance, changed to landing ships at the landing point, and forced a landing on an enemy shore with neither heavy equipment nor direct support from the artillery. To protect the landing soldiers, therefore, both battleship bombardment and air attack had to be provided at the same time. This operation led to the formation of a task-force team, which was composed of members of the different bureaucracies.

The U.S. victory at Guadalcanal is regarded as the turning point of World War II, and the beginning of the "organizational" victory of the U.S. military over the Japanese. While the bureaucratic Japanese military continued its use of the bayonet charge and hand-to-hand battle, the flexible U.S. military developed a new task-force organization, the Fleet Marine Force, to carry out landings on islands across the Pacific. Having established a base in the southern Pacific through the use of the Marines, the U.S. military started to carry out the bombing of mainland Japan by the Army's large bombers, which flew out from the occupied island bases.

In Search of a Synthesis—The Hypertext Organization

Just as the American military created a task force in addition to the traditional hierarchical structures of the Army and the Navy. A business organization should have a nonhierarchical, self-organizing structure working in tandem with its hierarchical formal structure. This point is particularly important for organizational knowledge creation. As business organizations grow in scale and complexity, they should simultaneously maximize both corporate-level efficiency and local flexibility.

In this section, we present an organizational design that provides a structural base for organizational knowledge creation. The central requirement for this design is that it provide a knowledge-creating company with the strategic ability to acquire, create, exploit, and accumulate new knowledge continuously and repeatedly in a cyclical process. The goal is an organizational structure that views bureaucracy and the task force as complementary rather than mutually exclusive. The most appropriate metaphor for such a structure comes from a "hypertext," which was originally developed in computer science.[7]

A hypertext consists of multiple layers of texts, while a conventional text basically has only one layer—the text itself. Texts on a computer screen may be paragraphs, sentences, charts, or graphics. Under a hypertext, each text is usually stored separately in a different file. When a text is needed, an operator can key in a command that pulls out all the texts on the computer screen at one time in a connected and logical way. A hypertext provides an operator with access to multiple layers. This feature allows anyone looking into the computer screen not only to "read through" the text, but to go down "into" it for further degrees of detail or background source material. He or she may even go "into" a different medium, such as video. For example, a hypertext version of, say, *Hamlet* might include video clips of different actors interpreting the "To be or not to be" speech in different ways. The essential feature of a hypertext is this ability to get "in" and "out" of multiple texts or layers.

These layers should be interpreted as the different "contexts" that are available. The layers put the knowledge of the hypertext document into a different context. To continue with the *Hamlet* example, the play itself is one context. The scholarly literature on the psychology of the character of Hamlet is another context, which enables the reader to interpret the play in a different light. Video clips of actors performing the "To be or not to be" speech provide yet another context, which helps the reader to transform her or his understanding of both the play and the scholarly literature. Thus, in terms of knowledge, each layer is really a different context. One example of a hypertext on the computer screen in shown in Figure 6-2.

Like an actual hypertext document, hypertext organization is made up of interconnected layers or contexts: the business system, the project team, and the knowledge base, as shown in Figure 6-3. The central layer is the "business-system" layer in which normal, routine operations are carried out. Since a bureaucratic structure is suitable for conducting routine work efficiently, this layer is shaped like a hierarchical pyramid. The top layer is the "project-team" layer, where multiple project teams engage in knowledge-creating activities such as new-product development. The team members are brought together from a number of different units across the business system, and are assigned exclusively to a project team until the project is completed. At the bottom is the "knowledge-base" layer, where organizational knowledge generated in the above two layers is recategorized and recontextualized. This layer does not exist as an actual organizational entity, but is embedded in corporate vision, organizational culture, or technology. Corporate vision provides the direction in which the company should develop its technology or products, and clarifies the "field" in which it wants to play. Organizational culture orients the mindset and action of every employee. While corporate vision and organizational culture provide the knowledge base to tap tacit knowledge, technology taps the explicit knowledge generated in the two other layers.

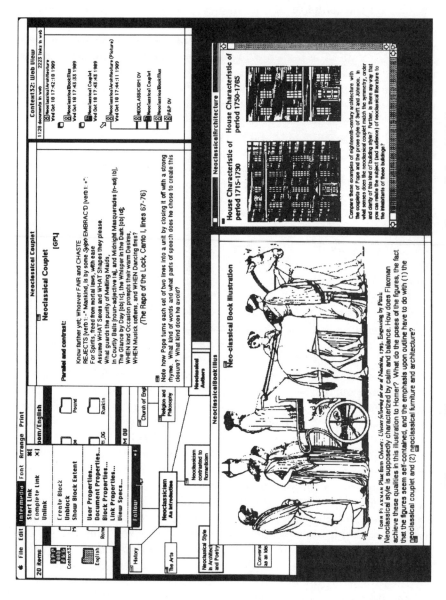

Figure 6-2. Hypertext on a computer screen. *Source: Bolter (1991).*

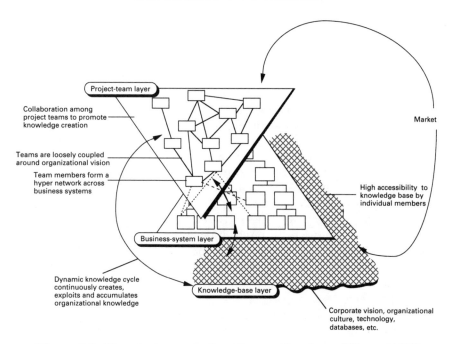

Figure 6-3. Hypertext organization. *Source: Nonaka and Konno (1993).*

What is unique about a hypertext organization is that three totally different layers or contexts coexist within the same organization. As with the *Hamlet* example, knowledge can reside within the business-system context, which may be analogous to the play itself. The project team provides another context, which may allow organizational members to view the traditional organizational context in a totally different light. As such, it may be analogous to the scholarly literature on Hamlet himself. The knowledge base is the third context in which knowledge can reside. It is here that knowledge created inside the two other contexts is stored and recontextualized. The knowledge base may be analogous to the video clips of speeches performed by different actors. The key characteristic of the hypertext organization is the ability of its members to shift contexts. They can move among the three contexts in order to accommodate the changing requirements of situations both inside and outside the organization. This ability offers the same flexibility as a computer operator moving easily through a hypertext document.

The process of organizational knowledge creation is conceptualized as a dynamic cycle of knowledge traversing easily through the three layers. Members of a project team on the top layer, who are selected from diverse functions and departments across the business-system layer, engage in knowledge-creating activities. Their efforts may be guided by the corporate vision presented by top management. Once the team completes its task, members move down to the knowledge-base layer and make an inventory of the knowledge created and/or acquired during their time with the project team. This inventory includes both successes and failures, which are documented and analyzed. After re-categorizing and recontextualizing the new knowledge acquired, team members return to the business-system layer and engage in routine operations until they are called again for another project. The ability to switch among the different contexts of knowledge swiftly and flexi-bly, so as to form a dynamic cycle of knowledge, ultimately determines the organizational capability for knowledge creation.

A hypertext organization, which is the dynamic synthesis of both the bureaucratic structure and the task force, reaps benefits from both. The bureaucratic structure efficiently implements, exploits, and accu-mulates new knowledge through internalization and combination, while the task force is indispensable for generating new knowledge through socialization and externalization. The efficiency and stability of the bureaucracy is combined with the effectiveness and dynamism of the task force in a hypertext organization.[8] Moreover, it adds an-other layer, the knowledge base, that serves as a "clearinghouse" for the new knowledge generated in the business-system and the project-team layers.

Needless to say, the knowledge content accumulated within the business-system layer is distinct from that generated in the project-team layer. To use the terminology developed in Chapter 3, bureau-cracy is more adept at accumulating operational knowledge (via in-ternalization) and systemic knowledge (via combination), while the project team generates conceptual knowledge (via externalization) and sympathized knowledge (via socialization). The role of the knowledge-base layer is to "mix" these different contents of knowledge and recate-gorize or recontextualize them into something more meaningful to the organization at large. A hypertext organization has the organizational capability to convert continuously and dynamically the different knowledge contents generated by the bureaucracy and the project team.

A hypertext organization should not be confused with a matrix struc-ture, which is used to achieve two or more different types of tasks in a conventional hierarchical organization.[9] Compared with the conven-tional matrix structure, a hypertext organization can be distinguished as follows:

1. In the matrix structure, an organization member must belong or report to two structures at the same time. In contrast, an organi-zation member in a hypertext structure belongs or reports to only one structure at one point in time. He or she is assigned to the project team during the project period or to the business system during "normal" times. Project members can therefore focus their attention solely on the ongoing project.

2. Organizational knowledge creation flows naturally from a hypertext organization, since each structure generates and accumulates new knowledge differently, while a matrix structure is not primarily oriented toward knowledge conversion.
3. In a hypertext organization, knowledge contents are combined more flexibly across layers and over time.
4. Since deadlines are set for the projects, the resources and energy of the hypertext organization can be used in a more concentrated manner to fulfill the goal of the project during the project period.
5. Since projects are placed under the direct control of top management, communication time and distance across top, middle, and lower management in the formal hierarchy can be compressed, resulting in a more thorough and in-depth dialogue across management levels. In a sense, a hypertext organization fosters middle-up-down management.

In addition, a hypertext organization has the organizational capability to convert knowledge from outside the organization. A hypertext organization is an open system that also features continuous and dynamic knowledge interaction with consumers and companies outside the organization. It is equipped with the capability to collect customer response to new products, find new trends in consumer needs, or generate new-product concept ideas with other companies.

The key characteristic of a hypertext organization is the ability of its members to shift contexts, moving easily in and out of one context into another. In the next section we will illustrate the hypertext organization by using two Japanese companies as examples. The first is Kao, which is still "in transition" from a matrix organization to a hypertext organization. At Kao, project members engage in specific projects while at the same time reporting to the business-system layer. They are not assigned exclusively to a project team. In contrast, Sharp represents a "more perfected" form of hypertext structure. An organization member stays in only one layer at any one time and shifts to another layer when the need arises.

Kao: An "In Transition" Case of a Hypertext Organization

We analyze Kao, Japan's leading household and chemical products maker, as an example of a hypertext organization still in transition. Having been established in 1887, Kao's businesses have expanded from toiletry products into cosmetics and floppy disks.[10] From the perspective of our theory, Kao qualifies as a hypertext organization because it utilizes three different layers, but is considered in transition because it is still structured as a matrix organization, with its project-team members reporting to two structures at the same time.

Kao's business-system layer is structured as flat as possible, which encourages active information sharing and direct employee interaction. It also utilizes a project-team approach to develop new products and solve organizational problems within the division structure, although the project team is not yet considered a stand-alone unit that employees can enter and leave. It also has the technological (explicit) and philosophical (tacit) knowledge bases that work to support and promote organizational knowledge creation. We shall now turn to describing each of these layers, with particular focus on the knowledge-creation process within each layer.

Business-System Layer: A Division System with Fluidity

Kao's business-system layer consists of a divisional system made up of 18 divisions, including the Home Product Division, Sanitary Product Division, and Chemical Division. Kao believes that direct communication among the employees of different divisions becomes limited in the conventional division system, and is thus striving to achieve active interaction among its employees. Kao also believes that direct interaction among employees generates creative ideas. But organizational members cannot interact equally when holding different amounts of information. Thus "information sharing" is regarded as the principle tenet that defines Kao's organization. Kao has built various mechanisms and support systems that assure the sharing of information within the business-system layer. They include "free access to information," "open floor allocation," "open meetings," and "fluid personnel change." These mechanisms and systems become the basis upon which tacit knowledge is shared or converted to explicit knowledge, and vice versa. We shall briefly describe each information-sharing mechanism below.

To assure "free access to information," computer systems have been introduced throughout the Kao organization, with all information being filed in a database. Through this system, anyone at Kao can tap into databases included in the sales system, the marketing information system (MIS), the production information system, the distribution information system, and the total information network covering all of its offices in Japan. The unique feature of this system is that any member, no matter what his or her position or to what section she or he belongs within the business system, has full access to the database (except for a limited amount of personnel information). In other words, anyone can get access to the rich base of explicit knowledge that exists within the business system through this "free access to information" system.

In the "open floor allocation" system, the divisions and functional groups within Kao are all configured around a large open space. Half of the executive floor space, for example, is occupied with an open space called the "decision-making room." In fact, executives rarely stay in their own offices. Divisional heads hold meetings at the round table located in one of the large open spaces. In the laboratories, researchers do not have their own desks, but share big tables. President Fumikatsu Tokiwa, a former researcher, explains the aim of this system as follows:

> R&D members have a natural tendency to gather into small groups, and isolate themselves from others. To interact, it does not even help to speak loudly if the offices are separated. So we tried to remove both the physical and mental walls at the same time.[11]

This kind of floor setup allows employees to share their tacit knowledge with others, or may trigger an externalization mode in the middle of a dialogue.

Information sharing and employee interaction are also accelerated through "open meetings." Any meeting at Kao is open to any employee, and top-management meetings are no exception. Any employee can attend the relevant portion of the meeting and make his or her opinion known. Through this practice, top management can acquire insights from those most familiar with the issues at hand, while employees can gain a better understanding of the general corporate policy. This kind of hands-on experience helps to mobilize all four modes of knowledge conversion.

What is known within Kao as the R&D conference is typical of these "open meetings." Through this conference, which is held every quarter, top management learns about research projects directly from the researchers, while research members gain an opportunity to voice their opinions directly to top management. This conference, which again is open to anyone outside of R&D, is regularly attended by some 1,800 people (out of a total of 7,000 employees).

Interaction among members with different experiences is also enhanced through the "fluid personnel change" system. For instance, researchers in one division are often transferred to other divisions or to other functional areas, such as sales or finance, on a "whoever is needed, wherever he or she is needed" basis. As a personnel director explains, "Ceaseless change is the basic way. Any member should experience at least three different positions in her or his first ten years within the company." This kind of active job-rotation system, especially among R&D people, enhances the accumulation and sharing of tacit knowledge and promotes interdisciplinary product development within the company. For example, Kao entered the cosmetics market in the mid-1980s with the introduction of a skin-care product called "Sofina" that resulted from the cooperative effort of people working in surface-active science and those in biological skin care.

As we have seen, Kao's organizational structure can be explained as a division system equipped with various mechanisms for active information sharing and direct employee interaction. Although it is a bureaucracy, the structure is flat, with all members of the organization being placed on equal footing and creating new knowledge through direct interaction of their respective functions. Its business system is sometimes described as a Japanese-style paperweight, which is shaped liked a large, circular coin with a small handle in the middle. The metaphor connotes the equal footing of all organizational members, with top management serving as the handle.

Project-Team Layer: Horizontal, Cross-Divisional Project Teams

Although Kao's organizational structure is basically a traditional division system structure, with daily work organized division by division, fast decision making and efficient resource allocation are achieved by treating each division as an independent profit center. However, when it comes to new-product development, marketing innovation, and human resource management issues, the divisions cooperate in a horizontal manner. Besides the vertical product divisions, Kao organizes three "horizontal" committees to deal with cross-divisional strategic issues. They are the Division Strategy Committee, Marketing Innovation Committee, and Human Resource Management Committee. We call Kao's organizational structure "in transition" because these committees are not totally outside of the business system. In other words, an organizational member is never solely committed to a project team; he or she is in both the business system and the committee at the same point in time.

The Division Strategy Committee, which meets twice a year and is attended by the vice presidents and division heads, determines which new products need to be developed by cross-divisional teams (see Figure 6-4). Ongoing cross-divisional projects, for example, include a hair treatment project for controlling hair hardness, a new cosmetics project for men's use, and an ultrathin paper products project for such products as diapers and sanitary napkins. Members of these teams come from the various divisions as well as from the R&D and production departments.

Kao's project-team activities are not limited to new-product development; they are applied widely throughout the entire organization, as in the case of the Marketing Innovation Committee. This committee meets two or three times a month and is attended by the product division's marketing-staff members as well as graphics engineers and market researchers, who operate outside the division. The committee examines common marketing issues across divisions, including effective market-research techniques, the appropriate advertising media mix, and environmentally conscious packaging. The committee forms Marketing Innovation Projects, which tackle these issues and develop appropriate recommendations.

The Human Resource Management Committee is another horizontal, cross-divisional committee, which meets once a month and is attended

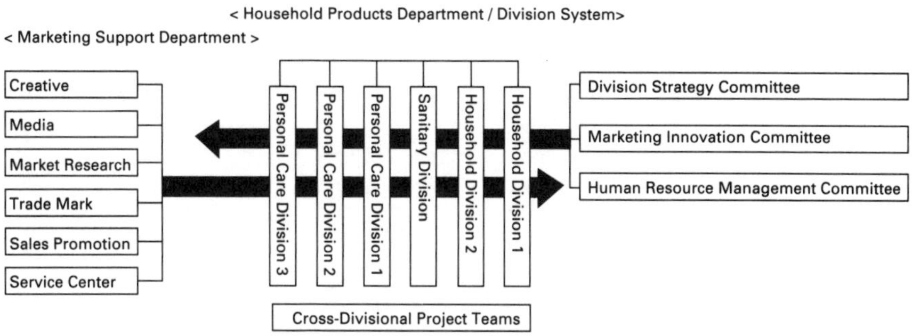

< Household Products Department / Division System>

Figure 6-4. Cross-divisional project teams at Kao. *Source: Kao Corp.*

by division heads. This committee reviews the overall status of human resource development across divisions, and is also responsible for selecting the appropriate members from each division for new-product and marketing-innovation projects.

Kao applies the idea of horizontal, cross-divisional team activities even to its corporate staff operation. Each "center" specialized in public relations, legal affairs, accounting/finance, or human resources carries out normal staff functions, but cross-center project teams are formed in order to deal with corporatewide issues, such as the reduction of fixed cost, risk management, working-hour reduction, and the simplification of corporate staff operation. In trying to reduce fixed cost, for example, the accounting/finance staff people work together with their colleagues in human resources and legal affairs.

Explicit and Tacit Knowledge Bases at Kao

The knowledge-creating activities conducted within the business-system and the project-team layers are captured and recontextualized in the corporatewide knowledge base. Explicit knowledge is captured and recontextualized under the "Five Scientific Areas," which provide Kao with a sense of direction regarding which new markets Kao should enter in the future. In addition, tacit knowledge generated in the two layers is accumulated and reconceptualized along the philosophical principles proposed by top management. This recontextualization fosters a unique organizational culture within Kao, which reorients the mindset of every employee.

"Five Scientific Areas" as an Explicit Knowledge Base

Kao believes that there are five key scientific areas vital to their current technology—fat and oil science, surface science, polymer science, biological science, and applied physics (see Figure 6-5). These five sci-

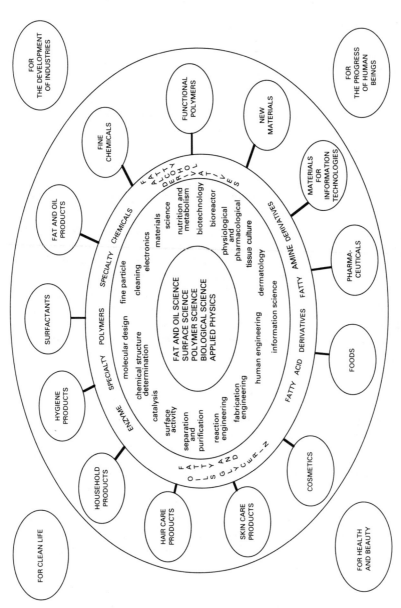

Figure 6-5. Kao's five scientific domains. *Source: Kao Corp.*

entific fields are closely related to Kao's historical development. The first, fat and oil science, dates back to Kao's soap production in 1923. The second scientific area was initiated after World War II, with the production of surface-active agent, such as a detergent, from fatty acids. The third area, polymer science, was established as a result of its studies on surface-active agents. Since these agents are applied to fiber and fiber is made from polymers, these two technologies are closely related. Biological science and applied physics have been developed recently as key scientific areas for the future.

Knowledge created in the business-system and project-team layers can be recategorized into these five scientific areas, allowing Kao to move into markets that at first glance may seem distant from its core business. These markets may seem far removed at the "product" level, but they may have very clear commonalities at the level of "basic science." This focus on science is what allows Kao to be in cosmetics and, at the same time, in computer floppy disks. As President Tokiwa explains, recontextualizing Kao's business along basic sciences has helped the company to move into new markets:

> To develop products, we used to categorize technological cores by products. But we found that it gave us a much wider vision if we regard technological cores as scientific knowledge. For instance, surface science is the study of surface tension. Surface-active agents are used in shampoos and detergents in order to activate surface tension. However, surface science is not only applicable to surface-active agents. For instance, skin cream can be looked at from a surface-science point of view as the surface between oil and skin. In that sense, skin cream is no longer a cosmetic. Another example is the floppy disk. It is a plastic film coated with magnet powder. We regard it as a type of surface and applied results from surface studies. Our business areas have expanded widely by shifting our approach from that of surface-active agents to the study of surfaces as a science. Although some say that Kao has entered mutually unrelated markets, different market segments do not necessarily mean different businesses. They are naturally related businesses from our point of view.[12]

Philosophical Principles as a Tacit Knowledge Base

At Kao, top management is very conspicuous. CEO Yoshio Maruta is called the "philosopher executive" because he is a devout student of Buddhism and expresses his philosophy openly. He insists that what executive management needs is not managerial theory, but rather a philosophy on how to guide an organization. Maruta's philosophy can be summarized in accord with three principles: (1) contribution to the consumer; (2) absolute equality of humans; and (3) the search for truth and the unity of wisdom. These philosophical principles, in turn, form the tacit knowledge base for Kao. They provide the context under which Kao's corporate culture is defined. Its strong corporate culture, in turn, affects the behavior of every Kao employee. We shall describe each of Maruta's philosophies below.

"Contribution to the consumer" means that the primary purpose of the corporation is not to receive profit or to increase market share, but to offer joy and satisfaction to consumers with products as the medium. Maruta's commitment to serving the customers better through knowledge can be seen in the following comment.

> The final goal of Kao is to utilize our knowledge into consumers' products. Increasing market share through competition is not the purpose. Kao will keep on contributing to the consumer according to the laws of the universe. There may usually be a certain gap between the knowledge we wish to provide and what the consumers wish to have. It happens because we usually see consumers' lifestyles from the corporate point of view, and cannot conceive actual consumer needs. Kao always has to stand from a consumers' viewpoint. (Maruta, 1988a, p. 5)

Maruta also believes that every human being has "equal ability" as long as restrictions are not imposed:

> Everyone in this world is equal in his capability. But those abilities are often restricted in society by others. That is the origin of the separation of people into those who control and those who are controlled. . . . This idea is applicable to a modern organization. Each person has equal creativity. If one member cannot give full play to his or her ability, there is something wrong with the organization or the individual's supervisor. . . . Management's task is to organize different individual's creative strengths. (Maruta, 1988b, p. 61)

Maruta argues that information differentials among employees should not become the source of authority or power. Since creative ideas result from interaction, information sharing becomes the fundamental basis of management. It is for this reason that information regarding Kao is available on computers on each floor, with every employee having access to this database.

Seeking "truth and the unity of wisdom," the third pillar of Maruta's philosophy, shows Kao's attitude toward knowledge creation. He says:

> The intelligence of a corporation does not come from the president nor top management. That must come from the gathering of all knowledge of all members. A big organization is separated into many sections. If that organization does not have the system to integrate the knowledge of each section, the newly created knowledge would be poor. Each section's knowledge does not mean the knowledge of the head officer. For example, a line operator can give a great idea for rationalization. The long-run prosperity of a corporation depends on whether it can integrate and accumulate these ideas as one.[13]

The knowledge gathered from organizational members is stored within Kao's tacit knowledge base, which is strongly influenced by Maruta's philosophical principles. This tacit knowledge base guides the behavior of Kao employees and serves as the key driver for its unique corporate culture.

Interaction with the Outside—Kao's ECHO System

As we have seen, Kao is in the process of moving into a hypertext form of organization, in which various forms of knowledge are converted among the three layers inside its organization. At the same time, Kao is equipped with mechanisms that allow knowledge interaction with customers outside the organization. Kao's ECHO System is one such example (ECHO stands for "Echo of Consumer's Helpful Opinion"). The ECHO System processes and analyzes customers' questions and complaints about Kao's products. Kao's operators all over Japan answer customers' phone calls using three subsystems—ECHO/Entry System, ECHO/Support System, and ECHO/Analytical System (see Figure 6-6).

The ECHO/Entry System enables an operator to input customers' questions and complaints according to predesignated key words and, in some complicated cases, in the form of sentences. Kao's operators handle up to about 250 phone calls a day, and over 50,000 phone calls a year.

The ECHO/Support System enables Kao's operators to respond to customers' questions quickly. For example, a mother may call in an emergency situation, asking what to do about a child who has swallowed detergent. In such a case, the Kao operator can reference the ECHO/Support System for a quick pictorial answer. Operators can also reference pictures of similar problems that have occurred in the past, such as the fading of clothes, staining of bathtubs, greasy stains on kitchen fans, and so on.

The ECHO/Analytical System enables the information collected through this system to be used anywhere throughout the Kao organization by the next morning. More than 350,000 consumer questions and complaints stored in the system can be analyzed and recalled, using 8,000 key words—for example, by customer name, by product, by department/division, by date, or by area. Information that may be useful in solving problems is often compiled into reports and sent to the relevant departments, including R&D, production, marketing, and sales.[14]

Sharp as a "Perfected" Hypertext Organization

In this section, we see how Sharp built a "perfected" form of hypertext organizational structure in order to create new knowledge at the organizational level.[15] Although knowledge creation takes place in different layers or contexts within Sharp, an organizational member stays in either the business-system layer or the project-team layer. It differs

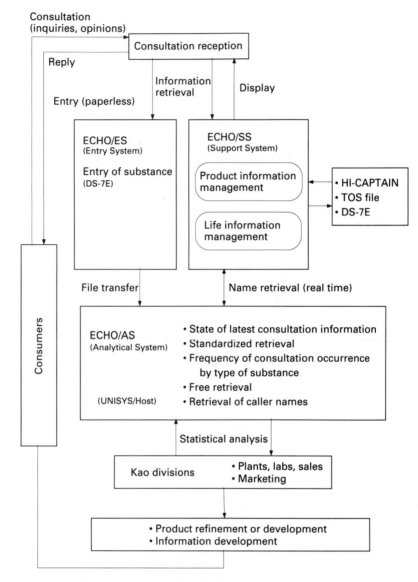

Figure 6-6. Kao's ECHO System. *Source: Kao Corp.*

from the transitional structure at Kao in that the project-team layer is fully developed and completely independent from the business-system layer. At the same time, Sharp is similar to Kao in that it has both an explicit knowledge base and a tacit knowledge base that serve as the third layer of a hypertext structure.

Since its foundation in 1912, Sharp has had a reputation for creating new products—from a self-adjusting belt buckle and Sharp pencil in the early years to liquid crystal projection TVs and electronic organizers today.[16] This reputation has been captured in the slogan of the company's founder, "Don't imitate." Its constant pursuit of creativity and originality led Sharp to formulate its R&D activities along the hypertext organizational structure. Our case study will focus on how knowledge is created within Sharp's R&D function through effective use of the three layers—business system, project team, and knowledge base.

The Business-System Layer: A Typical Hierarchy

Sharp's day-to-day R&D activities are organized in a typically traditional and hierarchical manner. The actual structure consists of the Corporate R&D Group, Business Group labs, and Business Division labs (see Figure 6-7). These three structures are separated on the basis of the time frame required for technological/product development. The Corporate R&D Group deals with long-term (3 or more years in the future) R&D themes; Business Group labs with mid-term (around 1.5 to 3 years) R&D themes; and Business Division labs with short-term (1.5 years or shorter) themes.

But these three structures are aligned as a traditional hierarchy, with research findings passed down the structures in a top-down fashion. Research findings at the Corporate R&D Group are transferred to the research laboratories of the nine Business Groups, then to the labs of each Business Division. During the product development process, rough prototypes are prepared in advance. Researchers at both the Business Group and the Business Division labs, who receive the prototypes, sometimes relocate to the Corporate R&D Group for a few months to improve their understanding of the research findings from the Corporate R&D Group. When research findings have to be utilized quickly for product commercialization, the Corporate R&D Group's researchers, in turn, sometimes move down to either the Business Group labs or the Business Division labs. Explicit knowledge concerning R&D is transferred efficiently and combined effectively under this kind of hierarchical structure.

Various meetings or conferences are used to coordinate the activities of the laboratories at the three levels (see Figure 6-8). They allow R&D members at Sharp to share knowledge not only within each level but also across the different levels. The first is the General Technology Conference, which is held once a month and is attended by the president, vice presidents, executive directors, and managers of the nine Business Group laboratories. They discuss what sort of R&D activities should be conducted at each laboratory for the upcoming one-year period. These discussions, which deal with the grand design of corporate R&D, often become heated and last as long as six hours, with a break for lunch. The second is the Laboratory Directors' Conference, which is

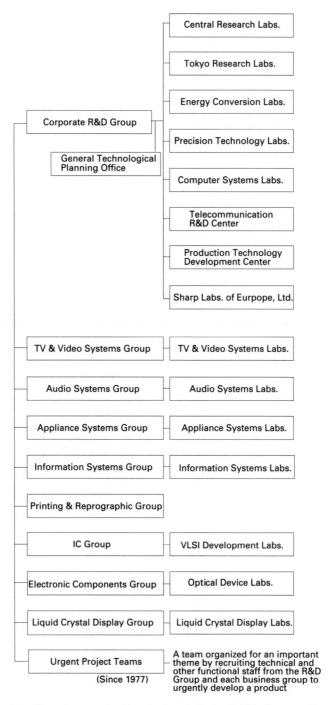

Figure 6-7. Sharp's organizational structure for R&D. *Source: Sharp Corp.*

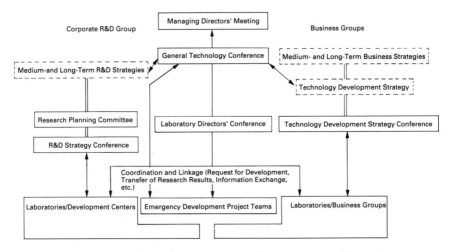

Figure 6-8. R&D conferences within Sharp. *Source: Sharp Corp.*

held once a month and is attended by managers of both the Business Group and the Business Division labs, the director of the Corporate R&D Planning Office, and the director of the Intellectual Property Office. The Laboratory Directors' Conference makes specific and detailed decisions, including when and how to transfer certain technology to the business groups and which collaborations are needed with an outside party. The third is the Technology Development Strategy Conference, which is held once a month in each Business Group. Participation in this conference is not necessarily limited to lab members of the Business Group, but can include members of the Product Planning Department and the Engineering Department, as well as selected individuals from the Corporate R&D Group. The Technology Development Strategy Conference is not merely a place for receiving technology from the Corporate R&D Group, but a place for deliberating actively on what kind of key technologies should be developed by each Business Group.

Project-Team Layer: The Urgent Project System

Sharp's R&D operations may have a traditional hierarchical structure, but when it comes to new-product development the company utilizes the task-force organization, which is a completely independent, parallel organizational structure. While normal product-development activities are carried out within each Business Division,[17] the strategically important product development projects are conducted under the "Urgent Project System."[18] Unlike the "in transition" hypertext structure at Kao, where project members retain their posts in their respective functional departments, the members of the Urgent Project System are relocated from their original departments and work exclusively for the project team.

The Urgent Project System gives its members, who could be recruited from any section or department within the company, the same "gold-badge" authority as corporate directors during the project period. The gold badge, which is a gold-colored nameplate, was called "kin-badge" ("kin" means "gold") in Japanese. "Kin" has the same sound as the first syllable of the word "urgent," which is "kin-kyu" in Japanese. Wearing the gold badge carries special significance not only for project members but for other employees at Sharp as well. Urgent Project members develop a priority product or technology within a year or two. But since it is managed directly under the president, the project budget is unlimited. People with the gold badge and their project are given top priority in using company facilities or equipment and in procuring materials. One Business Division manager describes the system as follows:

> The members are given the freedom to do whatever is necessary for development. There is always the possibility that they might fail, but they put their heart and soul into research and that's what produces products close to the innovative concept. (Numagami et al., 1991, p. 16)

In addition, members of the Urgent Project can be taken from anywhere in the company at any time. A department may be deprived of its best people for over a year. Needless to say, management has to make every effort during the initial stages to ensure that the system is enforced as originally intended. Each Business Division proposes projects that require companywide development efforts and completion in a brief period of time. These proposals are either adopted or rejected, or "justified," at the above-mentioned General Technology Conference, the highest decision-making meeting at Sharp.

To date, many successful products have been commercialized under the Urgent Project System. Examples include the electronic organizer, the liquid crystal projection TV, magneto-optical discs, and inverter-controlled air conditioners. Later we will take an in-depth look at how the electronic organizer was developed. This story brings the inner workings of a hypertext organization to life. Some 20 teams are involved in Urgent Projects today.[19]

The success of the Urgent Project System led to changes in Sharp's business system. Sharp recently started two strategy meetings—New Life Strategy Meeting and NEWING Product Strategy Meeting—in order to diffuse the Urgent Project idea widely within the entire organization. In the New Life Strategy Meeting, held once a month and attended by the president, vice presidents, and managers of the Business Group and the Business Division, the division managers explain new-product development plans. "Super Excellent (SE) Products" are selected as a result of this meeting. The requirements for an SE product are stringent. It should (1) be able to create a new market trend, (2) represent a completely new technology, (3) use completely new materials, and (4) employ completely new manufacturing methods.

The NEWING Product Strategy Meeting is also held monthly and is attended by 20 people, including the president, vice presidents, and managers of the Business Group and the Business Division. The word "NEWING" is an original coinage interpreted within Sharp to mean "efforts to create a new market." The candidates for new-product concepts are proposed by each Business Group or Business Division manager and reviewed for their originality and marketability. According to President Tsuji, the basic guideline of the meeting is that "we start with saying 'yes' rather than 'no' " to the suggested new ideas and concepts. This positive stance encourages new ideas and motivates development efforts. Attendees at the meeting describe it as "a really practical meeting; you get extremely exhausted after the meeting." Every meeting reviews two proposals, with discussions sometimes lasting more than six hours.

Once a product development plan is recognized as an SE product or a NEWING product, development work starts within the division. The authority given to the development team is similar to that given the Urgent Project, since development-team members receive direct support from the president and have the right to ask for whatever cooperation they need from within the firm. However, it differs from the Urgent Project in that the members basically stay "in" their original business-system layer and conduct other work during the development process.

Explicit and Tacit Knowledge Base at Sharp

Given the importance of both tacit and explicit knowledge, we need to think of the knowledge base in a far broader way than is traditional with most Western companies. In the case of Sharp, its explicit knowledge base can be described with the grand concept of "optoelectronics," which serves as a template for identifying useful and relevant new knowledge. Optoelectronics defines the field of research and resultant products in which Sharp wants to play. Sharp's tacit knowledge base can be symbolized with the slogan, "Don't imitate," which again serves as a template. Imbued with a tacit understanding of the imperative not to imitate, researchers at Sharp learn to distinguish what is really a "new product" from one that is not.

Optoelectronics as an Explicit Knowledge Base

Optoelectronics designates the technological field in which Sharp wants to put its stakes. Sharp believes that it should create its own field, combining "opto" (light, or photo vision) technology with microelectronics. Sharp wants to become a company uniquely positioned in this field.[20] Optoelectronics, in other words, is its corporate vision. (See Figure 6-9 for an illustration.)

Every knowledge generated in the business-system and project-team layers is recategorized and recontextualized with the corporate vision of optoelectronics in mind. It represents the image of the world that Sharp wants to live in, and is one of the key concepts describing what Sharp ought to be. Although its impact is felt throughout the company, it has a special bearing on researchers and engineers within Sharp. For example, Vice President Atsushi Asada comments on how the vision affects researchers and engineers:

> There is definitely a limit to what comes out spontaneously from one particular technology. Trying to bring a certain technology to a product limits the range of the researcher's view. Showing a concept in a more macroscopic way gives the researcher a greater degree of freedom. . . . All at once their mental horizon widens, and triggers a series of new proposals. A wider mental horizon immediately results in greater freedom for technology development.[21]

Much of the knowledge accumulated in the form of optoelectronics consists of knowledge created through the dynamic conversion of various knowledge contents. The essence of Sharp's strategy based on optoelectronics could be described as a dynamic conversion of component technologies and product concepts, as we can see in Figure 6-10. To use our terminology introduced in Chapter 3, component technologies can be interpreted as systemic knowledge (generated via combination) and product concepts as conceptual knowledge (created via externalization). By combining explicit knowledge (i.e., systemic knowledge) and by converting tacit knowledge into explicit knowledge (i.e., conceptual knowledge), Sharp has been successful in developing new technologies and products.

Optoelectronics also affects the tacit understanding of the imperative not to imitate, as described by President Tsuji:

> In narrowing down fields, optoelectronics and microelectronics became our priorities, and we started to think about how the component technologies originating from them could be merged into the "opto" business. . . . Being a manufacturer, we do all sorts of things, but if we are average in everything we do, we wouldn't be able to make an outstanding product. . . .[22]

"Don't Imitate" as a Tacit Knowledge Base

The founder's principle, "Don't imitate," represents Sharp's corporate culture. The principle forms the tacit knowledge base for Sharp, or a tacit understanding of the imperative not to imitate. President Tsuji explains that the purpose of the company since its foundation has always been the creation of unique product fields and concepts:

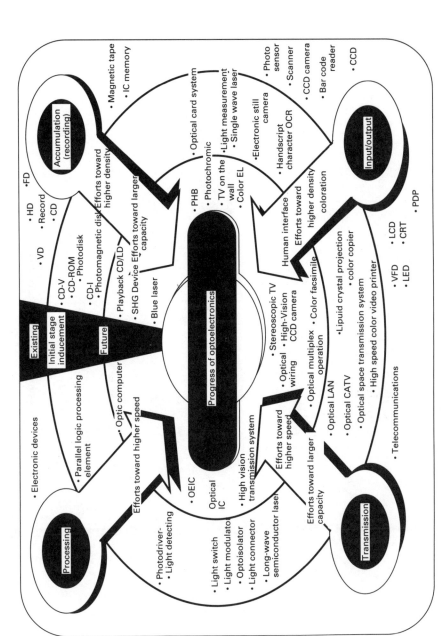

Figure 6-9. Development of optoelectronics technologies. *Source: Sharp Corp.*

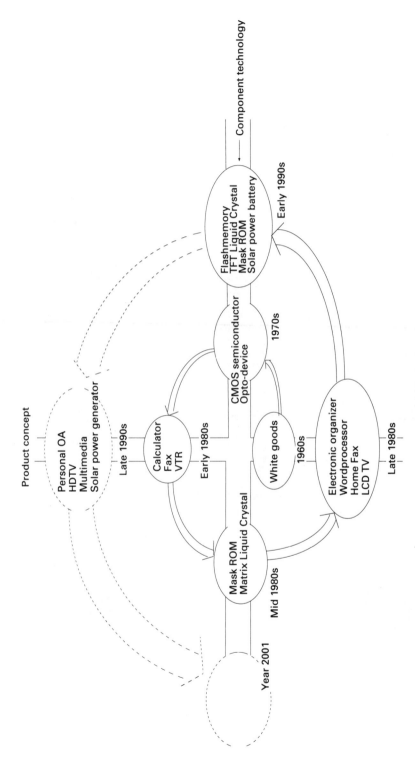

Figure 6-10. Dynamic spiral of component technology and product concept. *Source: Sharp Corp.*

Ever since the company's foundation, it has been our understanding that our major mission as a manufacturer was to develop our own technology and to make products based on that technology. I am the third president, but Mr. Hayakawa, who was the first, kept saying that we must make products that others will want to imitate. I think this thinking has taken root in the minds of our employees. My predecessor, President Saeki, has also said, "We can't contribute to society by making products just like those of other companies." The meaning of this was more or less the same, but it had a slightly different angle than what Mr. Hayakawa had advocated. I think this thinking has permeated the minds of the executives and employees over the years.[23]

The "Don't imitate" principle also serves as a guideline for Sharp's human resource development. President Tsuji considers the 1990s as a time period that will require a different kind of workforce, dominated by those equipped with creativity:

What I keep telling the top managers is to manage employees in such a manner as to allow them to develop their own ideas. I tell them they mustn't push ideas from the top down. . . . In my beginning-of-the-year address last year, I told the employees, "You know the saying, 'the nail that sticks out gets hammered down.' But what if the nail doesn't stick out, what do you think would happen? It would rot inside. So even if you might get struck, it's better to stick out than rot." . . .

And in my beginning-of-the-year address this year, I told them that they should all become *dragonflies*. A dragonfly has complex eyes, and it even has wings. I told them to absorb information with compound eyes and to experiment. I told them never to become a *flatfish* which has large eyes but only looks upwards. Our future tasks will be difficult tasks, but what is of great importance now is how to develop as many creative employees as possible. . . . These creative employees will challenge new things, and new entrepreneurs of a kind unknown before will arise from them. From all this, I believe that the image of a creative company will spontaneously emerge. . . .

I also said one more thing to our key personnel, and that was, "When you are driving a car, you may have to look into your rear-view mirror sometimes. But if you are speeding and on a winding road, it's more important to look ahead."[24]

As the words of President Tsuji indicate, "Don't imitate" has become a template for emphasizing the need to be creative. This tacit knowledge base fosters Sharp's corporate culture and influences the behavior of every employee at Sharp.

Interaction with the Outside—Sharp's Creative Lifestyle Focus Center

As we have seen, Sharp has nearly perfected a hypertext organization that allows knowledge to be converted among the three layers inside the company. In addition, it is equipped with an organizational mechanism for carrying out knowledge interaction with outside customers and companies. The Creative Lifestyle Focus Center, established in April 1985, is a case in point.[25] The center collects consumer opinions, interprets market data, and creates new-product concepts, which it disseminates to the planning sections of the various business divisions, as well as to the R&D sections.

The Creative Lifestyle Focus Center started various activities that enable Sharp to create new concepts based on inputs from consumers. One such example is the "Trend Leader System," which brings together about 600 "leading consumers," ranging from junior high school students to senior citizens in their seventies. Depending on the nature of the information needed for developing new products, relevant people clustered into "focus groups" are called into the center. Skilled interviewers elicit information from them that may remain tacit otherwise. This system, which started in 1985, enables Sharp to predict consumer trends ten years into the future.

A second example is the "Life Creator System," which was initiated in early 1990. It sets up an actual "living experiment" in which consumers are asked to touch and use potential new products in their still-incomplete stage. For instance, the center will hand over the lens-related parts of a video camera to children as well as to representatives of different industries, including a toy dealer, in hopes that they will cooperate and come up with a new-product concept. These and other living experiments are carried out under the "Life Creator System."

A Hypertext Organization in Action:
Sharp's Electronic Organizer

The development story of the electronic organizer brings out the inner workings of the hypertext organization. The significance of this story is the process by which the project shifts from the business-system layer to the project-team layer and back again into the business-system layer. As this criss-crossing takes place, organizational members involved in developing the electronic organizer also shift "in" and "out" of the two layers or contexts.

The origin of the electronic organizer, which started within the business-system layer, dates back to January 1985. Toshio Honda, the product development manager of the Calculator Division at that time, faced an urgent need to develop a new product:

> I strongly felt a sense of crisis about both the domestic and overseas calculator market at that time. In the mid-1980s, annual domestic production reached 20 million units and the Japanese market was almost saturated. In the overseas market, many NIES companies emerged as a competitive threat to Sharp. Given this situation, I came across the idea that Sharp should seek a market-creating product with the various technologies related to the calculator. (Komiya, 1988, p. 127)

Honda first promoted the product as a "calculator with an IC card for multipurpose use" and called it a "small information-management machine." His idea was based on the "system notebook," like Filofax, with pages that were replaceable as needed, that was popular among businessmen at that time. To bring his idea to fruition, Honda had to utilize technologies from outside the division—the new liquid crystal display technology and LSI technology—in addition to calculator technology. He also had to bring together many engineers from different fields within the company, which meant that the project plan needed the approval of the General Technology Conference, the highest R&D decision-making body within Sharp.

Honda developed the initial product concept so as to persuade top managers attending the meeting. He positioned the product as more than a successor to the calculator and called it "the tool to unite office automation and personal automation," which enabled information stored within the electronic organizer to be transferred to a computer through an IC card or telecommunication line. Honda pointed out that users of the electronic organizer would become potential customers for Sharp's computers and word processors.

Getting the Gold Badge

These efforts resulted in approval of the project plan at the General Technology Conference. A gold badge and a document stating an "official announcement of urgent directive" were given to eight members of "Urgent Project A1107" on June 1, 1985. This somewhat exaggerated announcement signified that a new-product development project, which would later introduce the world's first electronic organizer, officially started on that day under Sharp's Urgent Project System. The deadline for development was set at one year, and sales of the product were expected to start in October 1986.

The team, led by Hiroshi Nakanishi, then the engineering section manager at the Personal Machinery Division (the former Calculator Division), was composed of five members from the Personal Machinery Division, one engineer from the IC division, and one engineer from the Liquid Crystal Division of the Electronic Devices Group. The average age of the team members was 32, young relative to those working on other projects. As a result of the official announcement, these eight members were now officially "out" of the ordinary business-system layer and engaged exclusively "in" the Urgent Project team activity.

The interdivisional makeup of the team came in handy during the development process. The technology for incorporating LSI into a 2mm-thick IC card, for example, was developed by the member from the IC Division, while development of the clear panel touch-key was conducted mostly by the member from the Liquid Crystal Division. Nakanishi exercised his gold-badge power to develop the LSI necessary for the liquid crystal panel operation.

A year later, Urgent Project A1107 was completed as scheduled and a prototype machine was presented to top management at the General Technology Conference. President Tsuji examined the prototype at the meeting and rejected its commercialization without giving any detailed explanation. Urgent Project A1107 was officially over, and the young team members went back to their original business-system layers in disappointment.

Development Process Continues within the "Business System"

The team leaders, however, never gave up. Honda and Nakanishi put their heads together to analyze why the project was rejected. They found that the main reason for the rejection was the fact that Japanese characters, or *kanji,* could not be used on the product. Honda reflected:

> The results of the market research clearly backed up the need for using *kanji.* . . . However, we thought the product would become prohibitively expensive with such a function. (Komiya, 1988, p. 133)

Nakanishi made a similar comment:

> We were plagued by the concern that we would have serious trouble with a large number of specs and high power consumption if we incorporated *kanji* processing. (Komiya, 1988, p. 133)

Although the necessary corrective action was widely known, there was no *kanji*-processing expert within Nakanishi's division (Personal Machinery). And without the mighty gold badge, he could not request the assistance of engineers from other divisions. It was Nakanishi who came up with the idea of forming an intradivisional development team composed of 14 division members, including one *kanji*-processing expert recruited from the Computer Division through the intrafirm position-offering system.[26]

Even without the authority of the gold badge, the intradivisional development team succeeded in developing an electronic organizer with a *kanji*-processing function in two months. The product, which was called PA 7000, was introduced to the market in January 1987. It became a big success, selling over 5 million units by 1991 and taking more than a 70 percent share of the domestic market the same year.[27]

The product development of the electronic organizer illustrates the mechanisms by which Sharp continuously launches itself into new products and markets. It also shows how the Urgent Project System allowed its developers to take advantage of the Sharp system for key technologies.

We argued in this chapter that the hypertext organization is the ideal structure to bring about continuous organizational knowledge creation. A hypertext organizational structure enables an organization to create and accumulate knowledge efficiently and effectively by transforming knowledge dynamically between two structural layers—those of the business system, which is organized as a traditional hierarchy, and of the project team, which is organized as a typical task force. The knowledge generated in the two layers is then recategorized and recontextualized in the third layer, the knowledge base. We presented two case studies—Kao as an "in transition" and Sharp as a "perfected" hypertext organization—to illustrate how the new organizational structure we are proposing provides the best fit for creating knowledge continuously at the organizational level.

Notes

1. According to Weber, modern bureaucracy has the following characteristics: (1) fixed and official order by laws or administrative regulations; (2) hierarchy, that is, levels of graded authority; (3) management based upon written documents; and (4) operation based on specified/specialized work.

2. Burns and Stalker (1961) initiated contingency theory describing a bureaucratic structure as a mechanical system that works well only in a stable environment. On the other hand, an organic management system with a non-bureaucratic structure is more appropriate to an unstable environment. See Thompson (1967), Perrow (1967, 1973), Nonaka (1972), Galbraith (1973).

3. The concept of the task force evolved from that of the military operation. The "task-force principle" is used by the Navy and Marines to organize forces for specific purposes, while preserving a separate administrative organization for training and housekeeping. A task organization can function in a variety of organizational magnitudes, from campaigns of entire fleets throughout a war to a single ship on a one-time mission.

4. Mintzberg (1989, chap. 6) has proposed the "adhocracies," which contain "project structures" that can fuse the contributions experts have drawn from different specialties in order to form smoothly functioning creative teams.

D. Quinn Mills (1991) has claimed that what has always been accepted as formal hierarchy is actually disappearing in many larger, formerly bureaucratic settings. These institutions are shifting toward what he calls "cluster" organizations.

Another example of new organization concepts is an "infinitely flat" organization, an organization with innumerable outposts guided by one central "rules-based" or "computer-controlled inquiry" system (Quinn, 1992).

The "network" organization operates essentially without—or with only minimal—formal authority or "order-giving" hierarchies (Imai and Itami, 1984). This organization mode is sometimes described as a "spider's web" because of the lightness yet completeness of its interconnected structure (Quinn, 1992).

For some companies, the person having direct contact with the customer is so important that, rather than operate merely in a flat or network mode, they will literally invert their organizations, making all line executives, systems, and support staff in the company "work for" the front-line (Quinn, 1992).

Some highly innovative companies have found a special form of disaggregation—best described as a "starburst" or "satellite" organization—to be very effective. These companies constantly "split off" and "sell off" units, like shooting stars peeled from the core competencies of their parents (Sakakibara, Numagami, and Ohtaki, 1989).

Recently, some scholars have proposed the concept of internal market organization that internalizes market mechanism, as the transition from hierarchy (Halal, Geranmayeh, and Pourdehnad, 1993).

5. As for the structure of its fighting forces, the Japanese Imperial Navy, along with its air force, instituted an air force-led task force prior to the U.S. military's formation of one, but did not discard the conventional battleship-oriented structure and strategy until the end of the war. The Nagumo task force which was formed to attack Pearl Harbor, for example, arranged the battleships in a regular square style, with scattered warning ships outside the battleship perimeter. This system, however, was unable to defend the aircraft carrier from enemy fighters by anti-air guns and machine guns. Without a radar system, the aircraft carrier's only option was self-defense. The Japanese Imperial Army did not integrate the infantry, artillery, and aircraft, either. The infantry, conducting hand-to-hand combats, dominated the structure as its core, and the infantry and artillery were used separately in many battles.

6. For example, the U.S. Navy developed a circular anti-aircraft defense system in which nine warships, including battleships, cruisers, and destroyers, were located at regular intervals on the periphery. The formation had a radius of 1,500 meters, with an aircraft carrier at its center. The enemy planes rushing at the aircraft carrier were attacked from their sides and dive-bombers were shot when they came in at low altitude in order to launch torpedoes at a point of 1,500 meters from the targeted aircraft carrier.

7. For further discussion, see Nonaka et al., 1992.

8. It should be noted here that another critical factor for realizing this dynamic combination is the total coordination of time, space, and resource within an organization. A bureaucratic organization coordinates "requisite variety" and generates a "natural frequency" by "orchestrating" various rhythms (Jacques, 1979). As we have mentioned in Chapter 3, each task-force team creates its own "natural frequency" by synchronizing various rhythms brought into the field by members from diverse positions in a bureaucratic organization. The hypertext organization is an organizational structure that enables the orchestration of different rhythms, or "natural frequencies" generated by various product teams and hierarchical organization. It coordinates allocation of time, space, and resource within the organization so as to compose an organizational rhythm that makes organizational knowledge creation most effectively and efficiently. In this sense, a hypertext organization is a structural device to build "requisite variety," which is not secured solely by the middle-up-down management, into the organization.

9. The matrix-structure concept is a balance between two or more bases of grouping, for example, functional with market (or for that matter, one kind of market with another, say, regional with product). This is accomplished by the creation of a dual-authority structure—two or more managers, units, or individuals are made jointly and equally responsible for the same decisions.

10. Moreover, the company is currently planning to enter the food and printing markets.

11. Interviewed on May 21, 1991.

12. Interviewed on May 21, 1991.

13. Interviewed on March 27, 1991.

14. Kao has a comprehensive Strategic Information System (SIS), which is one of the most advanced in Japan, of which the ECHO System is only a part. Kao considers tacit information as important as information generated by the computer. For example, when sales of a local wholesale subsidiary drop, the head of the Sales Division and his staff will visit and observe the stores in the area to find out the causes of the sales decrease and jointly develop measures to overcome it.

15. This case study is based on Numagami, Nonaka, and Ohtsubo (1991).

16. The history of Sharp dates back to 1912, when an inventor and tinkerer Tokuji Hayakawa founded a small metal works in Tokyo. Hayakawa was an inventive person and always encouraged his employees to pursue creativity by saying, "Don't imitate. Make something that others will want to imitate." Today, Sharp is positioned uniquely within the consumer electronics industry in Japan.

17. In the case of product development within the business divisions, numerous meetings are held for product planning as a means to ensure cooperation and linkage among the engineering, marketing, and production sections. To begin with, the Product Planning Committee has been established to strengthen the link between marketing and product planning in the Business Division. The committee's aims are to refine the product concepts of the planning side by reviewing them from the marketing point of view. At the same time, the committee works to enhance marketing's sense of participation and involvement. The Plans and Programs Promotion Meeting, on the other hand, has been established to coordinate the efforts of the planning section with those of the production section. During these meetings, consideration is given to ways and means to convert product concepts into concrete products.

18. The Urgent Project System was developed based on the "734 Project," which was installed to develop the EL-805 calculator during the "calculator war" of the 1970s. Thanks to this project, Sharp won the "war" and became a leader in the industry (Sasaki, 1991).

In addition, some point out that the Urgent Project System is fashioned after Sharp's original development style. For instance, a member of the electronic organizer development team made the following comments:

> Ordinarily, our approach is to specialize in something first, and then have it backed up by an ordinary organization, rather than first establishing an organization to make things. There is, of course, the approach of setting up an organization first and then giving it some themes, but as we are working with a small number of people, it would be impossible to try to do everything. So, what we have done is to decide on the domain in which we want to specialize. Planning or engineering must run first. Only then does the product image begin to take form. If demand can be expected, then we make manpower increases. That is our pattern of approach. The Urgent Project just happens to openly manifest the above-described way of product development (Numagami, Nonaka, and Ohtsubo, 1991, p. 16).

19. The idea of an Urgent Project System has more recently been expanded into the product development system called "concurrent engineering." While each Urgent Project is accomplished with the completion of product develop-

ment, concurrent engineering involves not only a product development team, but also design, production, and testing, teams even before product commercialization. This system aims to shorten the development time as well as to prevent product defects and to increase productivity after the developed product has been commercialized. Examples of products developed under this system are Liquid Crystal View Cam (video camcorder) and Eco-A-Wash (washing machine using less water and detergent) (*Nikkei Sangyo Shimbun,* October 25, 1993; *Nikkei Information Strategy,* December 1993).

20. For example, the electronic organizer with a liquid crystal display was commercialized by Sharp based on its original ideas, and is still unmatched in terms of both product concept and component technologies. In the home telephone market, Sharp was the first in the industry to release a cordless telephone with an answering machine function. The CJ-A300 was released in September 1989 and sold 250,000 sets in four months. By virtue of this product, Sharp was able to double its market share from 9.5 percent in the previous year to 18.7 percent.

21. Interviewed on December 18, 1990.

22. Interviewed on January 29, 1991.

23. Interviewed on January 23, 1991.

24. Interviewed on January 23, 1991.

25. The beginning of this organization dated back to the oil crisis of the 1970s. The crisis triggered a change in consumer buying behavior. The baby boomers were already beginning to pick up on the "new family" style of living, but it was the oil crisis that converted the latent changes in their awareness into concrete changes in buying behavior. In view of this, in 1975, Masaki Seki, who was then executive director and had overall responsibility for the home electric appliance business, decided to reorient the business toward the development of differentiated products that were suggestive of a new lifestyle, in order to cope with the changes in consumers' sense of value. The idea was not only to stress the technical functions of a product but also to differentiate the product by adding some emotional value to it. Based on this idea, in 1976 Sharp began to put the "new life strategy" into practice. Numerous product groups, consisting of products in which color, shape, and function were comprehensively coordinated for use by the "new families" to whom they were targeted, were created under the "new life strategy."

26. Under the intrafirm position-offering system, a researcher at some Business Division labs can apply for a position offered by other division labs in which he or she is interested. The researcher can send application to Sharp's human resource development (HRD) department by mail, and then go through several interviews with managers of the HRD department and the designated division. This whole process will never be made public, except for the initial notice of the position offered and the subsequent announcement of the researcher named to the position. This system contributes to promoting motivation among researchers at Sharp along their own lines of interest.

27. *Nikkei Business,* August 19, 1991, pp. 10–23.

7

Global Organizational
Knowledge Creation

In the previous two chapters, we analyzed the management process and organizational structure most conducive to organizational knowledge creation. The knowledge-creating Japanese companies we encountered in the last four chapters—Honda, Canon, Matsushita, Kao, and Sharp—have gone increasingly global. This raises two questions. First, can the organizational knowledge-creation process used by these Japanese companies work outside of Japan? Second, what adjustments are necessary when Japanese companies start to work jointly with non-Japanese counterparts in a foreign country?

The very ethnic and cultural homogeneity that has facilitated the sharing of rich tacit knowledge among the Japanese has the potential of becoming a competitive disadvantage in the ethnically and culturally diverse global economy. Japanese companies may not be able to manage that diversity. But the two cases in this chapter show that the organizational knowledge-creation process used by Japanese companies can work on a global scale, although some adjustments are necessary. Japanese companies are flexible enough to adjust the knowledge-creation process by synthesizing Western approaches to organizational knowledge creation. Diversity provides a "natural" source of requisite variety for globalizing Japanese companies, which can take advantage of the heightened level of this enabling condition in a foreign environment.

This chapter focuses on how organizational knowledge creation takes place on a global scale. It will show the critical importance of socialization and externalization in global knowledge creation. The cases of the Nissan Primera and Shin Caterpillar Mitsubishi's REGA show how Japanese companies managed to learn or socialize non-Japanese tacit knowledge. Although both cases are focused on product development, findings may well apply to organizational knowledge creation across national boundaries in general.

Before presenting the two cases, we need to understand that differences between the Japanese and Western approaches to organizational knowledge creation do exist. The key differences are found in three areas. First, the interaction between tacit and explicit knowledge in the West tends to take place mainly at the individual level. Concepts tend to be created through the externalization efforts of top leaders (e.g., GE's Jack Welch) or product champions (e.g., 3M's Art Fry) and are then combined organizationally into archetypes of new products, services, or management systems. In Japan, on the other hand, the interaction of tacit and explicit knowledge tends to take place at the group level. Middle managers lead knowledge-creating project teams, which play a key role in sharing tacit knowledge among team members. This tacit knowledge interacts with explicit knowledge, such as a grand concept advanced by top management and information sent from the business front line. This intensive, human interaction produces mid-range concepts as well as concepts for target products, services, or business systems.

Second, Western business practices emphasize explicit knowledge that is created through analytical skills and through concrete forms of oral and visual presentation, such as documents, manuals, and computer databases. In terms of the knowledge-conversion modes, the Western strength lies in externalization and combination. Western-style knowledge creation can lead to the so-called "paralysis by analysis" syndrome. On the other hand, Japanese business people tend to rely heavily on tacit knowledge and use intuition, figurative (i.e., ambiguous) language, and bodily experience in knowledge creation. They are relatively weak in analytical skills, for which they compensate by frequent interaction among people (socialization). Another strength in Japanese-style knowledge creation is internalization. Once an archetype is created, high-quality tacit knowledge is quickly accumulated at the individual and organizational levels by mass producing or implementing an archetype. The emphasis on tacit knowledge in Japanese-style knowledge creation can lead to the so-called "group think" and the "overadaptation to past success"[1] syndromes.

Third, Western-style knowledge creation is receptive to certain enabling conditions, such as clear organizational intention, low redundancy of information and tasks (i.e., creative chaos is produced not by sequential performance of tasks but by the "natural" requisite variety), less fluctuation from top management, high autonomy at the individual level, and high requisite variety through individual "natural" differences. In contrast, Japanese-style knowledge creation is characterized by relatively ambiguous organizational intention, high redundancy of information and tasks (i.e., creative chaos through overlapping tasks), frequent fluctuation from top management, high autonomy at the group level, and high requisite variety through cross-functional project teams (Kagono et al, 1985). Figure 7-1 summarizes the differences between Japanese and Western knowledge-creating practices.[2]

We should bear these differences in mind when we address these two cases of organizational knowledge creation on a global scale, leading to the development of two successful products: Nissan's first global car,

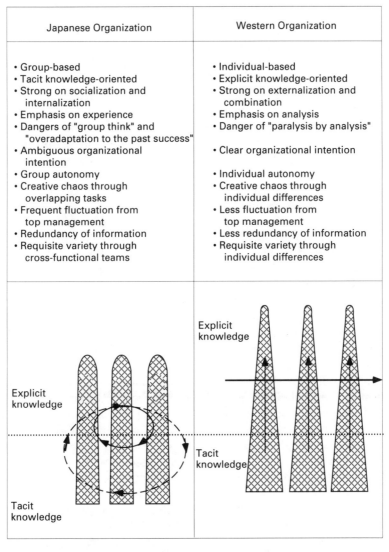

Figure 7-1. Comparison of Japanese-style vs. Western-style organizational knowledge creation.

Primera, and Shin Caterpillar Mitsubishi's REGA series of hydraulic shovels.

Nissan's Primera Project

In the first case, we look at how Nissan developed Primera, a "global car" that was originally targeted to the European market, where high performance is a critical factor, and then to the U.S. and Japanese markets, where users tend to ask for images, plush interiors, and a wider range of models and accessory options. To familiarize themselves with European users' expectations about performance, Nissan executives decided to embark on a massive exercise in socialization. It took the form of providing firsthand experience of the European automobile market, motoring culture, and road conditions to hundreds of Japanese employees in the early stages of the development project.

In April 1986, Nissan decided to develop a high-performance global car that was eventually named Primera. Being positioned as a global car, the car had to meet several qualifications. Top management decided that Primera had to: (1) be manufactured both in Japan and in Britain; (2) have 80 percent of its components emanate from Europe; and (3) be sold primarily in the European market and additionally in the U.S. and Japanese markets. All of these qualifications, which were unprecedented for Nissan, became the organizational intention set forth by top management.

This organizational intention introduced a considerable amount of fluctuation within the organization. To compensate for this, Nissan initiated an overall organizational system called the Product Strategy Division, under which the supervisor of a project development team coordinated cross-functional activities such as planning, design, testing, production, and marketing for a given model (see Figure 7-2). This system made the locus of responsibility clear for each model and, at the same time, provided considerable autonomy to the supervisor and the project team. The supervisor for the Primera project was Yasuhisa Tsuda.

Tsuda studied at the Berlin Technical College and had worked for Nissan in the United States, and therefore spoke German and English fluently. In the United States, he had headed Nissan's joint development of Santana with Volkswagen, which gave him firsthand experience of managing an international project. He also made frequent business trips to Europe, driving around in rented cars and gaining a good feel of consumer preferences there. Through such experiences he was able to internalize knowledge about international project management and socialize himself to tacit knowledge about the European automobile market, motoring culture, and road conditions. He also had been writing reports to his superiors on ideas that were based on these experiences, and even held informal study sessions on the European market. Through these efforts, Tsuda had developed his own "European

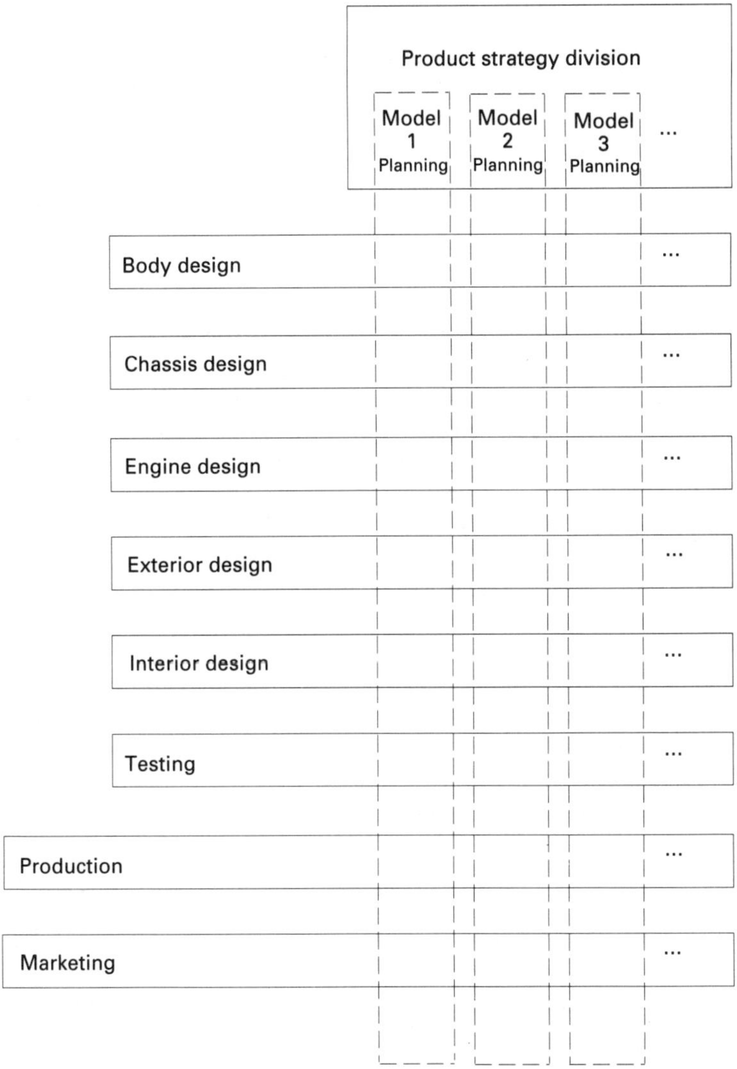

Figure 7-2. Organization for product development at Nissan.

Auto Theory," which helped shape the product concept for Primera and identify challenges that should be met to succeed in the European market.

Building a Development Team and Creating a Mid-Range Concept

Nissan recognized that in order to carry out a full-scale offensive in Europe, it had to acquire tacit and explicit knowledge about the European automobile market, culture, and road conditions. The obvious solution was to build a team around people who had already had some experience there. Eight Japanese managers were brought together under Tsuda. All of them had worked in Europe and shared tacit knowledge about the challenges confronting them, especially the recognition that existing Japanese models would not work in the European market. Yoshiharu Ohtake, one of the managers who was in charge of testing, said, "It was painfully obvious that Japanese models weren't right for the market. The desire to find a technical solution for this problem was rooted in me while I was in Europe."

Tsuda and his colleague, Shigeki Miyajima, devoted considerable time to developing a marketing strategy. They knew that given the nature of the European market and Nissan's stature within it, little would be gained if the new model was perceived as the only jewel in an otherwise lackluster crown. In addition to being a success in its own right, the new model had to boost Nissan's image and deepen its trustworthiness among European consumers. The name "Primera" was selected to reflect Nissan's desire to turn out a first-rate, blue-ribbon model that would spearhead its marketing effort throughout Europe.

Discussions with supervisors in charge of other Nissan models exported to Europe and with managers in the Overseas Sales Division in Japan gave rise to a concept that would serve as Nissan's image in the European market: "comfortable functionality." This mid-range concept spawned several ideas, such as a uniform insignia and front mask as well as more or less standardized layouts for the front panel, including switches, stereos, and heaters, that could be used across different Nissan models targeted for Europe.

Creating the Product Concept and Breaking It Down

Shigeru Sakai, one of the managers of the Primera project, developed the mid-range concept of "comfortable functionality" into a product concept for Primera by associating the car with the Autobahn. A conversation with the Chassis Design Team and an ensuing reflection resulted in a catchphrase, "Sure, fast, and comfortable on the Autobahn," as the product concept for Primera.

It was clear from the start of the project that Primera could not be a mere copy of other European models. In addition to having high performance standards exceeding those of competing models, Primera emphasized comfort as its distinguishing feature. This feature was further broken down into what Sakai called "Comfort 10," or 10 dimensions of comfort: space, ride, ventilation/air conditioning, texture/feel, sound, field of vision, visibility, operability, safety, and security (see Table 7-1 and Figure 7-3). To make the product concept clearer to those who were involved in the project and others concerned, Sakai compiled a 50-page catalog that included many sketches externalizing the mental model or image of Primera. It was the first time Nissan had com-

Table 7-1. Notes for Developing the Product Concept of Primera

---

Business Strategy *(where and how)*

• Turn a profit in Europe	- sales price and prime cost?
• Boost the image of Nissan models in Europe	- how?
• Change the image of Nissan models in Japan	
• Keep the production volume at NMUK	- avoid erosion of profit
• Target customers: UK companies and families	- profile of customers in aspects
German families	of family makeup, income, edu-
• Nissan's new middle-size models	cation, age, lifestyle, attitude

---

Product Strategy *(targets)*

    Selling points - *Worth the money?*
                     - How will purchase help enjoy life?

• Good feel	- A good feel is a sign of good quality
• Exterior design	- Functional beauty that does not sacrifice comfort
• Well-balanced functions	- Balances between engine performance and mileage, and between handling and ride

---

Vehicle Concept *(development objectives, target performances)*

    Sure, fast, and comfortable (or enjoyable) on the Autobahn

• Comfort and safety with driving at 160 km/h for an extended time

Maximum speed	- aerodynamics coefficient
High-speed stability	- suspension
Control stability	- antiskid
Quiet	- low wind noise, engine noise with little peak feeling
Operability	- layout of meters, switches, and pedals
Mileage	- weight, aerodynamics coefficient
Riding comfort	- seat form, suspension

• Interior comfort for the middle class
    Interior dimensions and trunk space for a middle-class family—packaging efficiency
    But exterior dimensions should be as compact as possible

Source: Nissan

piled a catalog of this kind before starting the product development process.

Communicating the Product Concept and Building Wider Support

The Primera project's efforts to clarify the product concept and its specific features at the beginning were not only new to Nissan but also a rejection of its conventional approach to product development, a process inundated with fluctuation and creative chaos. To break from the past, the top priority for the project team was to build wider support within the organization. The project-team members walked around the

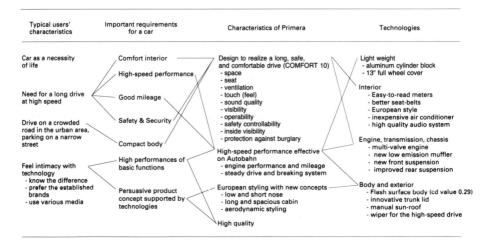

Figure 7-3. Analysis of the Primera concept. *Source: Nissan.*

company with a catalog in their hands to explain the specific requirements of a car that would succeed in the European market. But verbal explanations and rough sketches had their limitations. The full implication of driving on the Autobahn was lost on a person who had never driven on it.

To remedy this drawback, Nissan decided actually to send people to the Autobahn so that they could see and experience the situation for themselves. During the first three years of the Primera project, Nissan sent nearly 1,500 people from the planning, design, testing, production, and marketing departments to Europe to acquire tacit knowledge about the European automobile market, motoring culture, and road conditions. This experience helped to build a common understanding of the differences between the European and Japanese markets.

Gathering Information in Europe

The company's European Technology Liaison Office in Brussels served as an outpost for the Primera project. It provided people from Japan with rides in European cars so that they could personally experience what should go into a model designated for the European market, including performance requirements for the car's engine, cornering, and braking. Visitors from Japan quickly recognized a big difference between being told about something and experiencing it with their own bodies. It was a big shock to many of them, serving to magnify personal and organizational fluctuations. For instance, many engine specialists, who had been supremely self-assured before they left Japan, returned with crestfallen looks on their faces.

The outpost also functioned as an "information center" connecting

Europe and Japan. Examples of information sent to Japan included such general suggestions as "we need a seat that will prevent fatigue even on the 800-km (or 500-mile) haul from Belgium to Zurich," and such specific requirements as "the hazard-light button has to be in the center of the dashboard so that it can be pushed from the passenger seat as well." The outpost also arranged design clinics, which will be discussed below.

Designing Primera

From the beginning, the design team shared the need to "outengineer" the best European models, such as Mercedes Benz and BMW, while retaining the distinguished virtues of Japanese cars. Having studied European models for two years, the design team externalized four development objectives: (1) high performance, (2) cabin comfort, (3) distinctive design, and (4) top-quality luxury. The goal was to lead the world in all four areas.

Some members of the design team had already socialized themselves with European motoring culture and road conditions prior to joining the Primera project. For instance, Mikio Fujito, who was in charge of exterior design, had studied at the Royal College of Arts in London. He developed several design sketches during the project's early stages, with the assistance of two young designers sent to Europe from Japan. These sketches, which were drawn in Europe, were used to prepare one-quarter-scale clay models in Japan. Eight clay models were made and the four most promising ones were sent to the Liaison Office in Brussels.

These four clay models and other models prepared by local designers were subjected to tough screenings by the company's Brussels design clinics. More than 100 people, including designers, engineers, and dealers from both Europe and Japan, attended these clinics. They evaluated each scaled-down model, for example, on whether the design had a cold or warm feeling and whether the model looked slow or fast. The design clinics selected two clay models as a result of these evaluations.

The next step involved the preparation of full-scale clay models. The interior had to have ample headroom for four adults measuring 190 cm (or 6′3″) in height, but the exterior had to combine compactness with low air drag. This conflicting requirement meant achieving the largest possible cabin space within the most compact shell possible, while achieving the best possible aerodynamics. Once the actual prototype was completed, it was put through not only the ordinary battery of tests within Japan, but also test runs in Europe on a scale that far exceeded the norm. Specifically, the test runs in Europe logged 180,000 km (or 112,500 miles).

The Primera design team carried out frequent dialogues with the European Technology Liaison Office during development of the interior design. The aim was to develop the best interior design, which could provide comfort and pleasure regardless of the distance or speed, as well as visibility and operability. As part of the process, some designers went to Europe and took an 800-km (or 500-mile) ride in existing models, which was arranged by the Brussels office.

The engine went through rigorous testing as well. In the initial stages, team members of the Primera project went to Europe and ran tests to compare European and Japanese engines while they were in operation on the Autobahn. These tests helped to shed light on certain problems with the Japanese engine. To equal European models, the engine chamber had to deliver the same combustion efficiency at high rpm (revolutions per minute) as at medium or low rpm and remain cool even at high speeds. The problem was solved by developing a new engine—the SR20DE—for the Primera. While no car maker can afford to develop a new engine for each model, the strategic importance of Primera made it worth this investment. In addition to the engine, repeated runs on the test course in Japan revealed a need for suspension improvement, which led to the development of a new multilink suspension.

Timing couldn't have been better for the Primera project, as Nissan was undergoing an overall organizational reform, the main thrust of which was directed at changing the prevailing mindset of choosing the status quo for fear of failure. To use our terminology, fluctuation was introduced within the organization. The president at the time, Yutaka Kume, ordered such measures as delegation of authority to product supervisors to shorten the decision-making process and the interdepartmental rotation of personnel to increase diversity, which would enhance autonomy and requisite variety. As part of this reform, Nissan's engineers started their own bottom-up movement—called the 901 Campaign—to raise Nissan's technology level to the top of the world by 1990. Before this campaign began, only about 1 percent of some 700 engineers in the Engine Department went on overseas business trips. As part of the campaign, engineers were sent abroad in large numbers. The overseas trips took the engineers out of the Japanese environment, enhancing fluctuation and socialization, and thereby helping them increase their ability to assess car performance more objectively. These engineers played an important role in the quest for superior performance in the Primera project.

Forming the Yazaki Group

Another benefit of the campaign was the creation of a group of development-engineers-cum-test-drivers, whose role was to evaluate and communicate their bodily experiences to design engineers. A group of skilled test drivers called the Yazaki Group was formed, with Yoshiaki Yazaki serving as its leader.

A skilled test driver can externalize many of the quirks and problems of a new model within a few hours. It is far more difficult, however, to decide what should be corrected and how, especially when such
matters are strongly dependent on the local driving environment. The
person making the evaluation should have a deep tacit knowledge of
the target market that covers road conditions, driving styles, relevant
customs, and so on. To groom such evaluators, Nissan posted selected
engineers to some overseas markets for about a year to socialize, externalize, and internalize the local lifestyles and values. They were then
trained by Yazaki upon their return to refine their knowledge-
conversion skills.

Throughout Primera's development, the Yazaki Group refused to
compromise with the design engineers. To make a point, a Yazaki
group member would take design engineers along on test drives to give
them a bodily experience of a problem area in the prototype that did
not live up to the product concept. Yazaki required the design engineers to consider not whether Primera's performance was better than
those of major competing models, but whether it was the best in the
world. In this way, the evaluators and the designers came to share a
common understanding of the product concept. The Yazaki Group also
had frequent interactions with other members of the Primera team.
Shigeru Sakai, who was in charge of planning, recalled:

> I had a lot of contact with them. I was always off to the test course. They
> were the test pilots, and we were the designers and planners. As a plan-
> ner, I should listen to what pilots say. . . . I said "pilots" because I
> wanted to make the automobile equivalent of the Zero fighter. (Nonaka,
> 1992, p. 22)

Preparing for Production in Britain

The production people in Japan participated in the development project
at the early stage of concept development. It was not uncommon for
design engineers to produce drawings that could cause problems at the
manufacturing stage. Such problems could not be solved without the
vast reservoir of tacit knowledge acquired from working directly at
the plant, knowledge that was difficult to externalize into explicit language. The direct involvement in the early stage of people having this
tacit knowledge helped in the design of a high-quality product that
could be manufactured with more ease and efficiency.

As the new product moved closer to reality in Japan, attention
shifted to ensuring that Nissan Motor, U.K. (NMUK), which was responsible for production in Europe, would be ready for the planned
launch date. The quality of the Primera had to be up to the standards
of its Japanese production, while meeting the cost constraints applied
in Japan. Failure in this regard would jeopardize Nissan's entire European strategy.

While the basic design of Primera was completed in Japan, NMUK organized a task force to establish the necessary interface with local components suppliers. An earlier experience with another model manufactured at NMUK made it clear that components suppliers had to become involved in the project at an early stage. Consequently, NMUK was quick to establish links with local suppliers, while at the same time developing an effective method of knowledge transfer from Japan to NMUK.

Nissan tried as much as possible to replicate its Japanese operation in Britain, while recognizing the significance of cultural and other differences between the two national environments. The Japanese operation required few formal procedures and manuals, since the workers in Japan shared a relatively high amount of tacit knowledge. The following comment by a Japanese manager described the status quo in Japan:

> Much of the knowledge about production which Nissan has so painstakingly built up over the past several decades can, of course, be put into words and numbers. But much of it is locked up within the brains of individuals. (Nonaka, 1992, p. 28)

In contrast, British workers were more accustomed to having their duties and specific operating procedures articulated in explicit language. Therefore, Nissan codified its know-how on how to prepare for production of a new model into a manual and transferred it to NMUK.

To enhance socialization, NMUK sent some 300 middle-level British engineers and technicians to Japan to acquire the necessary production know-how through an on-the-job training program at a Japanese plant.[3] This program gave the U.K. operation a stronger knowledge base in production procedures, which proved to be useful in overcoming problems at the manufacturing stage. To further this exchange, Nissan frequently sent its Japanese engineers to Britain. As a result of these early preparations, production of Primera at NMUK started only six months after that in Japan.

Yet, NMUK had serious problems during the production startup stage when several suppliers failed to deliver workable parts on time. To improve this key process, NMUK sent Japanese engineers to each of the problematic suppliers for an extended period and succeeded in transforming these suppliers from its worst to its best. This transfer of Japanese engineers helped to establish trust and a long-term relationship between NMUK and its suppliers (see Womack and Jones, 1994, pp. 100–102).

Primera as a Global Car

As soon as Primera was introduced into the European market in 1990, it garnered a favorable market reaction, as evidenced by its sales trend. In the first four weeks after the model's debut, orders in Europe soared to 28,175 units. On an annual basis, 124,000 units were produced in Europe that year, exceeding the planned production volume of 100,000 units by a wide margin. Moreover, as of early 1994 Primera had won 19 best-car prizes throughout Europe.

Primera had a favorable reception in Japan and North America as well. In Japan, the targeted monthly production of 3,000 units for 1990 was easily surpassed as monthly sales averaged 5,030 units in 1990 and increased to 6,260 units in 1991. In North America, Primera was positioned as a luxury compact car and marketed through Nissan's Infiniti channel. It cleared its expected sales volume in North America as well, indicating that Nissan's vision for developing a global car was actually supported in the marketplace.

Implications of the Primera Case for Knowledge Creation

This case study shows that the Japanese approach to organizational knowledge creation works equally as well outside of Japan, although some adjustment is needed. The case highlights the much more vital importance of socialization for global knowledge creation than for domestic knowledge creation, especially when production is involved. It provides a good example of "cross-cultural socialization," a time-consuming and costly process that is indispensable to carrying out organizational knowledge creation across national boundaries.

In the Primera case, two rounds of socialization took place. The first round took the form of sending hundreds of Japanese engineers to Europe during the early stages of the project to gain tacit knowledge about the European car market, motoring culture, and road conditions. Nissan set up an information center in Brussels to facilitate this process. The second round of socialization, which was aimed at transferring manufacturing expertise from Japan to the British plant, took the form of sending some 300 British engineers and technicians to Japan to gain tacit knowledge about manufacturing practices. Nissan externalized the tacit knowledge that had been internalized over a long period of time at Japanese plants by compiling manuals to help the NMUK people learn Japanese manufacturing practices.

This case also shows the importance of mobilizing employees like Tsuda and Fujito, who had already socialized themselves in a foreign market and culture, as well as of training specialists, such as members of the Yazaki Group, who are adept at socializing tacit knowledge and externalizing it into explicit language. In our terms, they are the "knowledge specialists" in both socialization and externalization.

A less obvious but highly significant implication of the Primera case is the birth of a new approach to product development. As noted earlier, Japanese car manufacturers have been overlapping the development stages in what we called the "rugby style" to compress their new-product introduction lead time, enabling them to put out new models once every three or four years and to make minor changes about once every two years. In contrast, U.S. and European car manufacturers have taken a lot longer to come out with full model changes.[4] This ability to introduce new products with a shorter development cycle has long been considered a source of Japanese competitiveness. The overlapping approach can function with little organizational conflict because of the intensive socialization and resultant information redundancy among team members from the various functional departments. This vigorous exchange and sharing of information unites all the functional departments in pursuit of the common goal. The overlapping approach also involves the production department from an early stage of the project, which leads to the development of designs amenable to manufacturing. This process, in turn, results in short lead time and high quality of the product.

The rugby style, however, has its drawbacks. Since this approach entails problem solving by an interdepartmental pool of personnel who share the same space and time, the process is liable to give too much importance to preserving overall unity and conformance. In other words, it may lead to the risk of achieving a compromise or consensus around the lowest common denominator. Since the relative influence of the manufacturing and marketing departments is strong, the rugby approach hinders a relentless quest of technological potential.

In addition, the approach may not be conducive to setting clear-cut performance targets or standards at the outset for each functional department, since the development process is subject to constant change. BMW, Mercedes Benz, and other top-ranked European car makers still organize their development process by function (that is, department) and adhere to the phase-by-phase system to enable the pursuit of perfection and completeness by each department in each phase. This phased approach, however, necessarily lengthens the lead time, as well as requiring a great deal of effort to coordinate the various functional activities and ensure that an overall quality standard has been achieved in the final product (see Table 7-2 for a comparison of the Japanese and European styles of product development).

The argument above assumes that there is an intrinsic trade-off between performance and lead time. But Primera was able to achieve both, having been developed in less than four years just like other Japanese models, but still managing to meet the European standards of performance. What is more, Primera managed to meet both the local content target for production in Britain and the quality standards set by Nissan for its Japanese production.

Using metaphors from the world of sports, we have labeled the overlapping approach prevalent in Japan as "rugby" and the phased approach often used in the West as "relay." What the Primera case suggests is a third approach that can take advantage of both procedures.

Table 7-2. Comparison of Japanese-Style vs. European-Style Product Development of High-End Automobiles

	European-Style	Japanese-Style
Objective	Pursuit of superior performances	Adaptation to changing needs
Product appeal	Function (e.g., high-speed performance)	Image and quality
Product concept creation	Clear-cut decision at the initial stage, adhered to throughout the ensuing stages	Vague at the initial stage, modified and altered in ensuing stages in accordance with changes in needs
Flow of activities	Sequential approach	Overlapping approach
Ensuing process	Specific design targets fixed at the initial stage are pursued under a strict division of labor	Close cooperation among all departments concerned during the development
Organization	Organization according to function and often under a project leader with limited authority	Matrix- or project-team-type organization under a project leader with authority over the entire process from planning to production to sales
Strengths	Conducive to a relentless pursuit of superior performance, function, and high quality	Shorter lead time (3–4 years), high quality, and attuned to needs in the market
Weaknesses	Longer lead time (7–8 years), high development costs	Risk of compromise on a low level; not conducive to an all-out pursuit of superior performance

To continue using our sports metaphor, we have named the new style "American football." It achieves both short lead time and higher performance levels at the same time.

In the Japanese rugby style, a grand concept (i.e., business strategy), a mid-range concept, if any, and a product concept are gradually clarified through long and continuous interaction among project members. In the American football style, however, a grand concept, a mid-range concept, and the product concept are determined and clarified by a small number of project leaders through a thorough and intensive dialogue at the start of development. This process corresponds to the determination of the game plan and tactics before each play by the head coach and the offensive and defensive coordinators in American football. Determination of the concepts at this early stage is necessary because the frequent and face-to-face dialogue that is possible among all project members in the rugby approach is physically impossible to carry out on a global scale. Thus a clear division of labor is established, with teams formed for specialization in certain functions. In a sense, this division of labor is similar to an American football team with specialized units for offense, defense, and particular maneuvers.

Once the product concept is determined, all the functional departments move simultaneously, as in the rugby style, running together to meet the targeted cost, performance level, and launch date. First, large-scale socialization takes place, during which project members visit foreign markets to gain tacit knowledge. Second, an interdepartmental collaboration takes place to implement the overall business strategy, with departments sharing a common goal and a common information base. Third, all project members engage in evaluating or testing the prototype to judge whether the product concept has been realized.

In this way, the American-football approach to new-product development combines the benefit of a clear-cut division of labor among the functional teams, such as we encounter in relay, with the benefit of the entire team's running the entire distance, as in rugby. But the key to American football lies in making the comprehensive plan early in the game and in having the tactics decided by a few leaders who confer intensively among themselves.

In sum, the Primera case illustrates how a Japanese company created knowledge organizationally by having Japanese employees gain tacit knowledge associated with a foreign market through actual visits to Europe (socialization), and by making Japanese tacit knowledge associated with production know-how understood by foreigners (externalization). Because this case involves an international operation of a Japanese corporation, using Japanese knowledge-creating practices across national boundaries did not pose a serious problem. The next case involves a Japanese-U.S. joint venture. We shall see what difficulties could arise in synthesizing the Japanese and Western approaches to organizational knowledge creation on a global scale under such an arrangement.

Shin Caterpillar Mitsubishi's REGA Project

The second case takes the global knowledge-creation theme a step further. It is more than a story of a multinational company that developed a product for the global market and began to produce it in a foreign country. It is a story about two companies forming a joint venture to develop a global line of hydraulic shovels. The case shows that the newly formed Tokyo-based company, Shin Caterpillar Mitsubishi, surmounted many obstacles and successfully developed and marketed the REGA series of hydraulic shovels for the global market.

Historical Background

In 1963, Mitsubishi Heavy Industries, Ltd., of Japan and Caterpillar Inc. of the United States formed a joint venture company (Caterpillar Mitsubishi Corp.) to manufacture and sell Caterpillar products. At that time, Caterpillar viewed hydraulic shovels as a product with limited potential and decided not to enter the market. In 1970, however, the rapid growth of the market forced Caterpillar to reverse that decision. Although Caterpillar launched its first hydraulic shovel three years later in the United States, its contract with Mitsubishi prevented it from selling the product in Japan, which had emerged as the world's largest market for this type of product. In 1977, Caterpillar attempted to solve this problem by proposing a merger of its hydraulic shovel division with Caterpillar Mitsubishi, but met with a negative response from Mitsubishi. Mitsubishi did not want to pay a license fee for Caterpillar's technology, which was not at the leading edge, and feared that the American firm would exploit Mitsubishi's strengths as a leading producer of hydraulic shovels. The two sides could not compromise and the negotiation ended in failure.

During the 1980s both Mitsubishi and Caterpillar found good reason to reconsider their decision. Mitsubishi was eager to eliminate the unnecessary duplication of activities between its hydraulic shovel division and the tractor division of Caterpillar Mitsubishi. Meanwhile, Caterpillar suffered its first loss in half a century in 1983 and was facing stiff competition in the U.S. shovel market from Japan's largest construction equipment maker, Komatsu, which entered the market in 1982. This time around, Mitsubishi was more receptive to Caterpillar's proposal. After nine rounds of tough negotiation, a new joint venture, Shin Caterpillar Mitsubishi, was formed in July 1987. It pooled both companies' resources in the hydraulic shovel business. In addition, Caterpillar gained access to the Japanese market and Mitsubishi's technology, and Mitsubishi acquired a route to global expansion through Caterpillar's worldwide sales network.

Clashes Due to Differences in Product Development Approaches

The REGA series of "ultra-advanced" hydraulic shovels was Shin Caterpillar Mitsubishi's first attempt to develop a product for the global market. It was expected to be manufactured in Japan, the United States, and Europe. But differences in the Japanese and U.S. approaches to product development led to a number of clashes, which we will discuss below.

The first clash between the two approaches was about the relative importance of cost, quality, performance, and safety. In Japan, cost was considered the overriding factor, as evidenced by the frequently asked question, "What is the best quality we can achieve within the allocated cost?" In the United States, however, safety and performance were considered more important. The United States had strict product liability laws, and careful attention had be paid to safety. Caterpillar refused to budge on safety. Having done business in the litigation-prone U.S.

society, Caterpillar was nervous about the possibility of costly law-
suits. But the Japanese side wanted to eliminate any factor that increased costs and did not contribute directly to sales, especially since a
vicious price war was raging at the time in the Japanese construction
equipment market. The Japanese engineers insisted that Japanese
customers were extremely sensitive to price and quality. On the other
hand, the American engineers contended that Caterpillar's customers
would purchase a high-performance product even at a high price.

The second clash occurred over the problem of who should lead the
concept-creation process. In the United States, a marketing-led model
was prevalent, with opinions of the marketing department reflected
strongly in the development process. At Caterpillar, it was the marketing department that set the major specifications for a product. In Japan, however, a technology-led model was the norm, with the R&D
department taking the initiative. At Mitsubishi Heavy Industries, it
was the Engineering Department's planning section that determined
the specifications. One of Caterpillar's managers described the situation as follows:

> Mitsubishi's design and sales ideas focused on minimizing production
> costs. If a minimum cost could not be achieved, specifications should be
> changed and the sales price lowered. This would cause us to forego much
> of potential profits. . . . However, Caterpillar's profits do not derive from
> sales alone but also from parts sales and after-service by our sales organi-
> zation that brings together superior dealers and users. Over 50% of Cater-
> pillar's profits come from parts and services. Caterpillar always has a lot
> of marketing and design ideas. Mitsubishi doesn't, however; Mitsubishi
> makes their decisions on the basis of which design can be produced for the
> lower cost, and does not take after-service and other aspects into consider-
> ation. We found ourselves facing a completely culturally different concep-
> tual process. (Nonaka, Ohtsubo, and Fukushima, 1993, p. 12)

The third clash centered on how the development project should be
carried out. In the United States, each phase of a development process
was performed sequentially, like a relay. At Caterpillar, the development process consisted of four phases: concept making, prototyping, pilot running, and mass production. In contrast, the Japanese method
started with concept making, but prototyping, pilot running, and pre-
paring for mass production took place almost in parallel. Pilot running
started before the completion of prototyping, and the results of prototyping and pilot running were incorporated into the mass-production
system. The Japanese rugby style was effective in reducing development time. The product development cycle in Japan was usually between three and four years, while the cycle in the United States was
between five and ten years.

The fourth clash occurred about whether or not the design should be
standardized throughout the world. Caterpillar held firmly to the belief
that worldwide standardization brought about certain advantages,

such as interchangeability of parts. In addition, since Caterpillar owned its plants around the world, their layouts and manufacturing facilities were identical to those of its domestic facilities, which removed the potential problem of differences among plants in various countries. Thus Caterpillar insisted on worldwide standardization of both the design and the manufacturing process. But the Japanese side contended that its Akashi plant differed from Caterpillar's, making it difficult to implement standardization. Mitsubishi invited Caterpillar's two vice presidents for manufacturing to visit its Akashi plant; they were surprised at the differences between the Akashi plant and their own. As a result, Caterpillar reconsidered its policy of standardizing production diagrams.

Trying to understand these differences and reaching a compromise took a great deal of time during the REGA project. As these discussions proceeded, both sides came to realize that the factor hindering mutual understanding was not merely a language barrier, but differences in values and in approaches to problems. In the end, Caterpillar entrusted the overall approach of the REGA project to Shin Caterpillar Mitsubishi, on the conditions that the joint venture would make no compromise in performance and safety and that progress would be regularly reported to Caterpillar. Consequently, REGA was developed largely utilizing Japanese methods of product development.

Organizing the REGA Project

No special project team was formed for the REGA project. Members of the project retained their normal positions and wore a "second hat" for REGA. For example, a designer would work on REGA but also design non-REGA equipment in parallel. The Hydraulic Excavator Design Center, which was responsible for developing REGA, employed a matrix organization. One axis was the planning division, divided into three areas—large, medium, and small—according to the size of the hydraulic shovel being designed. The other axis was the design division, which was divided according to design components such as structure, hydraulic mechanism, electric and electronic system, and other equipment. Of the two axes, the planning division became the main axis, and its head managed the whole project.

How did U.S. and Japanese engineers work together within this scheme? From the beginning, both D. R. Larsen and Takeji Adachi, co-general managers of the Design Center, made a conscious effort to achieve good communication. Their desks were located next to each other. The two spent as much time together as possible, not only in their work but also in their private lives, by engaging in long discussions, visiting each other's homes, and traveling together. A close relationship developed between the two through these socialization efforts. In addition, there were two general managers and two vice general managers at the Design Center. In each case, one was Japanese and the other American. Like the top two, they had identical status and worked next to each other at adjacent desks. As of 1992, 21 American engineers were in residence at the Design Center.

This project was the first foreign experience for many of the American engineers. In fact, the majority of these engineers did not even have passports before coming to Japan. Larsen offered the following advice to these engineers: "Always think positively" and "Always keep the whole picture in sight." Yet, as soon as the American and Japanese engineers began working together, a major problem arose. The American engineers could not understand what the Japanese engineers were saying. Since American engineers were used to articulating their feelings, they kept asking "Why?" over and over again until the Japanese engineers felt cornered. Adachi, who had a shipbuilding background and was a complete amateur with hydraulic shovels, commented:

> Most Japanese become unable to answer if they are pushed with a series of why's. American engineers can always answer. An amateur, like I, can understand why Americans keep asking. (Nonaka, Ohtsubo, and Fukushima, 1993, p. 14)

On the other hand, Larsen made the following comment:

> What surprised me most on my first visit to Japan was the difference in logic process. . . . I have worked with French, Belgian, and German engineers. They possess a similar type of logic process. Therefore, we thought that the logic process would be the same. . . . We are still trying to determine how we can overcome this difference. (Ibid.)

The major source of difference in the "logic process" stemmed from the tendency of Japanese engineers to communicate on the basis of the tacit, experiential knowledge they shared. Few Japanese engineers were good at articulating their experience. The Japanese engineers at the Design Center realized that communication based on tacit knowledge would not work well with foreigners. Thus, achieving externalization became an important issue for the REGA project.

Standardizing REGA's Specifications for the Global Market

One of the most challenging problems in global product development is the trade-off between meeting different needs in different areas of the world and the pursuit of efficiency through standardization of products and production processes throughout the world. REGA was not only intended for the global market but also scheduled to be manufactured at the Akashi plant in Japan as well as at Caterpillar's Aurora plant in Illinois and the Gosselies plant in Belgium. Two steps were taken at the design and development stages to ensure some level of standardization among the three plants.

The first was the establishment of interplant meetings to enhance socialization. To manufacture REGA at the three different plants, it was imperative that the design drawings be standardized. This task was carried out at interplant meetings in which representatives from each plant met to discuss—often heatedly—topics ranging from purchasing to production to marketing. Experts on a given topic from each plant formed a team for each component (e.g., piping layout, power-train structure) to discuss how to produce a common product. The possibility of one plant with the lowest cost producing the entire component was also discussed.

This type of meeting was a new experience for both Caterpillar and Mitsubishi. Caterpillar gained a lot of from these meetings, since interplant communication had been poor until then. The Aurora plant had provided drawings to the Gosselies plant in the past, but engineers from the two plants had never met with each other until these interplant meetings. This fact alone made the interplant meetings valuable.

The second attempt at standardization was the development of the multiselection concept for the front, that is, the upper arm called a "boom," the lower arm, and the bucket. In the past, it had been considered sufficient for a single machine to have a single front of fixed size. In the case of REGA, however, 14 combinations were available for the front. This concept was developed by two American engineers at the Design Center in response to a problem concerning the best arm length for REGA in Japan. They discovered that the length considered optimal in the Japanese market differed from the lengths commonly used outside of Japan. They tested the idea with dealers throughout the world and decided to try marketing the variations. The idea of options for the arm and bucket was unique and eventually became REGA's main selling point.

Organizational Learning Through the REGA Project

Mitsubishi learned many things about development methods from the joint project. We shall describe as examples the use of design drawings and manuals.

The Akashi plant produced drawings based on a style originally used in shipbuilding, Mitsubishi Heavy Industries' mainstay business in the past. Design drawings for shipbuilding showed the completed form of a product, but all production design drawings were made at the plant. In fact, all aspects of the manufacturing process were delegated to the plant. Since the relationship between the design team and the plant was rather loose, the plant was allowed to modify or make additions to the drawings on-site. Even in cases in which nothing was wrong with a design, workers at the plant often changed specifications and prided themselves on not following the design drawings with which they were presented. Shin Caterpillar Mitsubishi inherited this "let the plant handle it" attitude from the Japanese parent company.

REGA's design drawings produced by the Design Center differed in several respects from those used previously at the Akashi plant. First, they conformed to Caterpillar drawing standards that were established worldwide. Second, they depicted not only the finished product but also all intermediate manufacturing processes. This meant that the drawings took about five times longer to produce than the drawings used previously. Third, American engineers added detailed written descriptions to the assembly procedure files. Once completed, these files covered some 950 separate procedures. One file containing 290 of these procedures was over five centimeters (or two inches) thick. This penchant for externalization helped REGA's cause, since drawings had to be developed that could be used anywhere in the world.

Mitsubishi also learned the importance of externalization from the joint project. Japanese engineers continued their effort to externalize their own tacit, experiential knowledge into something more explicit. Adachi recalled:

> Prior to the REGA project, Japanese engineers would design things as they like. Once a manager said, "I have decided X," no one would question him about it. Now, we had to explain this to non-Japanese clearly and unambiguously. Even though there was quite a bit of friction, we gained technical expertise, experience and know-how through working together. They became valuable assets. (Nonaka, Ohtsubo, and Fukushima, 1993, p. 18)

Manuals became one of the most concrete forms of capturing explicit knowledge. The value of manuals became particularly apparent in the replacement of engineers. When new American engineers came in to replace 15 of the 20 original engineers from Caterpillar, the newcomers had no more than two weeks to take over their predecessors' duties. Information in the manuals enabled them to complete the transfer of responsibilities within the allotted period. Makoto Deguchi, director and general manager of the Akashi plant, noted as follows:

> In Japan, technical expertise and know-how accumulate within individuals and there's a problem transferring them to others. That's why the same mistake would happen over and over again when a supervisor was replaced. But, we have eliminated this wastefulness and become able to transfer knowledge smoothly. (Ibid.)

Although it was still difficult for the Japanese to take over someone else's job with only two weeks of lead time, the project made them realize their lack of filing and presentation skills and the great need of training themselves to improve their externalization skills.

Itakura Goes to America

In December 1990, Adachi asked Noriyuki Itakura, who was a planning manager for large equipment at the time, to go to Caterpillar's Aurora plant in the United States. This turned out to be a golden opportunity for Itakura to blossom into a global "knowledge engineer," a key player in synthesizing the Japanese and Western approaches to organizational knowledge creation.

Itakura's first job was to act as a liaison, observing the production of a REGA pilot machine and reporting any technical problems to the Akashi plant. Itakura returned to Japan temporarily after six weeks but again found himself on a plane for America in September 1991. This time he came to work at the Aurora plant as a "product process supervising engineer" responsible for about 20 workers. His job was a mixture of engineering and production, since he worked with those on-site and resolved problems encountered during production based on design drawings sent from the Design Center. This type of work had never existed at Caterpillar before. Certainly it was unprecedented for the company to have a Japanese working in this capacity.

Itakura instituted a morning meeting held once a week for one hour, during which he externalized his way of thinking and his own experiences, particularly past mistakes he had made or witnessed. At first only Itakura spoke, but after about three months others began to participate. Several people started to challenge him, saying "That can't be right, Nori." Eventually, one hour was not enough and a special session was occasionally added. In this way, Itakura began to develop a two-way communication channel between himself and his staff.

In these morning meetings, Itakura often spoke about the proper mental attitude for a designer to have. Caterpillar designers seldom visited plants or actually touched the machines they developed. All responsibilities were clearly divided among sections, with operators working with the machines, lab personnel writing reports, and designers checking the reports. Itakura emphasized how important it was for designers to observe and touch the machines they develop, and explained the virtues of Japanese "on-the-job-site-ism" or "actual-experience-ism" to his American designers. In essence, he was stressing the importance of socialization.

Itakura was also surprised at first by the low level of cost consciousness among the design engineers at Caterpillar. In Japan, keeping costs within a predetermined target was considered a key concern from the inception of the design stage. In the United States, Itakura would be met with puzzled looks when he said anything like: "Well, if it's going to cost that much, we can't do it." To U.S. designers, "can" was purely a technical question completely unrelated to cost. To combat this lack of cost consciousness, Itakura called his staff together and spoke of his experience in reducing costs and working within cost limits at the Akashi plant. Although the cost-cutting scheme at the Akashi plant had been underway for ten years, it had only begun to prove effective in the last five years. In the first five years, it had largely been a repetition of trial and error. If a mistake was made, it would be reviewed, and problems would be identified and resolved one by one. Listening to his stories concerning the Akashi plant, his American staff engineers soon began to realize that these problems were the same ones confronting the Aurora plant.

Itakura also conveyed his experience in cost reduction to his immediate boss, D. M. Murphy. In a one-on-one meeting, he explained the history of the cost-cutting plan implemented at the Akashi plant. Murphy then arranged to have Itakura meet his top boss, E. D. Gramme, in February 1992. Armed with only his own experience and handwritten memos, Itakura again explained the cost-cutting plan. Itakura's recollection of this meeting was that he had "left a strong impression but wasn't completely understood."

Six months later, however, several Caterpillar staff members turned Itakura's explanation into a powerful piece of computer software. As part of its cost-reduction plan, Caterpillar produced a "cost-monitoring system" incorporating the cost-reduction and follow-up concepts Itakura had outlined. This system enabled Caterpillar to compare parts costs anywhere in the world and to track daily cost fluctuations. Thus the tacit knowledge accumulated in Japan was effectively documented and transformed into an explicit system by American computer skills. Itakura explained:

> Well, the idea was Japanese. But the ability to document or to compile manuals was definitely on their side. In Japan, you might find a kind of superman who can do a difficult job, which is convenient enough. But after he's gone, no one else can do it. In America, anyone can do the job as long as there's a manual. Documentation, the sharing of software, and building them into a business system are going to become important to manufacture the exact same product in many countries, while taking into account local conditions and cultures. In this respect, I think I learned the advantage of the American approach to documentation and software sharing. (Nonaka, Ohtsubo, and Fukushima, 1993, p. 25)

Itakura also learned the importance of managing diversity in the United States. Many Hispanics, African Americans, and women worked in his section, and he learned the necessity of giving special attention to minorities. Managers at the Aurora plant were required to report to their superiors every three months on what actions they had taken to cope with this issue. Itakura observed:

> Managing diversity is an extremely important question in the United States. America is thinking hard about how to manage people in the midst of diverse organizations, corporations, and races. But I think this issue is something Japan should also think about. When a company is going global, it naturally needs to consider the issue of managing diversity. (Nonaka, Ohtsubo, and Fukushima, 1993, p. 26)

It should be noted here that ethnic and cultural diversities are "natural" sources of requisite variety, one of the five enabling conditions for organizational knowledge creation.

Introducing REGA to the Market

In February 1992, Shin Caterpillar Mitsubishi held a press conference to announce the introduction of the REGA 300 series. REGA exceeded conventional hydraulic shovels in all aspects, including performance and safety. In addition to its smooth and comfortable operation, high power for digging and running, and comprehensive safety, one of REGA's striking features was its original design. A hydraulic shovel normally had the image of a dirty machine at a construction site, something completely unrelated to the world of design. But, REGA's exterior and operator cabin were designed by a firm that also designed the award-winning Diamante of Mitsubishi Motors. The design firm used the metaphor of a Japanese sword, which was represented by black lines on the sides of the machine.

Reaction to the design has been exceptionally favorable, especially when viewed from the rear angle. In Japan, it has been nicknamed *mikaeri bijin* (literally meaning a beautiful woman who is looking back), borrowing the title of a famous *ukiyoe* (or woodblock print). Photographs of equipment used in new-product announcements and catalogs are usually taken from the front. In the case of REGA, however, photographs emphasized the line of the Japanese sword along the sides of the machine. Adachi noted:

> The impact of this design was in fact much greater than expected. Now, customers who would never visit our company in the past come by just to see it. That's important to us. And even potential customers who used to tell us: "Sorry, we only use Komatsu," or "We have Hitachi," without even letting us in the door, will now say: "Please show it to us. Wow, this is really different. Can we get inside?" That's a big plus for us. (Nonaka, Ohtsubo, and Fukushima, 1993, p. 22)

Shin Caterpillar Mitsubishi invested a huge amount of money into the REGA series over a four-year period. The market has responded positively thus far, with sales exceeding the plan for 1992 and 1993. But the real value of this investment in time and money would come from how effectively the company made use of the knowledge it created during this project.

Implications of the REGA Case for Knowledge Creation

This case illustrates what can take place when Japanese and American engineers are placed on an equal footing to develop a global product. The project started out with more clashes than the Japanese-led Primera project, with two different value systems, patterns of engineering (or business) logic, and approaches to organizational knowledge creation colliding with each other. But it also shows what socialization can do to turn such possibly destructive clashes into immensely valuable chances for innovation.

The development of REGA represents a fascinating synthesis of Japanese and U.S. approaches to organizational knowledge creation. The synthesis is a synergy of Japanese and American strengths. Japanese strengths can be represented, for example, by the effective use of socialization (e.g., interplant meetings) and self-organizing teams (e.g., the rugby style of product development). American strengths, on the other hand, rest on externalization (e.g., iterative "why" questions, more specified design drawings, and standardized operation manuals) and combination (e.g., the cost-monitoring system).

We should also emphasize that both sides tried to overcome their weaknesses in knowledge creation and attempted to correct them through the four modes of knowledge conversion. Japanese engineers learned how to externalize tacit knowledge into explicit knowledge, and internalized it. American engineers learned how to socialize tacit knowledge from interaction with other people or direct experience on-site, and internalized it. Discovering and remedying weaknesses, both at the individual and organizational levels, hold the key to an effective organizational knowledge-creation process on a global scale.

Finally, the REGA case shows that for any organizational knowledge creation on a global scale to succeed, the following three conditions must be met. First, top management of the participating organizations should show strong commitment to the project. This visible support provides the first step in persuading project members to commit themselves to the project. Second, assigning capable middle managers to the project as "global knowledge engineers" is critical. The assignment of Itakura, for example, facilitated knowledge conversion within the joint venture. Third, participants in the project should develop a sufficient level of trust among themselves. Building trust requires the use of mutually understandable, explicit language and often prolonged socialization or two-way, face-to-face dialogue that provides reassurance about points of doubt and leads to willingness to respect the other party's sincerity.

These two case studies clearly show that the Japanese approach to organizational knowledge creation can be applied outside of Japan, and that the key adjustment needed is a prolonged phase of socialization and externalization. This adjustment is needed because it takes time for people from different cultures to share tacit knowledge. It also takes more time to build trust between people from different cultures.

Notes

1. As suggested in Chapter 6, overadaptation to past success was the single most important factor in the repeated defeats of the Japanese Imperial Army and Navy in World War II. Many Japanese companies seem to have maintained the same propensity.

2. For a comparison of knowledge management in the West (mainly USA) and Japan, see Hedlund and Nonaka (1993).

3. Although there is a huge body of literature on technology (i.e., knowledge) transfer across organizational or national boundaries, few studies stand out in relevance. Teece (1981), for example, argued as follows, citing Polanyi (1966):

> Know-how cannot always be codified, since it often has an important tacit dimension. Individuals may know more than they are able to articulate. When knowledge has a high tacit component, it is extremely difficult to transfer without intimate personal contact, demonstration, and involvement. Indeed, in the absence of intimate human contact, technology transfer is sometimes impossible. (p. 86)

Thus, Teece recognized the tacit dimension of knowledge and the need of socialization. Related to this article is von Hippel's (1994) concept of "sticky information." Contrary to the conventional economic view of information as costlessly transferrable, he observed that information is often costly or difficult to acquire, transfer, and use owing to attributes of information itself (e.g., tacitness) or information seekers (e.g., a lack of complementary information). He, too, argued the importance of tacit "information" and human skills, drawing on Polanyi (1958).

4. These differences in lead time seem to be shrinking as Japanese car makers have intentionally lengthened theirs during the latest recession after the explosion of the bubble economy, and U.S. and European car makers have learned concurrent engineering, whose basic idea was derived from the rugby approach.

8

Managerial and
Theoretical Implications

T he journey we embarked on is about to end. We started the journey with lofty goals: (1) to construct a new theory of organizational knowledge creation; (2) to provide a new explanation of
why certain Japanese companies have been successful at continuous
innovation; and (3) to develop a universal management model that con-
verges management practices found in Japan and the West. On reflection, we have taken a major step in achieving the first two goals. We
started to address the third goal in the previous chapter, but have not
yet given it a full treatment, which we intend to do below.

In this chapter we offer two sets of implications that are drawn from
our research. The first involves practical implications for business
practitioners interested in implementing a knowledge-creation program within their companies. The second is more conceptual in nature,
offering new insights about a universal model of management that
emerges out of the findings of our research.

A Summary of Our Major Findings

Before proceeding with our discussion of the two sets of implications,
it is important that we have a common understanding of what we have
been able to find out about organizational knowledge creation thus far.
The first step in understanding how organizational knowledge is created is to draw on a deep epistemological foundation to distinguish
between two types of knowledge—tacit and explicit knowledge. The in-

teraction of these two types of knowledge, which we called knowledge conversion, gave rise to the following four modes: socialization (from tacit to tacit), externalization (from tacit to explicit), combination (from explicit to explicit), and internalization (from explicit to tacit).

Second, we mentioned that this interaction between tacit and explicit knowledge is performed by an individual, not by the organization itself. We repeatedly emphasized that the organization cannot create knowledge devoid of individuals. But if the knowledge cannot be shared with others or is not amplified at the group or divisional level, then knowledge does not spiral itself organizationally. This spiral process across different ontological levels is one of the keys to understanding organizational knowledge creation.

As mentioned in Chapter 3, the socialization mode starts by building a team whose members share their experiences and mental models. The externalization mode is triggered by successive rounds of meaningful dialogue. Metaphors and analogies, which enable team members to articulate their own perspectives and thereby reveal hidden tacit knowledge that is otherwise hard to communicate, are often used in a dialogue. The combination mode is facilitated when the concept formed by the team is combined with existing data as well as with knowledge that resides outside the team to create more shareable specifications. The internalization mode is induced when team members begin to internalize the new explicit knowledge that is shared throughout the organization. That is, they use it to broaden, extend, and reframe their own tacit knowledge.

Third, the core of the organizational knowledge-creation process takes place at the group level, but the organization provides the necessary enabling conditions. The organization provides organizational contexts or devices that facilitate the group activities, as well as the creation and accumulation of knowledge at the individual level. We cited five conditions that are required at the organizational level to promote the knowledge spiral—intention, autonomy, fluctuation and creative chaos, redundancy, and requisite variety.

Fourth, our case studies suggest that the actual process by which organizational knowledge creation takes place is nonlinear and interactive. Our five-phase model of the process—which consists of sharing of tacit knowledge, concept creation, concept justification, archetype building, and cross-leveling of knowledge—differs from "horizontal" process models in that it moves cyclically and across levels. The first four phases move horizontally, but the fifth phase moves vertically, creating layers of activities at different organizational levels, as we saw in the Matsushita case.

The Matsushita case also showed that organizational knowledge creation is a never-ending, iterative process. Recall how the Home Bakery development went through a number of cycles involving the corporate organization at large. But the never-ending, circular process is not confined within the organization; it also takes place inter-organizationally. The knowledge created by the company mobilizes the tacit knowledge of others outside the organization, who convert it to explicit knowledge that will be fed back to the organization as environmental fluctuation. In most cases this interaction will take place between the product, service, or system that the company offers and customers, suppliers, distributors, and competitors.

Fifth, neither the top-down model of management nor the bottom-up model is particularly suited to foster dynamic interaction between tacit and explicit knowledge. The top-down model provides limited ability for the organization to realize socialization and externalization, and the bottom-up model is not particularly helpful in bringing about combination and internalization. Herein lies the limitation of these two models in bringing about the knowledge spiral across the four modes, as well as across the ontological levels. We proposed a new management process called middle-up-down management, which integrates the benefits of the top-down and bottom-up models and is the most fitting model for bringing about organizational knowledge creation.

Sixth, neither a formal hierarchy nor a flexible task force alone is the appropriate organizational structure in which knowledge creation can flourish. The hierarchical structure is effective in realizing the combination and internalization modes and the task-force structure is suited for the socialization and externalization modes. We proposed a hypertext organization as a new organizational structure most appropriate for the pursuit of both the efficiency of a hierarchy/bureaucracy and the flexibility of a task force. This does not mean that a hypertext organization is a prerequisite for organizational knowledge creation, but it is something that will facilitate the process.

Seventh, neither the Japanese nor the Western methodology of knowledge creation provides the complete solution. In the Western methodology, the interaction between tacit knowledge and explicit knowledge tends to take place mainly at the individual level, with a few individuals playing a critical role. While the interaction between tacit knowledge and explicit knowledge takes place at the group level in the Japanese methodology, its tendency is to overemphasize the use of figurative language and symbolism at the expense of a more analytical approach and documentation. We need to integrate the merits of both the Japanese and Western methodologies to develop a universal model of organizational knowledge creation. And since knowledge creation is at the heart of management in today's "knowledge society," that model will serve as the universal model for management at large.

Practical Implications

Any manager reading the popular press will realize that we have now entered the "knowledge society," in which knowledge is not just another resource alongside the traditional factors of production—labor, capital, and land—but the most critical resource. Managers will also perceive that the future belongs to "knowledge workers," those who use their heads instead of their hands, and the key to future prosperity lies in educating and training these workers. If companies will "train, train, train these knowledge workers, they will learn, learn, learn," goes the popular thinking.

This simplistic model will work if the company is concerned only with absorbing knowledge from somewhere and passing it along to individuals within the organization. But it will not work when the intent is to *create* knowledge, not only at the individual level, but at the group as well as the organizational level. In the simplistic case, knowledge moves laterally and in one direction, whereas knowledge moves in a spiral when creating organizational knowledge.

In this section we present seven guidelines a practitioner can adopt to implement an organizational knowledge-creation program within a company. Unfortunately, the process is not as simplistic as portrayed in the popular press, but it is guaranteed to be more effective. These guidelines, which will be discussed below, are as follows:

1. Create a knowledge vision.
2. Develop a knowledge crew.
3. Build a high-density field of interaction at the front line.
4. Piggyback on the new-product development process.
5. Adopt middle-up-down management.
6. Switch to a hypertext organization.
7. Construct a knowledge network with the outside world.

Create a Knowledge Vision

Top management should create a knowledge vision and communicate it within the organization. A knowledge vision should define the "field" or "domain" that gives corporate members a mental map of the world they live in and provides a general direction regarding what kind of knowledge they ought to seek and create. It is similar to organizational intention, and should serve as the foundation upon which the company's strategy is formulated. The essence of strategy lies in developing the organizational capability to acquire, create, accumulate, and exploit the knowledge domain. But at the present time, most companies have only products and services in mind when formulating their strategy. This preoccupation can be somewhat limiting, since products and, to a lesser extent, services have clear boundaries. In contrast, boundaries for knowledge are much more obscure, which helps to expand the competitive scope as well as the technological horizon of the company.

For example, the fact that Kao defines its knowledge domain as "surface science" enables the company, whose origin was in surface-active agents used in detergents, to move into new markets such as cosmetics and floppy disks. A skin cream can be looked at from a surface-science point of view as the surface between oil and skin, and floppy disk as a plastic film coated with magnet powder.

Similarly, both NEC and Sharp define their knowledge domain in terms of their core technologies. NEC, for example, includes pattern recognition and image processing as part of its core technologies and tries to match them with business activities through the "strategic technology domain" (STD) we saw in Chapter 3. Since STD links several core technologies to create a product concept, it not only represents a product domain but a knowledge domain as well. At Sharp, the core technology is "optoelectronics," which represents the image of the world Sharp wants to live in, and is one of the key concepts describing what Sharp ought to be. As we saw in Chapter 6, much of the knowledge accumulated in the form of optoelectronics consists of knowledge created through the dynamic conversion of various knowledge contents. The essence of Sharp's strategy based on optoelectronics could be described as a dynamic conversion of component technologies and product concepts.

A knowledge vision created by top management helps to foster a high degree of personal commitment from middle managers and front-line workers. It provides meaning to the daily tasks they are performing on the job and a sense of direction to the kind of knowledge they ought to be seeking. A knowledge vision also helps to restructure an existing knowledge system, which may be particularly useful during periods of transition. Without a vision, knowledge may be based solely on past experiences, especially successful ones. If the successful experiences of top management become the only criterion, it becomes difficult to turn to something new or different.

To foster a high degree of commitment from members of the organization, a knowledge vision should purposefully be left equivocal and open ended. A more equivocal vision gives members of the organization the freedom and autonomy to set their own goals, making them more committed to figuring out what the ideals of the top really mean.

In the not-too-distant future, top management will be evaluated not only by economic performance measures, but also on the quality of the knowledge vision it presents to constituents both inside and outside the company. The shift to the knowledge society will certainly accelerate this change. Someone at the top will have to be able to see the world from a knowledge perspective, mobilize the latent knowledge power held within the organization, and justify the knowledge created by the firm. Top managers should be aware that the height of their personal aspiration and their organizational intention will determine the quality of the knowledge the firm creates.

Develop a Knowledge Crew

Creating new knowledge starts with the individual. But as Robert Howard (1993) points out, "Creating new knowledge is not simply a matter of 'processing' objective information. In fact, it is a subjective and extremely personal activity (p. xvii)." Thus, knowledge creation starts from an individual's efforts to validate or justify her or his belief and commitment to the job and company; personal perspectives or "mental models" come into play as well. Highly subjective insights, intuitions, and hunches are at the root of knowledge creation and innovation.

To nurture rich insights and intuitions, a knowledge-creating company needs diversity in the pool of talents available within the company. This diversity enhances requisite variety, which is one of the enabling conditions, for the organization. We have already seen that a few of the crew members who worked for Nissan's Primera project had unusual backgrounds. Tsuda, one of knowledge engineers, had studied at Berlin Technical College and was fluent in both German and English. NMUK's Shigeki Miyajima had studied at the University of Glasgow and was married to a British national. And Mikio Fujito, an exterior designer, had studied at London's Royal College of Arts. These educational backgrounds, as well as these individuals' familiarity with the local scene, proved to be an asset in working with Europeans on the Primera project.

To ensure that the diverse pool of talents available within the company maintain their freedom and autonomy, the company should be able to offer diversity in career ladders as well. Attracting individuals with rich insights and intuitions can backfire if they can only be accommodated through a standardized and hierarchical career ladder. Most companies today have separate career ladders for a line manager and for a functional specialist. In addition to these two ladders, a separate ladder for a project leader should be established. A project leader is a kind of intrafirm entrepreneur with lots of frontier spirit. Project leaders get a kick out of trying something new and taking initiatives. But they are also skilled at coordinating and managing projects, generating new hypotheses or concepts, integrating various methodologies for knowledge creation, and communicating with team members and engendering their trust.

We have seen several people who would be ideal candidates to fill this role of project leader. Ikuko Tanaka of Matsushita, Hiroo Watanabe of Honda, and Hiroshi Nitanda of Canon come to mind on the domestic scene; Yasuhisa Tsuda of Nissan and Noriyuki Itakura of Shin Caterpillar Mitsubishi qualify as global project leaders. According to the three categories of knowledge crew we developed in Chapter 5—knowledge practitioners, knowledge engineers, and knowledge officers—they all fall into the category of knowledge engineers. We pointed out that knowledge engineers take the lead in converting knowledge, creating a modal spiral, and facilitating another spiral across different organizational levels. In this respect, they are the project leaders of the organizational knowledge-creation process. Having a separate career ladder for this group of "intrapreneurs" will send a clear-cut and positive message throughout the organization. In addition, it will provide a substantial boost to the actual implementation of the knowledge-creation effort.

A different performance-evaluation criterion should also be established for these project leaders. The traditional "penalty point" method of evaluation is not satisfactory for knowledge engineers charged with creating something new. For knowledge-creating companies, shifting the evaluation criterion from a negative to a positive method is a mandate; the same criterion should be applied to all crew members as well. Crew members should be evaluated in terms of how many new endeavors have been attempted. They should be allowed to make "meaningful failures," as at 3M, and given incentives to attain as much original experience as possible. To a certain extent, the awarding of the "gold badge" at Sharp has a similar effect of empowering crew members to carry out innovative projects without fear of being penalized. They are able to recruit anyone in the company to the project and to proceed with an unlimited budget.

Build a High-Density Field of Interaction at the Front Line

To nurture the highly subjective and personal mindset of individuals within the company, a knowledge-creating company should provide a place where a rich source of original experience can be gained—what we are calling a high-density field. A high-density field refers to an environment in which frequent and intensive interactions among crew members take place. It can be represented by the activities of the cross-functional new-product development teams we encountered throughout the book, including Honda's City, Matsushita's Home Bakery, Canon's Mini-Copier, Nissan's Primera, and Shin Caterpillar Mitsubishi's REGA. A high-density field also takes the form of group meetings such as Honda's *tamadashi-kai,* Canon's "camp session," and Sharp's "NEW-ING." Other examples include the once-a-week morning meetings held by Itakura of Shin Caterpillar Mitsubishi at Caterpillar's Aurora plant, during which he discussed his own thinking, experience, and past mistakes; Primera's test runs on the Autobahn; and the one-floor system at Kao, in which the walls of its R&D lab were removed to create a large open space to promote information sharing among lab researchers.

To repeat, our theory of knowledge creation is anchored to the very important assumption that human knowledge is created and expanded through the social interaction between tacit knowledge and explicit knowledge. The quintessential knowledge-creation process takes place when tacit knowledge is converted into explicit knowledge. In other words, our hunches, perceptions, mental models, beliefs, and experiences are converted to something that can be communicated and transmitted in formal and systematic language. A high-density field is the place where the conversion is triggered through some sort of dialogue. It is here that crew members begin constructing a common language and synchronizing their mental and physical rhythms.

Metaphors and analogies are often used in carrying out a dialogue among crew members. Since tacit knowledge is inexpressible, metaphors and analogies serve as the means of expression. But the language we use to express ourselves—such as "Automobile Evolution" in the case of the Honda City or "beer can" in the case of the Canon Mini-Copier—is often inadequate and sometimes inconsistent. Such discrepancies and gaps between image and expression help to promote interactions among individuals and often lead to collective reflection among them.

Crew members, especially those who are at the front line, carry out another kind of dialogue, namely a dialogue with the market. The market provides another high-density field, although the interaction is now between crew members and the outside world. A less obvious but equally important interaction takes place in this field, since knowledge is embedded in the market. The more mature the market, the more knowledge becomes tacit. Thus in a mature market, crew members have to interact much more intensively and frequently with the market, since the importance of the more qualitative type of information increases with maturity.

Piggyback on the New-Product Development Process

It is no coincidence that most of the cases illustrated in this book are anchored in new-product development projects. In addition to the projects at Honda, Matsushita, Canon, Nissan, and Shin Caterpillar Mitsubishi, we have made reference to new-product development projects at Sharp (electronic organizer), NEC (PC-8000), Mazda (new RX-7), Asahi Breweries (Super Dry), Fuji Xerox (FX-3500), and others.

Why such an overlap? The reason, very simply, is because the new-product development process happens to be the core process for creating new organizational knowledge. Organizational knowledge creation is like a "derivative" of new-product development. Thus, how well a company manages the new-product development process becomes the critical determinant of how successfully organizational knowledge creation can be carried out.

To manage the new-product development process successfully, companies should be mindful of the following three characteristics. First, companies must maintain a highly adaptive and flexible approach to new-product development. They must recognize that product development seldom proceeds in a linear and static manner. It involves an iterative, dynamic, and continuous process of trial and error. Probably the best illustration of this characteristic comes from the software industry. A recent study by Cusumano and Selby (1995) shows that software development utilizes an iterative and spiral approach. Software developers move around in phases, going among designing, coding, and testing as the project progresses. In addition, software developers test the product continuously as it is built and develop prototypes quickly, rather than testing primarily at the end of the development cycle. They also improve features continuously, introducing products in multiple-release cycles. Thus, it is important that companies maintain a highly adaptive and flexible approach toward managing the new-product development process.

Second, companies need to make sure that a self-organizing project team is overseeing the new-product development process. A project team takes on a self-organizing character as it is driven to a state of "zero information"—where prior knowledge does not apply. Ambiguity and fluctuation abound in this state. Left to itself, the process begins to create its own dynamic order. The project begins to operate like a startup company, taking initiatives and risks and developing its own agenda. At some point, the team begins to create its own concept. Companies must, therefore, be willing to give autonomy to the project team and, at the same time, tolerate fluctuation and creative chaos.

Third, companies need to encourage the participation of nonexperts in new-product development, which adds requisite variety to the process. Unlike the experts, who cannot tolerate mistakes even 1 percent of the time, the nonexperts are willing to challenge the status quo. Companies should, therefore, be prepared to tolerate and anticipate mistakes. Engineers at Honda, for example, are fond of saying, "A 1 percent success rate is supported by mistakes made 99 percent of the time."

Adopt Middle-up-down Management

The process of organizational knowledge creation is often triggered by a sense of urgency or crisis within the organization. We have seen that creative chaos can be generated internally by setting challenging organizational goals that are far beyond the current capability of the firm, or by promoting "reflection-in-action," in which the company encourages its crew members to doubt and negate the existing cognitive/behavioral premises.

One of the most effective ways of managing creative chaos, in our opinion, is middle-up-down management. In this model, top management articulates the vision or dream for the company, while front-line employees down in the trenches look at reality. The gap between dream and reality is narrowed by middle managers who mediate between the two by creating middle-range business and product concepts. In doing so, they synthesize the tacit knowledge of both top management and front-line employees, make it explicit, and incorporate it into new technologies, products, and programs.

In our view, middle managers play a key role in the organizational knowledge-creation process. They have a lot of knowledge, being positioned at the intersection of the vertical and horizontal flows of information in the company, which qualifies them to serve as team leaders. But our view is not in accord with the badgering they have been receiving recently in the West, where middle managers have been portrayed as "cancer" and a "disappearing breed." In contrast, in a knowledge-creating company they are positioned as the "knot," "bridge," and "knowledge engineers."

Switch to a Hypertext Organization

In order for a company to qualify as a knowledge-creating company, it must have the organizational capability to acquire, accumulate, exploit, and create new knowledge continuously and dynamically, and to recategorize and recontextualize it strategically for use by others in the organization or by future generations. Unfortunately, conventional organizational structures are not flexible enough to perform all of these functions. A hierarchy is the most efficient structure for the acquisition, accumulation, and exploitation of knowledge, while a task force is the most effective structure for the creation of new knowledge. Recategorizing and recontextualizing the knowledge generated in these two structures or layers necessitates the establishment of a third layer we called the knowledge base. This layer does not exist as an actual organizational entity, but is embedded in corporate vision, organizational culture, or technology. Corporate vision and organizational culture tap tacit knowledge, whereas technology taps the explicit knowledge generated in the two layers.

A switch to a hypertext organization, which accommodates all three layers, is by no means easy. To use a computer metaphor, all three layers of text are stored separately in a separate file and can be pulled out on the screen as needed. To convince managers who have an either-or mentality that they should view hierarchy and task force as complementary rather than mutually exclusive is a challenge in itself. To overlay another layer (knowledge base) on top of the two and say "You can be in any one of these three layers at any one point in time" may be asking too much. But this ability to switch from one layer to another is fundamentally the core feature that distinguishes the hypertext organization from conventional structures. Within a hypertext, crew members can traverse through the three layers, but can be in only one layer at any one given point in time.

Although it is not easy, the switch to a hypertext is necessary, primarily for two reasons. First, it makes the life of crew members a lot easier, because they have to be in only one layer at a time. Since they will not have to perform dual functions, as in a matrix organization, being in one layer at a time will improve crew members' endurance. Second, the quality of knowledge tapped by the organization increases, since a specialization of sorts takes place. The business-system layer in a hierarchy specializes in acquiring, accumulating, and exploiting explicit knowledge, while the task force deals primarily with tacit knowledge and creates new knowledge through a conversion process. The knowledge-base layer, in a sense, focuses on storing and reinterpreting both tacit and explicit knowledge.

Switching to this kind of loose and flexible organization may take some time. The decision to switch will require the vision and commitment of top management. Those who are currently resisting should bear in mind that one Japanese company, Sharp, has already made that switch, with Kao on its way to doing the same. To use another computer metaphor, these companies will be on the "Windows" operating system, pulling multiple files onto the screen dynamically, while the rest will be operating like a static MS-DOS system.

Construct a Knowledge Network with the Outside World

Creating knowledge is not simply a matter of processing objective information about customers, suppliers, competitors, channel members, the regional community, or the government. Crew members also have to mobilize the tacit knowledge held by these outside stakeholders through social interactions. Tapping the mental maps of customers is a typical example of this activity.

Most customers' needs are tacit, which means that they cannot tell exactly or explicitly what they need or want. Asked "What do you need or want?," most customers tend to answer the question from their limited explicit knowledge of the available products or services they acquired in the past. This tendency points to the critical limitation of the one-way questionnaire format employed in traditional market research.

A much more interactive methodology involving direct two-way communication offers better promise. The way NEC developed its personal computer is a case in point. Recall how the new-product development process was kicked off by the sales of Japan's first microcomputer kit, the TK-80, and the establishment of the BIT-INN service center in Akihabara. Customers ranging from high school students to professional computer enthusiasts visited BIT-INN and shared their experiences of using the TK-80. The continued dialogue and insights that NEC gained eventually led to its best-selling PC-8000 personal computer. Another example of direct communication comes from the apparel industry. Leading apparel companies in Japan, such as Onward-Kashiyama, Renown, and Sanyo, send their own sales force to the selling floors of major department stores to engage in meaningful dialogue with customers.

For direct communication to be effective, it helps to have the actual products or prototypes on hand. They project a much stronger image of the message the company is trying to convey than words alone. Sharp, Microsoft, and Apple, for example, all have their product development team members take their prototypes into the marketplace and ask for spontaneous impressions or reactions from customers on the street to the new product idea or concept. Matsushita Electric's bicycle division went a step further by devising a tool called a "fitting scale" that articulates how a customer feels while riding a bicycle prototype at one of its store locations, and translates the customer's feeling of "best fit" into specifications that the factory can understand.

But on occasion, one comes across creative customers who are adept at externalizing their tacit needs. Mobilizing the knowledge of this small group of creative customers or "opinion leaders" is critical to the knowledge-creation process. Sharp, for example, established two "customer boards" to involve these leading-edge customers in its new-product development process. As mentioned earlier, the first board, called the "Trend Leader System," organized 600 leading customers, ranging from junior high school students to senior citizens in their 70s, as outside staff members. Sharp clustered these customers into small groups and collected valuable information that enabled the company to predict consumer trends 1 to 10 years into the future. The second board, known as the "Life Creator System," involved leading customers in various live experiments, the objective of which was to create a better quality of life.

Theoretical Implications

We have repeatedly emphasized that the focus of this book is on knowledge *creation*, not on knowledge per se. From our perspective, knowledge *creation* fuels innovation, but knowledge per se does not. In other words, the process by which new knowledge is created within the organization—in the form of new products, services, or systems—becomes the cornerstone of innovative activities. That process is *dynamic*, producing two different kinds of knowledge spirals. The first spiral takes place at the epistemological dimension across the four modes of knowledge conversion—socialization, externalization, combination, and internalization—as we saw in Figure 3-3. Another spiral takes place at the ontological dimension, where knowledge developed at the individual level is transformed into knowledge at the group and organizational levels, as shown in Figure 3-5. Although each dimension produces a dynamic spiral, the truly dynamic nature of our theory can be depicted as the interaction of the two knowledge spirals over time. It is this dynamic process that fuels innovation.

Organizational knowledge is also created through an *interactive* process. Interactions in the epistemological and ontological dimensions bring about the two spirals mentioned above. At the epistemological dimension, it is the interaction across the four modes that produces a spiral when time is introduced as the third dimension. At the ontological dimension, the iterative and continuous interactions across, say, the project-team level, the divisional level, and eventually the corporate or inter-organizational levels over time, produce a spiral that can be visualized as moving from left to right and back again to the left.

The key to our theory lies in understanding the nature of the conversion behind the dynamic and interactive process of knowledge creation. We encountered a number of conversions throughout the book. The most visible and important, of course, is the conversion of tacit knowledge into explicit knowledge and vice versa, which we referred to as knowledge conversion. Other examples of conversion include a managerial conversion of top-down style and bottom-up style into middle-up-down management, or an organizational conversion of bureaucracy and task force into a hypertext structure.

The starting point toward building a conversion is to recognize the need to transcend beyond dichotomies. We discovered a strong propensity in the West to view the world in terms of a dichotomy. This intellectual tradition can be traced back to the Cartesian dualism or split, as we saw in Chapter 2. A is pitted against B, resulting in the "A vs. B" model. The debates over subject vs. object, mind vs. body, rationalism vs. empiricism, and scientific management vs. human relations reflect this intellectual tradition. The danger, in our opinion, is to view the building blocks of organizational knowledge creation in the same light. In our view, tacit knowledge and explicit knowledge, for example, are not opposing ends of a dichotomy, but mutually complementary entities. They interact with and interchange into each other to create something new. The same holds true for top-down and bottom-up management, as well as for bureaucracy and task force. In all these cases, what appear to be opposite ends of a dichotomy interact with each other to create a synthesis. In other words, our model looks at A *and* B simultaneously.

The dynamic and simultaneous interaction between two opposing ends of "false" dichotomies creates a solution that is new and different. In other words, A and B create C, which synthesizes the best of A and B. C is separate and independent of A and B, not something "in-between" or "in the middle of" A and B. It corresponds to middle-up-down management, which is created by taking the best of top-down and bottom-up, and to hypertext, which is created by synthesizing bureaucracy and task force. In both cases, C is created by pursuing A and

B simultaneously. Our approach has been to take the best of two worlds and create something new from their dynamic interaction. In other words, a dynamic, interactive, and simultaneous conversion process involving A and B creates C, a synthesis of the two.

Our approach is in stark contrast to the either-or approach prevalent in the West. In an A vs. B model, a dialectic process is used to seek an answer in either one of the two opposing sides of the dualism (i.e., either A or B). But how a synthesis occurs in the dialectic process is not clear. A "boxing of logic" takes place in the dialectic process, with both sides being represented by explicit knowledge. As in boxing, one winner (i.e., either A or B) emerges after the confrontation. In our approach, the synthesis occurs through a transformation, or what we called a knowledge conversion, between not only explicit and explicit knowledge, but between tacit and explicit as well as between tacit and tacit. This transformation takes place through both confrontation and collaboration.

We have encountered a number of "false" dichotomies throughout the book. In this final section, we will focus on the following seven dichotomies, which are listed approximately in the order in which they appeared in the book:

1. Tacit/explicit
2. Body/mind
3. Individual/organization
4. Top-down/bottom-up
5. Bureaucracy/task force
6. Relay/rugby
7. East/West

These dichotomies form the basis upon which our theory of organizational knowledge creation was constructed. For each dichotomy, we take the two seemingly opposing concepts, integrate them dynamically, and build a synthesis. We will discover that the essence of knowledge creation is deeply rooted in the process of building and managing syntheses, which take place through a conversion process. The seven syntheses that we will discuss below represent the "something new" this book has to offer. Our hope is that they will shed some new light for researchers engaged in the study of innovation.

Tacit/Explicit Dichotomy

Recall our earlier observation that the history of Western epistemology can be seen as a continuous controvesy over which type of knowledge—tacit or explicit—is more truthful. While those in the West tend to emphasize the importance of explicit knowledge, the Japanese put more emphasis on tacit knowledge. The critical assumption underlying our model of knowledge creation favors the Japanese view that human knowledge is created and expanded through social interaction between tacit and explicit knowledge.

This assumption enabled us to postulate four different modes of knowledge conversion—socialization, externalization, internalization, and combination. Three of these modes have already been discussed in writings on organization theory to some extent. Socialization, for example, is similar in content to theories of group processes and organizational culture; combination has its roots in the information-processing paradigm; and internalization is closely related to the learning organization. But we felt that externalization, which has been somewhat neglected in the literature, holds the key to knowledge creation. It is in this mode that tacit knowledge, which is personal, context-specific, and therefore hard to formalize and communicate to others, is converted into knowledge that is transmittable and articulable, such as words or numbers. We also discovered the importance of using metaphors and analogies, especially when we cannot find adequate expression through analytical methods of deduction or induction, as a means of converting tacit knowledge into explicit knowledge.

Each of the four modes of knowledge conversion yields a knowledge content that is distinct from the others. As we briefly discussed in Chapter 3, socialization yields "sympathized" knowledge, such as mental models and technical skills. Externalization yields "conceptual" knowledge, as in the concept of the "Tall Boy" at Honda. Combination yields "systemic" knowledge, such as a prototype or a new component technology. Internalization yields "operational" knowledge about project management, production process, or policy implementation.

These four knowledge contents represent C, the four syntheses of the four modes of knowledge conversion, that resulted from the interaction between A and B, the two types of knowledge. In other words, "something new" is created by having tacit and explicit knowledge interact with each other.

Body/Mind Dichotomy

Embedded in Western epistemology is the tradition of separating the body from the mind, which has been referred to as the Cartesian split or dualism. Descartes argued that the ultimate truth can be deduced only from the real existence of a "thinking self," which was made famous by his phrase, "I think, therefore I am." He assumed that the "thinking self" is independent of body or matter, because while a body or matter does have an extension we can see and touch but does not think, a mind has no extension but thinks. Thus, according to the Cartesian dualism, true knowledge can be obtained only by the mind, not the body.

This epistemological tradition still lives today, as seen in the fascination with the "systems thinking" developed by Peter Senge (1990), originator of the learning organization. The focus of the learning organization is clearly on learning with the mind, not with the body. As we mentioned earlier, Senge even says that trial-and-error learning is a delusion, since the most critical decisions made in an organization have systemwide consequences stretching over years and decades, a time frame that makes learning from bodily experience an impossibility.

In contrast, we have placed strong emphasis on the importance of bodily experience. We have argued, for example, that the most powerful learning comes from bodily experience. A child learns to eat, walk, and talk through trial and error; he or she learns with the body, not only with the mind. But learning represents only one of the interactions in the knowledge-creation framework. Learning by doing is equivalent to internalization, which is the conversion of explicit knowledge into tacit knowledge. The remaining three modes of knowledge conversion place equal importance on acquiring knowledge from pure or direct experience. One gains subjective insights, intuitions, and hunches from bodily experience.

We have argued that personal and physical experience is equally as valuable as indirect, intellectual abstraction. For example, recall how being a "man of action" was considered to contribute more to one's character than mastering philosophy and literature in medieval *samurai* education. The synthesis of the two opposing sides of the dualism was dubbed "the oneness of body and mind" by Eisai, one of the founders of Zen Buddhism in medieval Japan. This philosophy lives on in Japan, making it easier to build a synthesis (C) of two seemingly opposing concepts—body and mind (A and B)—than in the West.

Individual/Organization Dichotomy

As we have pointed out, knowledge is created only by individuals. An organization cannot create knowledge on its own without individuals. It is, therefore, very important for the organization to support and stimulate the knowledge-creating activities of individuals or to provide the appropriate contexts for them. Organizational knowledge creation should be understood as a process that "organizationally" amplifies the knowledge created by individuals and crystallizes it at the group level through dialogue, discussion, experience sharing, or observation.

Recall how the new-product development team at Honda argued and discussed what Hiroo Watanabe's slogan might possibly mean, before coming up with a metaphor of its own, "man-maximum, machine-minimum." This example illustrates the central role self-organizing teams play in the knowledge-creation process. They provide a shared context in which individuals can carry on a dialogue, which may involve considerable conflict and disagreement. But as we mentioned earlier, it is precisely such a conflict that pushes individuals to question existing premises and to make sense of their experiences in a new way. This kind of dynamic interaction facilitates the transformation of personal knowledge into organizational knowledge.

It should be clear from the above discussion that an individual and an organization are not at the opposing ends of a dichotomy. The individual is the "creator" of knowledge and the organization is the "amplifier" of knowledge. But the actual context in which much of the conversion takes place is at the group or team level. The group functions as the "synthesizer" of knowledge. The more autonomous, diverse, and self-organizing the team, the more effectively it will function as a synthesizer. Thus the dynamic integration of individuals (A) and the organization (B) creates a synthesis in the form of a self-organizing team (C), which plays a central role in the knowledge-creation process. It provides a shared context in which individuals can interact with each other. Team members create new points of view through dialogue and discussion.

Top-down/Bottom-up Dichotomy

The top-down model and the bottom-up model of management have long been viewed as two opposing ends of the management-process spectrum. The implicit assumption behind the top-down model is that only top managers are able and allowed to create knowledge. Moreover, the knowledge created by top management exists to be processed or implemented. In contrast, the bottom-up model assumes that knowledge is created by entrepreneurially minded front-line employees, with very few orders and instructions coming from top management. Certain individuals, not a group of individuals interacting with each other, create knowledge, since there is relatively little dialogue among members of the organization.

We have concluded that neither model is adequate as a process for managing knowledge creation. For one thing, the top-down model is suited for dealing with explicit knowledge, but not tacit knowledge, while the reverse holds true for the bottom-up model. Because of this limitation, the two models can carry out only partial knowledge conversions—the top-down model is focused on combination and internalization, and the bottom-up model on socialization and externalization. Another obvious limitation of the two models is the neglect of middle managers in both. In top-down management, middle managers process a lot of information, but seldom get involved in creating knowledge. In bottom-up management, the knowledge creator is clearly the entrepreneurial individual at the front line of the organization, with middle managers playing a minimal role.

Again, the middle-up-down model provides the synthesis for the two extreme ends of the dichotomy. In this model, knowledge is created by middle managers, who are often leaders of a team or a task force, in a process involving a spiral interaction between the top and front-line employees, as we saw in Figure 5-1. The model puts middle managers at the very center of synthesis building. Knowledge is created neither through A nor B, but through C, which synthesizes the best of two worlds.

Bureaucracy/Task-Force Dichotomy

Bureaucracy and task force are two opposing organizational structures that have been around a long time. Bureaucracy, which is a highly formalized, specialized, and centralized structure, works well in conducting routine work efficiently on a large scale. The task force, on the other hand, is flexible, adaptive, dynamic, and participative, and is particularly effective in carrying out a well-defined task that needs to be completed within a certain time frame.

But neither structure is well suited for fostering organizational knowledge creation. Bureaucracy hobbles individual initiative because of its strong propensity for control and can be dysfunctional in periods of uncertainty and rapid change. It is not suited to acquire, create, exploit, and accumulate tacit knowledge. The task force, because of its temporary nature, is not all that effective in exploiting and transferring knowledge continuously and widely throughout the entire organization. Neither is it particularly suited to tap explicit knowledge.

A hypertext structure, which is a synthesis of bureaucracy and task force, reaps benefits from both. The bureaucratic structure efficiently implements, exploits, and accumulates new knowledge through internalization and combination. The task force, on the other hand, is indispensable in generating new knowledge through socialization and externalization. The efficiency and stability of the bureaucracy are combined with the effectiveness and dynamism of the task force within a hypertext organization. In this respect, A and B are seen as complementary, rather than mutually exclusive.

In addition, a hypertext organization contains a third organizational layer, called the knowledge base, in which the organizational knowledge generated in bureaucracy and task force is recategorized and reconceptualized in accord with the firm's corporate vision, organizational culture, or technology. As mentioned earlier, corporate vision helps to calibrate the direction in which the firm should develop its technology or products, and clarifies the domain in which it wants to compete. Organizational culture calibrates the mindset and action of every employee. Technology taps the explicit knowledge generated in bureaucracy and task force, while corporate vision and organizational culture tap the tacit knowledge created in the two other layers. In this way, a hypertext structure (C) recategorizes and synthesizes the knowledge generated in A and B through a process of continuous interaction.

Relay/Rugby Dichotomy

We positioned the sequential "relay" approach to new-product development and the overlapping "rugby" approach as though they were at opposite ends of a dichotomy in Figure 3-7. Under the relay approach, new-product development proceeds sequentially from phase to phase—concept development, feasibility testing, product design, development process, pilot production, and final production—with one group of functional specialists passing the baton to the next group. In relay, functions are specialized and segmented, with division of labor being the norm. One of its major drawbacks is the long lead time to develop products; on the other hand, the phase-by-phase approach enables the pursuit of perfection and completeness by each group of functional specialists in each phase, often leading to high performance standards.

Under the rugby approach, the product development process emerges from the constant interaction of a multidisciplinary team whose members work together from start to finish. In our 1986 *Harvard Business Review* article (Takeuchi and Nonaka, 1986), we argued that the rugby approach was essential for companies seeking to develop new products quickly and flexibly. The constant interaction of team members encouraged them to challenge the status quo, implement trial and error, and stimulate new kinds of learning. The rugby approach worked well, to use terminologies developed in this book, because of the intensive socialization process and the resulting information redundancy among team members from various functional areas. But as we pointed out in Chapter 7, it may run the risk of compromising performance standards in an effort to preserve overall group unity and conformance.

But we saw in the previous chapter that the relay and rugby approaches need not necessarily be positioned as opposite ends of a dichotomy. An intrinsic trade-off between performance gained from the relay approach and speed achieved through the rugby approach can be avoided by resorting to the "American-football" approach, which capitalizes on the advantages of both relay and rugby. The American-football approach, which was partially utilized in the development of the Nissan Primera in Europe, can simultaneously attain both exceptionally high performance standards and short lead time. In order to develop a car in two locations several thousand miles apart, the Primera team members could not physically carry out the constant face-to-face interactions they were accustomed to in the rugby approach. Thus they had to clarify the overall strategy and develop concrete mid-range and product concepts before starting the project. Decisions were made at the outset by a few project leaders who engaged in intensive dialogues, just as the overall game plan and specific tactics in American football are determined by the head coach and the offensive and defensive coordinators.

Once the product concept was determined, several functional departments carried out concurrent activities under a clear division of labor. These departments are analogous to the specialized units in American football. Each department operated in a rugby-like fashion, with the team going the entire distance as a unit, passing the ball back and forth among themselves as well as with other teams. While each team was off and running, the project leaders conferred among themselves to achieve the interdepartmental collaboration that was essential to the success of the project. In this manner, American football not only capitalized on the advantages of both the relay and rugby approaches, but signaled a clearly new approach to product development.

East/West Dichotomy

We started our journey, thinking that a wide gap existed between the ways Japanese and Western companies approached organizational knowledge creation. By the time we reached Chapter 7, we had compiled a long list of differences, which was presented in Figure 7-1. Does this suggest Rudyard Kipling's "East is East, and West is West, and never the twain shall meet"?

The experiences at Nissan when it developed Primera and at Shin Caterpillar Mitsubishi when it developed REGA, however, carry some hope that a synthesis of the Japanese and Western approaches to organizational knowledge creation may indeed be possible. To create a synthesis, both sides must realize two simple facts. Both sides must first realize that differences do exist. Figure 7-1, which summarizes the points of contention into 11 areas, is a good place to start. At first glance, the gap appears too wide to contemplate any kind of synthesis. But the root of the differences can actually be boiled down to the two dimensions that we identified in Chapter 3—the epistemological and the ontological. Epistemologically, the difference should be obvious by now: Westerners tend to emphasize explicit knowledge and the Japanese tend to stress tacit knowledge. Ontologically, Westerners are more focused on individuals, while the Japanese are more group-oriented.

Second, both sides must realize that they have their weaknesses as well as their strengths and be willing to learn from the other side. Epistemologically, Western companies should start paying more attention to the less formal and systematic side of knowledge and begin focusing on highly subjective insights, intuitions, and hunches that are gained through experience or the use of metaphors or pictures. The reverse could be said of Japanese companies, which need to make better use of advanced information technology, software capabilities, and computerized management systems to accumulate, store, and disseminate explicit knowledge throughout the organization. Of course, gaining access to either tacit or explicit knowledge alone will not create new knowledge; a conversion from one type of knowledge to the other has to take place within the organization. This requirement highlights the importance of the ontological dimension. Western companies need to learn how to amplify or crystallize knowledge at the group level through dialogue, discussion, experience sharing, and observation. Japanese companies, on the other hand, need to learn how to build up stronger capabilities at the individual level, not only at the top but throughout the organization. A clearer statement of organizational intention by top management, a higher level of autonomy for each front-line employee, and a larger pool of knowledge engineers with diversified backgrounds and externalization skills will help to reduce the fluctuation and redundancy inherent in the Japanese process and make it easier to implement knowledge creation on a global scale.

This kind of mutual learning is already taking place. In both the Primera and REGA projects, Japanese engineers learned the importance of documentation and manuals from their Western counterparts. In addition, Japanese managers in the REGA project learned how American strength in computer software could enhance externalization. As we saw in Chapter 7, a staff member at Caterpillar turned the verbal explanation of a Japanese manager on how to cut costs into a cost-monitoring system, which enabled the company to compare parts costs anywhere in the world and to track daily cost fluctuations. Western managers, on the other hand, learned the importance of socialization from the Japanese. At Nissan, for example, 300 British engineers and technicians were sent to Japan to gain firsthand experience of Japanese manufacturing practices. At Shin Caterpillar Mitsubishi, socialization took the forms of: (1) Larsen and Adachi, the two top managers, having their desks next to each other and spending as much time together as possible, both on and off work; (2) interplant meetings to improve communication across plants in Japan, the United States, and Belgium; and (3) morning meetings instituted by Itakura once a week, in which he shared his own experiences or urged American engineers actually to touch the machines for whose construction they were responsible.

These simple realizations go a long way toward paving the road for establishing an East-West synthesis of organizational knowledge creation. Our contention is that this synthesis is already taking place, both in the East and the West. We need only look at two entrepreneurial companies—Microsoft and Seven-Eleven Japan—for evidence. In our opinion, both have succeeded in incorporating the "best of two worlds."

Microsoft is known as an American company that is run like a Japanese company. Like many other American companies, it has, for example, a sophisticated electronic mail (E-mail) system that enables everyone in the company to exchange explicit knowledge. A front-line employee receives an average of 50 messages a day, with managers receiving about 100 messages, and the CEO, Bill Gates, receiving as many as 200 messages a day through E-mail. In addition, Microsoft uses its E-mail system to carry out "virtual meetings," in which a group of people sit down in front of personal computers and exchange not only data but also vocal messages, graphs, pictures, and video. Microsoft's software developers try to elicit as much tacit knowledge as possible in a process reminiscent of the hands-on product development approach utilized among Japanese companies. They take a prototype to market, have customers try it out, get a feel for what the customers like and dislike about the product, and gain insights on how to improve it. This trial-and-error process can be repeated several times before a product is finally introduced to the market.

Seven-Eleven in Japan is run like an American company. This convenience store chain makes extensive use of manuals (i.e., quintessential explicit knowledge) for store operation, employee training, and franchisee recruiting, which it learned from U.S. 7-Eleven and adapted to Japanese conditions. The company also has Japan's best retail information system. It enables not only store owners but also part-time employees to access detailed point-of-sales (POS) data and to place orders through hand-held computers called "graphic order terminals." When placing orders, they hypothesize what items would sell well, how much, and how to sell them, based on their beliefs and experiences as well as on POS data, advice of "field counselors" from Seven-Eleven Japan's local offices, information about weather forecasts, local events, and others. Each hypothesis is tested by an actual order and confirmed by POS data. Successful hypotheses are collected by the field counselor, and a selected one is reported at a weekly meeting at the headquarters, which is attended by all field counselors, top management, and headquarters staff. The hypothesis is tested throughout the stores in the following weeks. By utilizing this system that elicits the front-line knowledge, the company has become Japan's most profitable retailer and is now teaching the system to U.S. 7-Eleven, which it acquired in 1991.

We believe that the future belongs to companies that can take the best of the East and the West and start building a universal model to create new knowledge within their organizations. Nationalities will be of no relevance, as we will no longer identify the key characteristic of successful companies as being Japanese, American, or European. Success in the new "knowledge society" will be judged on the basis of knowledge-creating capabilities. To become knowledge-creating companies, managers in the East and West need to build and manage multiple conversions, spirals, and syntheses, and not be content simply to carry out a unidimensional boxing match. The key lies in multiple transformations across multiple dimensions, or what we will call hyertransformations. Hypertransformation will necessarily involve a dynamic, interactive, and simultaneous process, as we have seen in this final section of the book. In the final analysis, companies that can orchestrate a hypertransformation, and do it quickly, will gain sustainable competitive advantage in this fast-changing corporate environment. The speed by which conversions, spirals, and syntheses take place, therefore, will be a key capability in the future.

Our hope is that Japanese companies have become less of an enigma to Westerners. For most of the past 50 years, Japanese companies existed in an environment in which the only certainty was uncertainty. Although they allowed themselves to relax a little during the "bubble" economy, they are currently facing an economy in which the only certainty is again uncertainty. To cope with this uncertainty, they are turning themselves into knowledge-creating companies on a global scale. They will emerge stronger from the current recession, since the seeds for continuous innovation have already been sewn. Japanese companies have taught us that innovation can be achieved by continuosly creating new knowledge, disseminating it widely through the organization, and embodying it quickly in new technologies, products, and systems. This knowledge-creating process is no longer an enigma. This process is also no longer endemic to Japanese companies. It is universal.

REFERENCES

Aaker, D. A. 1989. Managing Assets and Skills: The Key to Sustainable Competitive Advantage. *California Management Review,* 31, no. 2:91–106.

Anderson, J. R. 1983. *The Architecture of Cognition.* Cambridge, MA: Harvard University Press.

Argyris, C. 1964. *Integrating the Individual and the Organization.* New York: John Wiley & Sons.

———. 1993. *Knowledge for Action: A Guide to Overcoming Barriers to Organizational Change.* San Francisco: Jossey-Baas.

Argyris, C., and D. A. Schön. 1978. *Organizational Learning.* Reading, MA: Addison-Wesley.

Ashby, W. R. 1956. *An Introduction to Cybernetics.* London: Chapman & Hall.

Austin, J. L. 1962. *How to Do Things with Words.* Oxford: Oxford University Press.

Ayer, A. J. 1984. *Philosophy in the Twentieth Century.* New York: Vintage Books.

Badaracco, J. L., Jr. 1991. *The Knowledge Link: How Firms Compete through Strategic Alliances.* Boston: Harvard Business School Press.

Barnard, C. I. 1938. *The Functions of the Executive.* Cambridge, MA: Harvard University Press.

Bateson, G. 1973. *Steps to an Ecology of Mind.* London: Paladin.

———. 1979. *Mind and Nature: A Necessary Unity.* New York: Bantam Books.

Berger, P. L., and T. Luckmann. 1966. *The Social Construction of Reality.* Garden City, NY: Doubleday.

Block, P. 1987. *The Empowered Manager: Positive Political Skills at Work.* San Francisco, CA: Jossey-Bass.

Bolter, J. D. 1991. *Writing Space: The Computer, Hypertext, and the History of Writing.* Hillsdale, NJ: Lawrence Erlbaum Associates.

Borucki, C. C., and P. Byosiere. 1991. Toward Global Business Leadership: Emerging Middle Managerial Roles in Five American MNCs. Paper presented at the 12th Annual International Conference of the Strategic Management Society, London.

Boulding, K. E. 1983. System Theory, Mathematics, and Quantification. In *The Study of Information,* ed. F. Machlup and U. Mansfield, pp. 547–550. New York: John Wiley & Sons.

Brown, J. S. 1992. *Reflections on the Document.* Mimeograph, Xerox Palo Alto (CA) Research Center.

Brown, J. S., and P. Duguid. 1991. Organizational Learning and Communities-of-Practice: Toward a Unified View of Working, Learning, and Innovation. *Organization Science,* 2, no. 1:40–57.

Burns, T., and G. M. Stalker. 1961. *The Management of Innovation.* London: Tavistock.

Buzzell, R. D., and B. T. Gale. 1987. *The PIMS Principles: Linking Strategy to Performance.* New York: The Free Press.

Campbell, J. P., M. Dunnette, E. E. Lawler III, and K. E. Weick. 1970. *Managerial Behavior, Performance, and Effectiveness.* New York: McGraw-Hill.

Cannon-Bowers, J. A., E. Salas, and S. Converse. 1993. Shared Mental Models in Expert Team Decision Making. In *Individual and Group Decision Making,* ed. N. J. Castellan, Jr., pp. 221–246. Hillsdale, NJ: Lawrence Erlbaum Associates.

Cohen, M. D., J. G. March, and J. P. Olsen. 1972. A Garbage Can Model of Organizational Choice. *Administrative Science Quarterly,* 17, no. 1:1–25.

Cohen, M. D., and L. S. Sproull. 1991. Editor's Introduction. *Organization Science,* 2, no. 1.

Condon, W. S. 1976. An Analysis of Behavioral Organization. *Sign Language Studies,* 13.

Conger, J. A., and R. N. Kanungo. 1988. The Empowerment Process: Integrating Theory and Practice. *Academy of Management Review,* 3:471–482.

Cusumano, M., and W. Selby. 1995. *Microsoft Secrets.* New York: The Free Press.

Daft, R. L., and K. E. Weick. 1984. Toward a Model of Organizations as Interpretation Systems. *Academy of Management Review,* 9, no. 2:284–295.

Dancy, J. 1985. *Introduction to Contemporary Epistemology.* Oxford: Basil Blackwell.

Davis, R. 1986. Knowledge-Based Systems. *Science,* 231:957–963.

Dewey, J. 1929. *The Quest for Certainty.* New York: G. P. Putnam.

Dierickx, P. A., and K. Cool. 1990. Asset Stock Accumulation and Sustainability of Competitive Advantage. *Management Science,* 35, no. 12:1504–1511.

Dodgson, M. 1993. Organizational Learning: A Review of Some Literatures. *Organizational Studies,* 14:375–394.

Donnellon, A., B. Gray, and M. G. Bougon. 1986. Communication, Meaning, and Organized Action. *Administrative Science Quarterly,* 31:43–55.

Dopson, S., and R. Stewart. 1990. What is Happening to Middle Management? *British Journal of Management,* 1:3–16.

Dretske, F. 1981. *Knowledge and the Flow of Information*. Cambridge, MA: MIT Press.

Drucker, P. F. 1991. The New Productivity Challenge. *Harvard Business Review,* Nov.–Dec.: 69–79.

———. 1993. *Post-Capitalist Society*. Oxford: Butterworth Heinemann.

Duncan, R., and A. Weiss. 1979. Organizational Learning: Implications for Organizational Design. In *Research in Organizational Behavior,* ed. B. M. Staw, Vol. 1, pp. 75–123. Greenwich, CT.: JAI Press.

Emig, J. 1983. *The Web of Meaning*. Upper Montclair, NJ: Boynton/Cook.

Fiol, C. M. 1994. Consensus, Diversity, and Learning in Organizations. *Organization Science,* 5:403–420.

Fransman, M. 1993. Information, Knowledge, Vision and Theories of the Firm. JETS paper, Institute for Japanese-European Technology Studies, University of Edinburgh.

Fujikawa, Y., and H. Takeuchi. 1994. Shin-seihin no "Yosou-gai no Seikou" ga Motarasu Kyosou-yuui (Competitive Advantage Through Unexpected Success in New Product Development. *Japan Marketing Journal,* 14, no. 2: 47–57 (in Japanese).

Gadamer, H. 1989. *Truth and Method*. 2nd ed., trans. J. Weinsheimer and D. G. Marshall. New York: Crossroad.

Galbraith, J. 1973. *Designing Complex Organizations*. Reading, MA: Addison-Wesley.

Gelwick, R. 1977. *The Way of Discovery: An Introduction to the Thought of Michael Polanyi*. Oxford: Oxford University Press.

Gerth, H. H., and C. W. Mills. 1972. *From Max Weber: Essays in Sociology*. New York: Oxford University Press.

Gibson, J. J. 1979. *The Ecological Approach to Visual Perception*. Boston, MA: Houghton Mifflin.

Gill, J. H. 1974. Saying and Showing: Radical Themes in Wittgenstein's *On Certainty. Religious Studies,* 10.

Gleick, J. 1987. *Chaos*. New York: Viking Press.

Gouldner, A. W. 1954. *Patterns of Industrial Bureaucracy*. Glencoe, IL: The Free Press.

Graumann, C. F. 1990. Perspectival Structure and Dynamics in Dialogues. In *The Dynamics of Dialogue,* ed. I. Markova and K. Foppa, pp. 105–126. New York: Harvester Wheatsheaf.

Gruber, T. R. 1989. *The Acquisition of Strategic Knowledge*. San Diego, CA: Academic Press.

Guth, W. D., and I. C. Macmillan. 1986. Strategic Implementation Versus Middle Management Self-Interest. *Strategic Management Journal,* 7:313–327.

Halal, W. E., A. Geranmayeh, and J. Pourdehnad. 1993. *Internal Markets: Bringing the Power of Free Enterprise INSIDE Your Organization*. New York: Wiley.

Harvard Business School. 1985. *General Electric 1984: Case Study*. Boston, MA: Harvard Business School.

Hayek, F. A. 1945. The Use of Knowledge in Society. *American Economic Review,* 35, no. 4:519–530.

Hedberg, B. 1981. How Organizations Learn and Unlearn. In *Handbook of Organizational Design,* ed. P. Nystrom and W. Starbuck, Vol. 1, pp. 3–27. New York: Oxford University Press.

Hedlund, G. 1986. The Hypermodern MNC—A Heterarchy? *Human Resource Management,* 25, no. 1:9–35.

Hedlund, G., and I. Nonaka. 1993. Models of Knowledge Management in the West and Japan. In *Implementing Strategic Process: Change, Learning and Cooperation,* Lorange, P. et al. eds., pp. 117–144. Oxford: Basil Blackwell.

Hirata, M. 1993. Howaito-kara no Chiteki-kakushin (Intellectual Productivity Innovation Among White-collar Workers). *Business Review,* March: 40–53 (in Japanese).

Hogg, M. A., and D. Abrams, eds. 1993. *Group Motivation: Social Psychological Perspectives.* New York: Harvester Wheatsheaf.

Howard, R. 1993. *The Learning Imperative: Managing People for Continuous Innovation.* Boston: Harvard Business School Press.

Huber, G. P. 1991. Organizational Learning: The Contributing Processes and the Literatures. *Organization Science,* 2, no. 1:88–115.

Huck, V. 1955. *Brand of the Tartan: The 3M Story.* New York: Appleton-Century-Croft.

Imai, K., and H. Itami. 1984. Interpenetration of Organization and Market. *International Journal of Industrial Organization,* no. 2:285–310.

Imai, K., I. Nonaka, and H. Takeuchi. 1985. Managing the New Product Development Process: How Japanese Companies Learn and Unlearn. In *The Uneasy Alliance: Managing the Productivity-Technology Dilemma,* ed. K. B. Clark, R. H. Hayes, and C. Lorenz, pp. 337–381. Boston, MA: Harvard Business School Press.

Itami, H. 1987. *Mobilizing Invisible Assets.* Cambridge, MA: Harvard University Press.

Iwabuchi, A. 1992. *Canon-hatsu: Kyosei Keiei no Subete (Canon: All About Its Symbiotic Management).* Tokyo: Ko Shobo (in Japanese).

Jacques, E. 1979. Taking Time Seriously in Evaluating Jobs. *Harvard Business Review,* September–October:124–132.

Jantsch, E. 1980. *The Self-Organizing Universe.* Oxford: Pergamon Press.

Johnson, L. W., and A. L. Frohman. 1989. Identifying and Closing the Gap in the Middle of Organizations. *Academy of Management Executive,* 3:104–114.

Johnson-Laird, P. N. 1983. *Mental Models.* Cambridge: Cambridge University Press.

Jordan, J. N. 1987. *Western Philosophy: From Antiquity to the Middle Ages.* New York: Macmillan.

Kagono, T., I. Nonaka, K. Sakakibara, and A. Okumura. 1985. *Strategic vs. Evolutionary Management.* Amsterdam: North-Holland.

Kaplan, R. E. 1984. Trade Routes: The Manager's Network of Relationships. *Organizational Dynamics,* Spring:37–52.

Kobayashi, T. 1985. *Tomokaku Yattemiro (In Any Case, Try It).* Tokyo: Toyo Keizai Shimposha (in Japanese).

Kohno, H. 1992. *Matsushita ni Okeru Shippai no Kenkyu (A Study of Failure at Matsushita).* Tokyo: Yell (in Japanese).

Komiya, K. 1988. Sharp no Kin-bajji-butai Denshi-techou o Umidasu (Sharp's "Kin-badge" Task Force Invented an Electronic Organizer). *Purejidento* December: 124–133 (in Japanese).

Kraut, A. I., P. R. Pedigo, D. D. McKenny, and M. D. Dunnette. 1989. The

Role of the Manager: What's Really Important in Different Management Jobs. *Academy of Management Executive,* 3, no. 4:286–293.

Kumakura, C. 1990. *Nihonjin no Hyogenryoku to Kosei (Expression Capabilities and Personalities of the Japanese.* Tokyo: Chuo Koronsha (in Japanese).

Lakoff, G., and M. Johnson. 1980. *Metaphors We Live By.* Chicago, IL: University of Chicago Press.

Leonard-Barton, D. 1992. Core Capabilities and Core Rigidities: A Paradox in Managing New Product Development. *Strategic Management Journal,* 13:111–125.

Levitt, B., and J. G. March. 1988. Organizational Learning. *Annual Review of Sociology,* 14:319–340.

———. 1990. Chester I. Barnard and the Intelligence of Learning. In *Organization Theory: From Chester Barnard to the Present and Beyond,* ed. O. E. Williamson, pp. 11–37. New York: Oxford University Press.

Levitt, T. 1991. *Marketing Imagination.* New York: The Free Press.

Likert, R. 1961. *New Patterns of Management.* New York: McGraw-Hill.

Machlup, F. 1983. Semantic Quirks in Studies of Information. In *The Study of Information,* ed. F. Machlup and U. Mansfield, pp. 641–671. New York: John Wiley & Sons.

Magami, H. 1990. Canon. *Jinzai Kyoiku,* October:80–85 (in Japanese).

March, J. G. 1978. Bounded Rationality, Ambiguity and the Engineering of Choice. *Bell Journal of Economics,* 9:587–608.

March, J. G., and J. P. Olsen. 1976. *Ambiguity and Choice in Organizations.* Oslo, Norway: Universitestforlaget.

March, J. G., and H. A. Simon. 1958. *Organizations.* New York: John Wiley & Sons.

Marshall, A. 1965. *Principles of Economics.* London: Macmillan.

Maruta, Y. 1988a. Shohisha eno Houshi—Sono Rinen to Senryaku (Serving the Customer—Vision and Strategy). *Business Research,* June:3–8 (in Japanese).

———. 1988b. Soshiki no Eichi o Kessyusuru Keiei (Management by Mobilizing Organizational Knowledge). *Business Review,* December: 61–69 (in Japanese).

Maturana, H. R., and F. J. Varela. 1980. *Autopoiesis and Cognition: The Realization of the Living.* Dordrecht, Holland: Reidel.

Mayo, E. 1933. *The Human Problems of an Industrial Civilization.* New York: Macmillan.

McCulloch, W. 1965. *Embodiments of Mind.* Cambridge, MA: The MIT Press.

McGregor, D. 1960. *The Human Side of Enterprise.* New York: McGraw-Hill.

Merton, R. K. 1940. Bureaucratic Structure and Personality. *Social Forces,* 18:560–568.

Mills, D. Q. 1991. *Rebirth of the Corporation.* New York: John Wiley & Sons.

Minnesota Mining and Manufacturing Company. 1977. *Our Story So Far.* St. Paul, MN: Minnesota Mining and Manufacturing Company.

Mintzberg, H. 1973. *The Nature of Managerial Work.* New York: Macmillan.

———. 1989. *Mintzberg on Management: Inside Our Strange World of Organizations.* New York: The Free Press.

———. 1994. *The Rise and Fall of Strategic Planning.* New York: Free Press.

Morgan, G. 1986. *Images of Organization.* Beverly Hills, CA: Sage.

Moser, P. K., and A. V. Nat. 1987. *Human Knowledge.* Oxford: Oxford University Press.

Nakamura, Y. 1967. *Tetsugaku Nyumon (Introduction to Philosophy).* Tokyo: Chuo Koronsha (in Japanese).

Neisser, U. 1976. *Cognition and Reality.* San Francisco, CA: W. H. Freeman.

Nelson, R. R., and S. G. Winter. 1977. In Search of a Useful Theory of Innovation. *Research Policy,* 6, no. 1:36–77.

—————. 1982. *An Evolutionary Theory of Economic Change.* Cambridge, MA: Harvard University Press.

Nisbet, R. A. 1969. *Social Change and History: Aspects of the Western Theory of Development.* London: Oxford University Press.

Nishida, K. 1990. *An Inquiry into the Good,* trans. M. Abe and C. Ives. New Haven, CT: Yale University Press.

Nitobe, I. 1899. *Bushido: The Soul of Japan.* Philadelphia: Leeds and Biddle.

Nonaka, I. 1972. Organization and Market: Exploratory Study of Centralization vs. Decentralization. Ph.D. diss., Graduate School of Business Administration, University of California, Berkeley.

—————. 1985. *Kigyo Shinka-ron (Corporate Evolution: Managing Organizational Information Creation).* Tokyo: Nihon Keizai Shimbun-sha (in Japanese).

—————. 1987. Managing the Firms as Information Creation Process. Working paper, Institute of Business Research, Hitotsubashi University. In *Advances in Information Processing in Organizations,* ed. J. Meindl, R. L. Cardy, and S. M. Puffer, Vol. 4, pp. 239–275. Greenwich, CT: JAI Press, 1991.

—————. 1988a. Creating Organizational Order Out of Chaos: Self-Renewal of Japanese Firms. *California Management Review,* 30, no. 3:57–73.

—————. 1988b. Toward Middle-Up-Down Management: Accelerating Information Creation. *Sloan Management Review,* 29, no. 3:9–18.

————— 1989. Organizing Innovation as a Knowledge-creation Process: A Suggestive Paradigm for Self-renewing Organization. Working Paper, University of California at Berkeley, No. OBIR-41.

—————. 1990a. Redundant, Overlapping Organizations: A Japanese Approach to Managing the Innovation Process. *California Management Review,* 32, no. 3:27–38.

—————. 1990b. *Chishiki-souzou no Keiei* (A Theory of Organizational Knowledge Creation). Tokyo: Nihon-Keizai-Shimbunsha (in Japanese).

—————. 1991. The Knowledge-Creating Company. *Harvard Business Review,* November–December:96–104.

—————. 1992. *Nissan: Development of Primera.* Tokyo: Nomura School of Advanced Management, Case Study SMIP-92-01 (CN), (in Japanese).

—————. 1994. A Dynamic Theory of Organizational Knowledge Creation. *Organization Science,* 5, no. 1:14–37.

Nonaka, I., H. Amikura, T. Kanai, and T. Kawamura. 1992. Organizational Knowledge Creation and the Role of Middle Management. Paper presented at the Academy of Management Conference, Las Vegas, August 11.

Nonaka, I., P. Byosiere, C. C. Borucki, and N. Konno. 1994. Organizational Knowledge Creation Theory: A First Comprehensive Test. *International Business Review,* special issue.

Nonaka, I., and N. Konno. 1993. Chisiki Besu Soshiki (Knowledge-Based Organization). *Business Review,* 41, no. 1:59–73 (in Japanese).

Nonaka, I., N. Konno, T. Tokuoka, and T. Kawamura. 1992. Soshiki-teki Chishiki Sozou o Takameru Haipa-tekisuto Soshiki (Hypertext Organization for Accelerating Organizational Knowledge Creation). *Diamond Harvard Business,* August–September:12–22 (in Japanese).

Nonaka, I., T. Ohtsubo, and M. Fukushima. 1993. Shin Caterpillar Mitsubishi: Development of REGA. Unpublished case study (in Japanese).

Norman, D. A. 1988. *The Psychology of Everyday Things.* New York: Basic Books.

Numagami, T., I. Nonaka, and T. Ohtsubo. 1991. *Sharp.* Tokyo: Nomura School of Advanced Management, Case Study SMIP-91-16-(CN) (in Japanese).

Numagami, T., T. Ohta, and I. Nonaka. 1989. Self-renewal of Corporate Organizations: Equilibrium, Self-sustaining, and Self-renewing Models. Working Paper, University of California at Berkeley. No. OBIR-43.

Ohmae, K. 1982. *The Mind of the Strategist.* New York: McGraw-Hill.

Orr, J. E. 1990. Sharing Knowledge, Celebrating Identity: Community Memory in a Service Culture. In *Collective Remembering,* ed. D. Middleton and D. Edwards, pp. 169–189. Newbury Park, CA: Sage.

Pascale, R. T., and A. G. Athos. 1981. *The Art of Japanese Management.* New York: Simon & Schuster.

Penrose, E. T. 1959. *The Theory of the Growth of the Firm.* Oxford: Basil Blackwell.

Perrow, C. 1967. A Framework for the Comparative Analysis of Organizations. *American Sociological Review,* 32:194–208.

———. 1973. *Complex Organizations: A Critical Essay.* 2nd ed. New York: Random House.

Peters, T. J. 1987. *Thriving on Chaos.* New York: Alfred A. Knopf.

———. 1992. *Liberation Management.* London: Macmillan.

Peters, T. J., and R. H. Waterman, Jr. 1982. *In Search of Excellence.* New York: Harper & Row.

Pfeffer, J. 1981. Management as Symbolic Action. In *Research in Organizational Behavior,* ed. L. L. Cummings and B. M. Staw, Vol. 3, pp. 1–52. Greenwich, CT: JAI Press.

Piaget, J. 1974. *Recherches sur la Contradiction.* Paris: Presses Universitaires de France.

Pinchot, G., III. 1985. *Intrapreneuring: Why You Don't Have to Leave the Corporation to Become an Entrepreneur.* New York: Harper & Row.

Polanyi, M. 1958. *Personal Knowledge.* Chicago: University of Chicago Press.

———. 1966. *The Tacit Dimension.* London: Routledge & Kegan Paul.

Porter, M. E. 1980. *Competitive Strategy.* New York: The Free Press.

———. 1985. *Competitive Advantage.* New York: The Free Press.

———. 1990. *The Competitive Advantage of Nations.* New York: The Free Press.

Prahalad, C. K., and G. Hamel. 1990. The Core Competence of the Corporation. *Harvard Business Review,* May–June:79–91.

Prigogine, I., and I. Stengers. 1984. *Order out of Chaos: Man's New Dialogue with Nature.* New York: Bantam Books.

Quinn, J. B. 1992. *Intelligent Enterprise: A Knowledge and Service Based Paradigm for Industry.* New York: The Free Press.

Reich, R. B. 1991. *The Work of Nations*. New York: Alfred A. Knopf.

Richards, I. A. 1936. *The Philosophy of Rhetoric*. Oxford: Oxford University Press.

Roethlisberger, F. J., and W. J. Dickson. 1939. *Management and the Worker*. Cambridge, MA: Harvard University Press.

Romer, P. M. 1986. Increasing Returns and Long-Run Growth. *Journal of Political Economy,* 94:1002–1037.

———. 1990a. Are Nonconvexities Important for Understanding Growth? *American Economic Review,* 80, no. 2:97–103.

———. 1990b. Endogenous Technical Change. *Journal of Political Economy,* 98, no. 5, pt. 2:S71–S102.

Rosch, E. H. 1973. Natural Categories. *Cognitive Psychology,* 4:328–350.

Roszak, T. 1986. *The Cult of Information*. New York: Pantheon Books.

Russell, B. 1961. *A History of Western Philosophy*. London: Unwin Hyman.

———. 1989. *Wisdom of the West*. New York: Crescent Books.

Ryle, G. 1949. *The Concept of Mind*. London: Hutchinson.

Sakakibara, K., T. Numagami, and S. Ohtaki. 1989. *Jigyo Sozo no Dainamikusu (Dynamics of Business Creation)*. Tokyo: Hakuto Shobo (in Japanese).

Sasaki, T. 1991. Erekutoronikusu no Jidai to Tomoni (My Life with the Electronics Age). *Business Review,* December: 98–109 (in Japanese).

Scheflen, A. E. 1982. Comments on the Significance of Interaction Rhythm. In *Interaction Rhythms,* ed. M. Davis. New York: Human Sciences Press, pp. 13–21.

Schein, E. H. (1985). *Organizational Culture and Leadership*. San Francisco, CA: Jossey-Bass.

Schön, D. A. 1983. *The Reflective Practitioner*. New York: Basic Books.

Schumpeter, J. A. 1951. *The Theory of Economic Development*. Cambridge, MA: Harvard University Press.

———. 1952. *Capitalism, Socialism and Democracy*. 4th ed. London: George Allen & Unwin.

Searle, J. R. 1969. *Speech Acts: An Essay in the Philosophy of Language*. Cambridge: Cambridge University Press.

Selznik, P. 1949. *TVA and the Grass Roots*. Berkeley, CA: University of California Press.

Senge, P. M. 1990. *The Fifth Discipline: The Age and Practice of the Learning Organization*. London: Century Business.

Shannon, C. E., and W. Weaver. 1949. *The Mathematical Theory of Communication*. Urbana, IL: University of Illinois Press.

Shiozawa, S. 1990. *Matsushita Keiei Runessansu (Management Renaissance at Matsushita)*. Tokyo: President-sha (in Japanese).

Simon, H. A. 1945. *Administrative Behavior*. New York: Macmillan.

———. 1969. *The Science of the Artificial*. Boston, MA: MIT Press.

———. 1973. Applying Information Technology to Organization Design. *Public Administration Review,* 33:268–278.

———. 1986. Keieisha no Yakuwari Saihomon (The Functions of the Executive Revisited). In *Banado (Barnard),* ed. K. Kato and H. Iino, pp. 3–17. Tokyo: Bunshindo (in Japanese).

Singley, M. K., and J. R. Anderson. 1989. *The Transfer of Cognitive Skill*. Cambridge, MA: Harvard University Press.

Slater, R. 1991. *The New GE*. Homewood, IL: Business One Irwin.

Spender, J. C. 1993. Competitive Advantage from Tacit Knowledge? Unpacking the Concept and Its Strategic Implications. Graduate School of Management, Rutgers University, New Brunswick, NJ. Mimeographed.

Squire, L. R. 1987. *Memory and Brain*. New York: Oxford University Press.

Stalk, G., P. Evans, and L. E. Shulman. 1992. Competing on Capabilities: The New Rules of Corporate Strategy. *Harvard Business Review*, March–April:57–69.

Stewart. R. 1967. *Managers and Their Jobs*. London: Macmillan.

Takeuchi, H. 1988. Gaining Competitive Advantage Through Global Product Development. *Hitotsubashi Journal of Commerce and Management*, 26, no. 1:21–52.

———. 1991. Small and Better: The Consumer-driven Advantage in Japanese Production Design. *Design Management Journal*, Winter: 62–69.

———. 1994. *Besuto Prakutisu Kakumei (Best Practice Revolution)*. Tokyo: Diamond-sha (in Japanese).

——— (forthcoming). Chi no Souzou ni Yoru Kasutama Ritenshon (Customer Retention Through Knowledge Creation). *Business Review*, 41, no. 3 (in Japanese).

Takeuchi, H., and I. Nonaka. 1986. The New New Product Development Game. *Harvard Business Review*, Jan.–Feb.: 137–146.

Takeuchi, H., and J. Quelch. 1983. Quality is More Than Making a Good Product. *Harvard Business Review*, July–Aug. 139–145.

Takeuchi, H., and M. E. Porter. 1986. Three Roles of International Marketing in Global Strategy, in Porter, M. E. ed., *Competition in Global Industries*, pp. 111–146. Boston: Harvard Business School Press.

Takeuchi, H., and Y. Fujikawa. 1993. Shohin-siborikomi-gensho ni Miru Nihon-kigyo no Senryaku-kadai (Product Pruning: A Strategic Challenge for Japanese Companies), *Japan Marketing Journal*, 12, no. 2:4–14 (in Japanese).

Takeuchi, H., and Y. Ishikura. 1994. *Ishitsu no Manejimento (Managing Heterogeneity: The Path to Global Management)*. Tokyo: Diamond-sha (in Japanese).

Taylor, F. W. 1911. *The Principles of Scientific Management*. New York: Harper and Brothers.

Teece, D. J. 1981. The Market for Know-How and the Efficient International Transfer of Technology. *Annals of the American Academy of Political and Social Science*, 458:81–96.

Teece, D. J., G. Pisano, and A. Shuen. 1991. Dynamic Capabilities and Strategic Management. Working paper, Center for Research in Management, University of California, Berkeley.

Thompson, J. D. 1967. *Organization in Action*. New York: McGraw-Hill.

Tichy, N., and S. Stratford. 1993. *Control Your Destiny or Someone Else Will*. New York: Doubleday.

Tobe, R., Y. Teramoto, S. Kamata, T. Sugino, H. Murai, and I. Nonaka. 1984. *Shippai no Honshitsu (The Essence of Failure)*. Tokyo: Diamond-sha (in Japanese).

Toffler, A. 1990. *Powershift: Knowledge, Wealth and Violence at the Edge of the 21st Century*. New York: Bantam Books.

Tregoe, B. B., et al. 1989. *Vision in Action*. New York: Kemper-Tregoe Inc.

Varela, F. J., E. Thompson, and E. Rosch. 1991. *Embodied Mind: Cognitive Science and Human Experience.* Cambridge, MA: MIT Press.

von Foerster, H. 1984. Principles of Self-Organization in a Socio-Managerial Context. In *Self-Organization and Management of Social Systems,* ed. H. Ulrich and G. J. B. Probst, pp. 2–24. Berlin: Springer-Verlag.

von Hippel, E. 1994. "Sticky Information" and the Locus of Problem Solving: Implications for Innovation. *Management Science,* 40, no. 4:429–439.

Waldrop, M. M. 1992. *Complexity: Life at the Edge of Chaos.* New York: Simon & Schuster.

Weick, K. E. 1969. *The Social Psychology of Organizing.* Reading, MA: Addison-Wesley.

———. 1979. *The Social Psychology of Organizing.* 2nd ed. Reading, MA: Addison-Wesley.

———. 1991. The Nontraditional Quality of Organizational Learning. *Organization Science,* 2, no. 1:116–124.

———. 1993. The Collapse of Sensemaking in Organizations: The Mann Gulch Disaster. *Administrative Science Quarterly,* 38:628–652.

Westley, F. R. 1990. Middle Managers and Strategy: Microdynamics of Inclusion. *Strategic Management Journal,* 11:337–351.

Winograd, T., and F. Flores. 1986. *Understanding Computers and Cognition: A New Foundation for Design.* Reading, MA: Addison-Wesley.

Winter, S. G. 1988. On Coase, Competence and the Corporation. *Journal of Law, Economics and Organization,* 4, no. 1:163–180.

Womack, J. P., and D. T. Jones. 1994. From Lean Production to the Lean Enterprise. *Harvard Business Review,* March–April:93–103.

Wooldridge, B., and S. W. Floyd. 1990. The Strategy Process, Middle Management Involvement, and Organizational Performance. *Strategic Management Journal,* 11:231–241.

Yamanouchi, T. 1991. Prodakuto Pranningu: Canon no Pasonaru Kopia (Product Planning: Canon Personal Copier). In *Maketingu: Riron to Jissai (Marketing: Theory and Practice),* ed. K. Tanouchi, pp. 335–355. Tokyo: TBS Britanica (in Japanese).

Yanagida, K. 1986. *Katsuryoku no Kouzou Senryaku-hen (The Structure of Corporate Vitality: Strategy).* Tokyo: Kodansha (in Japanese).

Yuasa, Y. 1987. *The Body: Toward an Eastern Mind-Body Theory,* trans. S. Nagatomi and T. P. Kasulis. Albany, NY: State University of New York Press.

Zimmerman, B. J. 1993. The Inherent Drive to Chaos. In *Implementing Strategic Processes: Change, Learning and Cooperation,* Lorange P. et al. eds., pp. 373–93. Oxford: Basil Blackwell.

INDEX

Aaker, D. A., 55n
Abductive reasoning, 30, 66, 86
Abe, Masao, 52n
Abrams, D., 92n
Absolute Spirit (Hegel), 24–25
Action
  in Japanese concept of human being, 30
  and knowledge
    in organizational knowledge creation
      theory, 58–59, 90n
    Western concept of, 26–27
  relationship to language, 92n
ACTION 61 reorganization plan
      (Matsushita). See Matsushita
      Electric Industrial Company
ACT model (Anderson and Singley), of
      cognitive psychology, 61–62, 91n
Adachi, Takeji, 215–16, 218, 244
Adaptation, in organizational learning
      theory, 45, 55n
Adaptive learning (Senge), 44–45
Adhocracies (Mintzberg), 161, 193n
Administrative Behavior (Simon), 38
AE-1 camera (Canon). See Canon,
      development of AE-1 camera
Age, of engineers, in development of
      Canon Mini-Copier, 148
Air Force, Japanese, 194n

Akashi plant (Shin Caterpillar-
      Mitsubishi), 215–19
Ambiguity
  in new-product development process,
      232
  role in organizational knowledge
      creation, 14, 79–80
  in top-down management model, 125
American football approach, to product
      development, 211–12, 242–43
Amikura, H., 158n
Amphibious operations, U.S. development
      in World War II, 165–66, 194n
Analog knowledge, 60, 61t
Analogy, role in knowledge conversion,
      13, 64–67, 71, 225, 231
  examples of, 65–66, 66t, 92n
Analytic philosophy, 26
Anderson, J. R., 61–62
Answer Center (General Electric [GE]),
      69
Apparel companies, Japanese, salesperson
      contact with customers in, 153,
      235
Apple Computer, use of customer
      feedback at, 89, 235
Apprenticeship, as socialization, 63
  example of, 63–64

257

Values (*cont'd.*)
  in organizational knowledge creation
    theory, 59, 80
  in organizational intention, 74–75
  top management responsibility for
    establishing, 156
Varela, F. J., 52*n*–53*n*, 76, 91*n*
Variety, requisite. *See* Requisite variety
Virtual corporation concept, 11
Virtual meetings, at Microsoft, 245
Vision
  in business strategy, 41, 54*n*, 227
  construction into knowledge, in
    organizational knowledge creation
    theory, 59
  corporate
    in combination, 68–69
    in hypertext organization, 167, 169,
      233, 241
    Matsushita's reestablishment of, 114–
      16
    at Sharp, 186
    top management responsibility for,
      156–57
  as element of corporate strategy, 74, 87
  equivocality of, 157, 228
  intentionally ambiguous, 79–80
  knowledge, 227–28
  in middle-up-down management model,
    129
  in top-down management model, GE
    example of, 131–32, 135
Volkswagen, 200
Voluntary individuals concept
    (Matsushita)
  development as corporate vision, 87,
    114–16
  operationalizing of, 116–20
von Foerster, H., 93*n*
von Hippel, E., 49, 223*n*

Wakabayashi, Naoki, 97
Waldrop, M. M., 94*n*
Watanabe, Hiroo, 12, 65, 70, 78, 80, 92*n*,
    129, 154, 229, 239
Waterman, R. H., Jr., 42, 137
Weaver, W., 58
Weber, Max, 125, 161, 193*n*
Weick, Karl, 39–40, 45, 55*n*, 93*n*, 158*n*
Weiss, A., 55*n*
Welch, Jack, 130–35, 150–51, 158*n*–159*n*,
    198

Western companies, suggestions for
    learning from Japanese
    knowledge-creation approaches,
    243–44
Western Electric, Hawthorn experiments
    at, 36
Western epistemology, 21–27, 51*n*. *See
    also* Knowledge creation,
    organizational, Western approach
    to
  versus organizational knowledge
    creation theory, 58
  versus Polanyi's theory of knowledge,
    60
Western philosophical tradition, versus
    Japanese intellectual tradition,
    20–21, 28–32
Westley, F. R., 158*n*
William of Occam, 51*n*
Winograd, T., 78
Winter, S. G., 34–35
Wittgenstein, Ludwig, 26–27, 52*n*, 91*n*
Womack, J. P., 208
Wooldridge, B., 158*n*
Work-hour reduction, effects of,
    Matsushita example, 117–20
Work-Out program (GE), 133, 159*n*
World War II, U.S. and Japanese military
    organizational structures during,
    160–66
Writing, as externalization, 64
Wundt, Wilhelm, 52*n*

Xerox, 10. *See* Fuji Xerox

Yamamoto, Kenichi, 157
Yamawaki, Toshihaya, 112
Yamanouchi, Teruo, 140, 142, 149
Yanagida, K., 97
Yazaki, Yoshiaki, 206
Yazaki Group, 153, 206–7, 209
Yoshida, Hiroshi, 77*t*
Young employees, and development of
    Canon Mini-Copier, 148, 150
Yuasa, Y., 29–30

Zen Buddhism, influence on Japanese
    concept of knowledge, 29–30, 239
Zero information, state of, 232